"These nineteenth- and early-twentieth-century biographies, now republished by Chelsea House, reveal an unsuspected significance. Not only are a good many of them substantively valuable (and by no means entirely superseded), but they also evoke a sense of the period, an intimacy with the attitudes and assumptions of their times."
                                    —*Professor Daniel Aaron*

Other titles in this Chelsea House series:

NATHANIEL HAWTHORNE
GEORGE E. WOODBERRY

INTRODUCTION BY
RICHARD POIRIER

American Men and Women of Letters Series

GENERAL EDITOR
PROFESSOR DANIEL AARON
HARVARD UNIVERSITY

CHELSEA HOUSE
NEW YORK, LONDON
1980

Cover design by Stanley Dunaj

Library of Congress Cataloging in Publication Data

Woodberry, George Edward, 1855-1930.
   Nathaniel Hawthorne.

   (American men and women of letters)
   Reprint of the 1902 ed. published by Houghton
Mifflin, Boston, issued in series: American men
of letters.
   1. Hawthorne, Nathaniel, 1804-1864. 2. Novel-
ists, American--19th century--Biography.
I. Series. II. Series: American men of letters.
PS1881.W6   1980   813'.3 [B]   80-23480
ISBN 0-87754-154-X

Chelsea House Publishers
Harold Steinberg, Chairman & Publisher
Andrew E. Norman, President
Susan Lusk, Vice President
A Division of Chelsea House Educational Communications, Inc.
133 Christopher Street, New York 10014

CONTENTS

THE VISITABLE PAST
Daniel Aaron

THE TWENTY-FIVE BIOGRAPHIES of American worthies reissued in this Chelsea House series restore an all but forgotten chapter in the annals of American literary culture. Some of the authors of these volumes—journalists, scholars, writers, professional men—would be considered amateurs by today's standards, but they enjoyed certain advantages not open to their modern counterparts. In some cases they were blood relations or old friends of the men and women they wrote about, or at least near enough to them in time to catch the contemporary essence often missing in the more carefully researched and authoritative later studies of the same figures. Their leisurely, impressionistic accounts—sometimes as interesting for what is omitted as for what is emphasized—reveal a good deal about late Victorian assumptions, cultural and social, and about the vicissitudes of literary reputation.

Each volume in the series is introduced by a recognized scholar who was encouraged to write an idiosyncratic appraisal of the biographer and his work. The introductions vary in emphasis and point of view, for the biographies are not of equal quality, nor are the writers memorialized equally appealing. Yet a kind of consensus is discernible in these random assessments: surprise at the insights still to be found in ostensibly unscientific and old-fashioned works; in some instances admiration for the solidity and liveliness of the biographer's prose and quality of mind; respect for the pioneer historians among them who made excellent use of the limited material at their disposal.

The volumes in this American Men and Women of Letters series contain none of the startling "private" and "personal" episodes modern readers have come to expect in biography, but they illuminate what Henry James called the "visitable past." As such, they are of particular value to all students of American cultural and intellectual history.

Cambridge, Massachusetts
Spring, 1980

INTRODUCTION
TO THE
CHELSEA HOUSE EDITION

Richard Poirier

Early in this study of Hawthorne we come upon a passage that illustrates the unique virtues and charms of its author, the critic, poet, and teacher of American literature George E. Woodberry (1855-1930). He is telling us about Hawthorne's early reading, which included Shakespeare, Milton, and James Thomson, and that the first book Hawthorne bought as a boy with his own money was *The Faerie Queene*. These are obligatory notations in a literary biography, but along with them, quite casually offered, is the information that he often read while lying on the floor, "when not playing with cats—the only boyish fondness known of him." And he read the more, the passage continues, because "while vigorous enough now" (he had been lamed playing ball at age nine and was bothered by the injury until at least age twelve), "two outward circumstances that most affected his boyhood, the monotony of his mother's sorrow" (her husband died in 1808, when Nathaniel was four) "and his own protracted physical disability, must have given him touches of gravity and delicacy beyond his years. It is noticeable that nothing is heard of any boyfriends; nor did he contract such friendships, apparently, before his college days."

We can hear in this passage the affectionate, even avuncular voice of someone who knows his subject intimately, so intimately that no one item impresses itself upon him as a "secret" destined for revelation. It is the voice of a man always so confidently close to the material that he does not italicize any of it for public notice. When, for example, he comes to those twelve years Hawthorne famously spent as a sort of recluse, he characteristically emphasizes that the seclusion was neither as important nor as mysterious as many have supposed, nor as absolute as Hawthorne himself chose later to remember it. When he returned home with a diploma from Bowdoin College, he found that in emulation of his mother, who remained in prolonged mourning for her husband, each member of his family elected to live apart from the others, though in the same house. The custom of staying most of the time in a room of your own had spread from his mother to his favorite elder sister, Elizabeth, who later went off to be a much-honored schoolteacher in Boston, and to his youngest sister, Louisa. Hawthorne, with no clear idea of what he wanted to do with his life, fell naturally into the habit of isolation to which circumstances invited him in any case, including the taking of meals alone in his room. Nonetheless, he went for frequent walks in the town and traveled during the twelve years, as on a visit to his college friend Horatio Bridge, in Augusta, Maine. He is even reported to have challenged to a duel a man who mistreated a woman of his acquaintance, prompting from Woodberry the wry observation that "Hawthorne's solitude in Salem must have been less complete than has been represented. ..."

More significant than any period of personal reclusiveness, episodes of which are common enough among writers, is that for a protracted period he kept secret—from the general public, that is—his identity as a writer. Even his letters to friends like Bridge tended to be signed "Oberon," some eidolon of himself that crops up also in certain of the early stories, like "The Devil in Manuscript." In the twelve years after he left college not a single published article appeared in his own name. He preferred instead to identify himself as, say, "the author of 'The Gentle Boy'" or "the author of 'The Gray Champion.'" This shyness of authorship, this refusal to assume authority, this suppression of identity is a phenomenon among certain writers and remains a vexing question of contemporary theory in our own day; Woodberry in 1902 was not obliged to be solemnly speculative about it in Hawthorne's case. Instead he proceeds as if in deference to Hawthorne's own indecisiveness, writing about him as if he were someone not necessarily destined to become a genius of American literature, someone who might as easily have remained nearly anonymous. This seems to me a rewarding and refreshing approach. He finds it in fact rather "singular" that as a practical way of life "Hawthorne should have undertaken to live by his pen, or been allowed to do so by his friends" —who included his classmate Franklin Pierce, later to be president of the United States—"but he was indulged at home, the young lord of the family. ... He probably drifted, more or less, into authorship, partly through a dilatory reluctance to do anything else, and partly led on by the hope of a success with some one of his tales which would justify him."

Woodberry does not infer from the events of Hawthorne's life what Hawthorne's own experience of them would or should have been. This laudable circumspection depends upon a reading of the life and of the work that has convinced him of something about Hawthorne that may sound peculiar to us now, even possibly begrudging, but that is rather more persuasive, I think, than other accounts prove to be. Speaking of the six tales in which, as he sees it, Hawthorne's originality is most characteristically expressed—"Egotism, or The Bosom Serpent," "The Minister's Black Veil," "Young Goodman Brown," "The Birthmark," "Rappaccini's Daughter," "The Artist of the Beautiful"—he makes the preliminary and unexceptionable point that they are all in one way or another about the idea of isolation or solitude, and that while the themes of sin, conscience, and evil are implicit, they await his later works in order to become central. But he goes on to insist that "from the beginning he had no message, no inspiration welling up within him, no inward life of his own that sought expression. He was not even introspective." Imagine Hawthorne alone and apparently deep in thought, Woodberry seems to say, and he would in all likelihood be revealing no more than his "great capacity for idleness." He had "apparently no intellectual life," and when it came to conviviality he had a special liking for the kind of working-class

people he met at the Boston Coal Wharf
when he was a weigher and gauger at the
Salem Custom House, and around the dock
areas of Liverpool, where he served in the
American consulate on an appointment from
President Pierce. With such New England writers as Emerson and Margaret Fuller he had a
polite but never friendly relationship, and
though Melville made a great effort to be his
friend and wrote most admiringly of his work,
Hawthorne did not, for reasons Woodberry
never explores, reciprocate the warmth of feeling. Though as a man of letters and a diplomat
in England he might have found it easy to introduce himself to anyone in the literary
world, he did not bother to make the acquaintance of Dickens, Thackeray, Carlyle, George
Eliot or, until being neighbors in Italy made it
impossible to avoid them, the Brownings. "His
thoughts and affections found their exercise in
the domestic circle," observes Woodberry, who
gives the most admiring account of Hawthorne's
extraordinary devotion to his wife and children, "just as his eyes were engaged with the
look of landscape, the incidents of the road,
and the changes of the weather."

This is not the romantic view of Hawthorne,
or of the American artist of the first half of the
nineteenth century, that still informs twentieth-

century criticism. Woodberry's Hawthorne is not the lonely figure alienated by the barrenness of an American society that can offer no nourishing social texture for the novel. Woodberry, unlike Henry James in his earlier study of Hawthorne for the English Men of Letters series, or, still earlier, James Fenimore Cooper in *Home As Found,* offers no catalog of the items "missing" from American life by way of sustenance for a novelist. Quite the reverse. He is not at all persuaded that American society, however provincial, was deficient in what it had to offer. In fact, his book came at a point in American criticism when he, among others, felt the need to claim that American writers did function within a society substantial enough to support the fictional enterprise, and to claim further that a writer like Hawthorne was not averse to exploiting these possibilities for the writing of realistic fiction. From the beginning, according to this account, Hawthorne was, by intention at least, a realistic writer. The early "Sights from a Steeple," "like so much of Hawthorne's writing, has a curious accent of the school reader, as if it were meant for that, so well is it adjusted to ready comprehension, so mild in its interests, so matter-of-fact yet playful in fancy is its substance, and so immediate is its village charm."

When we read such an opinion, it is especially important once again to remember the sound of Woodberry's voice in this book and thus to be aware that when he talks this way it is with none of the self-promoting condescension that makes James's characterizations of Hawthorne and of pre-Civil War American society interesting less for what they tell us about either of these than for what they tell us of James's "anxiety of influence" where Hawthorne is concerned. Woodberry is anxious instead to appropriate Hawthorne to some version of American historical reality. He is so committed to establishing a reciprocal and above all cordial relationship between Hawthorne and his immediate social circumstances that at a number of points he chastises the author—for the sketch of the Custom House that precedes *The Scarlet Letter,* for example, and for local portraiture in *The House of the Seven Gables,* where he "stooped to literary revenge on his humble associates by holding them up to personal ridicule."

More recent criticism has made readers skeptical of a view of Hawthorne's work that takes anything as necessarily referential or "matter-of-fact." No one who has read even so tiny a story as "The Wives of the Dead" with proper attention to its extraordinarily complicated design, its irresoluble play on confusions of identity and "doubles," will agree with Woodberry that it is an example of "the slightness of Hawthorne's attempt in the earlier pieces." But to find Woodberry deficient in his estimates of one or another of the works only makes it the more surprising that his general accounts of Hawthorne remain so vital and instructive, once we read him with due respect to his, as well as to Hawthorne's, complications of mind. For example, while he claims that Hawthorne has "no inward life" searching for a way to express itself, he also claims that he has "a transcendent sense of the reality of the soul's life with God." This may seem contradictory, but only because for most readers this late in the twentieth century "spirituality" or "the moral life" or "the soul"—to mention some of the items of obvious interest to Hawthorne— are not considered "real." When credited at all, they are thought to be products of the very introspection denied to the author. As Woodberry reminds us, he was himself closer to a time, and Hawthorne closer still, when "spirituality" and the existence of the soul were among the "facts" of life. They had in the consciousness a place no less powerful than sexuality does now, something people "see" whenever they look at the manifestations of life

around them. Woodberry, in a beautiful and
vivid phrase, claims for Hawthorne "an historical consciousness that was latent, like clairvoyance." In his bones he felt like a "public"
man in Salem not only by virtue of his job at
the Custom House but also as a descendant of
the Hathornes who settled there in 1637.
Salem was supportive of his confidence of
place and sense of self; it could be said that it
was the only spot where he might have been a
recluse without also feeling unaccounted or un-
cared for. "Salem," Woodberry writes, "was a
true center of the old times; and a young imagination in that town and neighborhood, already
disposed to writing prose romance, would feel
the charm of historical association and naturally catch impulses from the past, especially if,
as in the case of Hawthorne, the history of his
ancestors was inwoven within its good and
evil." It is therefore possible on the one hand
to say, as Woodberry does of the scene of *The
Scarlet Letter,* that "such a village and such a
tragedy never existed" and to claim at the same
time that the story has an "intense reality."

Because Woodberry wants especially to hon-
or Hawthorne's "remorseless adherence to his
own impressions," it is incumbent upon him to
be especially inquisitive and complicated about
those elements in Hawthorne that seem less a

matter of "impressions" than of literary con-
trivance, namely his symbolism and his allegory. He ascribes to Scott the literary influence
that fixed Hawthorne's attention on specific
objects, like the letter *A*, and that incited at
the same time an interest in the history of his
own country. But by insisting on the "remorseless" reality of such an object for Hawthorne,
and for the reader, Woodberry is able also to
account for its extraordinary resonance. It becomes like some feature of a long-familiar
scene that grows strange in direct proportion to
the intensity with which it is stared at. Thus, in
"Lady Eleanor's Mantle," Hawthorne has "fully seized the power of the physical object,
plainly sensible to all as a matter of fact, to
serve as the medium for moral suggestion often
difficult to put into words, of that sort whose
effect is rather in the feelings than in the
thought; and this, without turning the object
into an expressed symbol." So also with the
pink ribbons worn in the cap of Young Goodman Brown's wife and later found by him in
the forest where the party of the devil has been
meeting. This, too, is a physical object, but because of the workings of Hawthorne's style we
cannot always be sure that it is not also an
imagined object. "The story," Woodberry
writes with a common sense that might have

saved later explicators a good deal of unreward-
ing labor, "is one of those whose significance is
felt to contain mystery which Hawthorne
meant to remain in its dark state." When it
comes to Hawthorne's allegory, Woodberry is
again directed by his realistic predilections to a
view at once sensible but, in application, suited
to the provocatively evasive refinements of
Hawthorne's writing. "The allegorizing method," he writes, "though it appears with greater
or less influence, is not employed with any exclusiveness but takes its place with other resources of his art."

Woodberry is too astute a critic to leave it at
that. He knows that Hawthorne's allegory and
his realistic disposition exist in a reciprocally
modifying relationship, and he applauds one result of this—"the indefiniteness and mystery of
effect." But this, in turn, prompts from him a
quite serious criticism of what he calls Hawthorne's "inartistic didacticism," a moralism
that sometimes gets into the fiction as a sort of
afterthought to prevent a story or passage from
simply dissolving altogether into contradictions
and indecisiveness. Perhaps for that reason, the
study is most sympathetic in discussing works
brief enough to allow for the most intimate
play of these various elements. These are the
tales and *The Scarlet Letter*—which, he con-

vincingly argues, was "the climax of his tales."
About *The House of the Seven Gables, The
Blithedale Romance,* and *The Marble Faun* he
tends to be less sympathetic because the prin-
ciples of coherence are not as easily visible to
him. There is no clear evidence, that is, of the
creative interplay in the larger works between
realistic elements and other "vital germs of
thought, emotion, and action ... that are
loosed into activity and grow of themselves."

With a tentativeness and delicacy as appropriate to Hawthorne's life as to his work,
Woodberry's study offers that rare gift in critical biography—not a psychological theory of
character and creation, but rather a sense of
what Hawthorne was probably like to those
who knew him best among his friends, someone like President Pierce, who was his companion on the final trip to Vermont where Hawthorne died. So that while we are given less
biographical material than we are apt to get
from the massive biographies written in our
own century, it can be argued that we are given
more by way of sympathetic comprehension.
Woodberry's Hawthorne is someone who at
some point refused to be Wakefield, the man in
the story so named who chose to disappear but
to remain in the neighborhood where he once
occupied a place. In yet another instance of

critical decorum, Woodberry, declining to read
the story as having any such biographical possibility, remarks, quite aptly all the same, that
"the element of life's contingency, the nearness
of an event [Wakefield's being discovered] that
might happen but never does, is what makes
the strangeness of this curious study." And yet
Woodberry is aware, without any pronounced
vanity at his awareness, that early and late
Hawthorne was in danger of disappearing off
the page or out of historically consequential
life. His suspicion reveals itself not only in the
biographical account but, quite indirectly, in
one or another of his brilliant summaries of
Hawthorne's habitual practices as a writer.
"Probably in no one point is Hawthorne's peculiarity so obviously marked," he writes, "as
in the persistency with which he clings to the
physical image. . . . and doubtless he especially
valued its function to afford by its crude definiteness a balance to the tenuous and impalpable, the vagueness, refinement, and mystery, to
which it is the complement, in his art; he gains
reality by its presence for what else, as a whole,
might seem too insubstantial, too much a part
of that shadow world in which he dreaded to
dwell altogether." What most interests Woodberry are the positive manifestations of that
dread—Hawthorne's conviviality with family,

working-class people he did not fear, old friends from college days, and, at last, with the audience he imagined in and for his work, an audience of immense sophistication.

New York, New York
July, 1980

AUTHOR'S PREFACE
TO THE
1902 EDITION

THE narrative of Hawthorne's life has been partly told in the autobiographical passages of his writings which he himself addressed to his readers from time to time, and in the series of "Note Books," not meant for publication but included in his posthumous works; the remainder is chiefly contained in the family biography, "Nathaniel Hawthorne and his Wife" by his son Julian Hawthorne, "Memories of Hawthorne" by his daughter, Mrs. Rose Hawthorne Lathrop, and "A Study of Hawthorne," by his son-in-law, George Parsons Lathrop. Collateral material is also to be found abundantly in books of reminiscences by his contemporaries. These are the printed sources of the present biography.

The author takes pleasure in expressing his thanks to his publishers for the ample material they have placed at his disposal; and also to Messrs. Harper and Brothers for their permission to make extracts from Horatio Bridge's "Personal Recollections of Nathaniel Hawthorne," and

to Samuel T. Pickard, Esq., author of "Hawthorne's First Diary," and to Dr. Moncure D.
Conway, author of "Nathaniel Hawthorne" (Ap-
pleton's), for a like courtesy.

COLUMBIA COLLEGE, April 1, 1902.

NATHANIEL HAWTHORNE

NATHANIEL HAWTHORNE

I.

FIRST YEARS.

THE Hathorne family stock, to name it with
the ancient spelling, was English, and its old
home is said to have been at Wigcastle, Wilton,
in Wiltshire. The emigrant planter, William
Hathorne, twenty-three years old, came over in
the Arbella with Winthrop in 1630. He settled
at Dorchester, but in 1637 removed to Salem, where
he received grants of land; and there the line continued generation after generation with varying
fortune, at one time coming into public service
and local distinction, and at another lapsing again
into the common lot, as was the case of the long
settled families generally. The planter, William
Hathorne, shared to the full in the vigor and
enterprise of the first generation in New England.
He was a leader in war and peace, trade and politics, with the versatility then required for leader-
ship, being legislator, magistrate, Indian fighter,
explorer, and promoter, as well as occasionally a
preacher; and besides this practical force he had

a temper to sway and incite, which made him reputed the most eloquent man in the public assembly. He possessed — and this may indicate another side to his character — a copy of Sir Philip Sidney's "Arcadia," certainly a rare book in the wilderness. He was best remembered, both in local annals and family tradition, as a patriot and a persecutor, for he refused to obey the king's summons to England, and he ordered Quaker women to be whipped through the country-side.

The next generation, born in the colony, were generally of a narrower type than their fathers, though in their turn they took up the work of the new and making world with force and conscience; and the second Hathorne, John, of fanatical memory, was as characteristically a latter-day Puritan as his father had been a pioneer. He served in the council and the field, but he left a name chiefly as a magistrate. His duty as judge fell in the witchcraft years, and under that adversity of fortune he showed those qualities of the Puritan temperament which are most darkly recalled; he examined and sentenced to death several of the accused persons, and bore himself so inhumanely in court that the husband of one of the sufferers cursed him, — it must have been dramatically done to have left so vivid a mark in men's minds, — him and his children's children. This was the curse that lingered in the family memory like a black blot in the blood, and was ever after used to explain any ill luck that befell the house.

The third heir of the name, Joseph, was a plain farmer, in whose person the family probably ceased from the ranks of the gentry, as the word was then used. The fourth, Daniel, "bold Hathorne" of the Revolutionary ballad, was a privateersman, robust, ruddy of face, blue-eyed, quick to wrath, — a strong-featured type of the old Salem ship-master. His son, Nathaniel, the fifth descendant, was also bred to the sea, a young man of slight, firm figure, and in face and build so closely resembling his famous son — for he was the father of Hawthorne — that a passing sailor once recognized the latter by the likeness. What else he transmitted to his son, in addition to physique, by way of temperament and inbred capacity and inclination, was to suffer more than a sea-change; but he is recalled as a stern man on deck, of few words, showing doubtless the early aging of those days under the influence of active responsibility, danger, and the habit of command, and, like all these shipmasters — for they were men of some education — he took books to sea with him. He died at Surinam in 1808, when thirty-two years old. He had married Elizabeth Clarke Manning, herself a descendant in the fifth generation of Richard Manning, of St. Petrox Parish, Dartmouth, whose widow emigrated to New England with her children in 1679. Other old colonial families that had blended with the Hathornes and Mannings in these American years were the Gardner, Bowditch, and Phelps stocks, on the one side, and the Giddings, Potter, and Lord, on the other. Of such descent, Nathaniel Hawthorne, the second child and only son of this marriage, was born at Salem, July 4, 1804, in his grandfather Daniel's house, on Union Street, near the wharves.

The pleasant, handsome, bright-haired boy was four years old when his mother called him into her room and told him that his father was dead. She soon removed with him and his sisters, of whom Elizabeth was four years older and Louisa two years younger than himself, to her father's house in the adjoining yard, which faced on Herbert Street; and there the young mother, who was still but twenty-seven, following a custom which made much of widows' mourning in those times, withdrew to a life of seclusion in her own room, which, there or elsewhere, she maintained till her death, through a period of forty years; and, as a perpetual outward sign of her solitude, she took her meals apart, never eating at the common table. There is a touch of mercy in life which allows childhood to reconcile itself with all conditions; else one might regret that the lad was to grow up from his earliest memory in the visible presence of this grief separating him in some measure from his mother's life; it was as if there were a ghost in the house ; and though early anecdotes of him are few and of little significance, yet in his childish threat to go away to sea and never come back again, repeated through years, one can

but trace the deep print of that sorrow of the un-
returning ones which was the tragedy of women's
lives all along this coast. His mother cared for
him none the less, though she was less his companion, and there seems to have been no diminu-
tion of affection and kindness between them,
though an outward habit of coldness sprang up as
time went on. He had his sisters for playmates
at first, and as he grew up, he was much looked
after by his uncles. His first master was Dr.
Worcester, the lexicographer, then just graduated
from Yale, who set up a school in Salem; and,
the lad being lamed in ball-playing, the young
teacher came to the house to carry on the lessons.
The accident happened when Hawthorne was nine
years old, and the injury, which reduced him to
crutches, continued to trouble him till he was
twelve, at least, after which, to judge by the fact
that he attended dancing-school, he seems to have
entirely recovered from it. The habit of reading
came to him earlier, perhaps because of his con-
finement and disability for sports in these three or
four years; he was naturally thrown back upon
himself. He is seen lying upon the floor habitually, and when not playing with cats — the only
boyish fondness told of him — reading Shakspere,
Milton, Thomson, the books of the household, not
uncommon in New England homes, where good
books were as plenty then as all books are now;
and on Sundays, at his grandmother Hathorne's,
across the yard, he would crouch hour after hour

over Bunyan's "Pilgrim's Progress," that refuge
of boyhood on the oldtime Sabbaths.   It is recollected that, by the time he was fourteen, he had
read Clarendon, Froissart, and Rousseau, besides
"The Newgate Calendar," a week-day favorite;
and he may be said to have begun youth already
well versed in good English books, and with the
habit and taste of literary pleasure established as
a natural part of life.   "The Faërie Queene" was
the first book he bought with his own money.   He
was vigorous enough now; but the two outward
circumstances that most affected his boyhood, the
monotone of his mother's sorrow and his own protracted physical disability, must have given him
touches of gravity and delicacy beyond his years.
It is noticeable that nothing is heard of any boy
friends; nor did he contract such friendships, apparently, before college days.

In the fall of 1818, when Hawthorne was fourteen years old, the family removed to Raymond,
in Maine, where the Mannings possessed large
tracts of land.   The site of this township was
originally a grant to the surviving members and
the heirs of Captain Raymond's militia company
of Beverly, the next town to Salem, for service in
the French and Indian war; and Hawthorne's
grandfather, Richard Manning, being the secre-
tary of the proprietors, who managed the property
and held their meetings in Beverly, had toward
the close of the century bought out many of their
rights.   After his death the estate thus acquired

was kept undivided, and was managed for his children by his sons Richard and Robert, and finally at any rate, more particularly by the latter, who stood in the closest relation to Hawthorne of all his uncles, having undertaken to provide for his education. He had built a large, square, hip-roofed house at Raymond, after the model common in his native county of Essex, as a comfortable dwelling, but so seemingly grand amid the humble surroundings of the Maine clearing as to earn the name of "Manning's folly;" and, about 1814, he built a similar house for his sister, near his own, but she had not occupied it until now, when she came to live there, at first boarding with a tenant. It was pleasantly situated, with a garden and apple orchard, and with rows of butternut-trees planted beside it; and perhaps she had sought this retirement with the hope of its being consonant with her own solitude. The country round about was wilderness, most of it primeval woods. The little settlement, only a mill and a country store and a few scattered houses, lay on a broad headland making out into Sebago Lake, better known as the Great Pond, a sheet of water eight miles across and fourteen miles long, and connected with other lakes in a chain of navigable water; to the northwest the distant horizon was filled with the White Mountains, and northward and eastward rose the unfrequented hill and lake country, remarkable only, then as now, for its pure air and waters, and presenting a vast solitude. This was the Maine home of Hawthorne, of which he cherished the memory as the brightest part of his boyhood. The spots that can be named which may have excited his curiosity or interested his imagination are few, and similar places would not be far off anywhere on the coast. There was near his home a Pulpit Rock, such as tradition often preserves, and by the Pond there was a cliff with the usual legend of a romantic leap, and under it were the Indian rock-paintings called the Images; but the essential charm of the place was that in all directions the country lay open for adventure by boat or by trail. Hawthorne had visited the scene before, in summer times, and he revisited it afterward in vacations, but his long stay here was in his fifteenth year, the greater part of which he passed in its neighborhood.

The contemporary record of these days is contained in a diary [1] which has been regarded as Hawthorne's earliest writing. The original has never been produced, and the copy was communicated for publication under circumstances of mystery that easily allow doubts of its authenticity to arise. The diary is said to have been given to him by his uncle Richard "with the advice that he write out his thoughts, some every day, in as good words as he can, upon any and all subjects,

---

[1] Hawthorne's First Diary, with an account of its discovery and loss. By Samuel T. Pickard. Boston: Houghton, Mifflin & Co. 1897. The volume has been withdrawn by its editor in consequence of his later doubts of its authenticity.

as it is one of the best means of his securing for
mature years command of thought and language,"
— these words being written on the first leaf with
the date, " Raymond, June 1, 1816." Whether
this inscription and the entries which follow it are
genuine must be left undetermined; there is nothing
strange in Hawthorne's keeping a boy's diary,
and being urged to do so, in view of his tastes
and circumstances, and it would be interesting to
trace to so early a beginning that habit of the
note-book that was such a resource to him in
mature years ; but the evidence is inconclusive.
Whether by his hand or not, the diary embodies
the life he led in this region on his visits and
during his longer stay; the names and places, the
incidents, the people, the quality of the days are
the same that the boy knew, wrote of in letters of
the time, and remembered as a man; and though
the story may be the fabrication of his mulatto
boy comrade of those days, it is woven of shreds
and patches of reality.   After all, the little book
is but a lad's log of small doings, — swapping
knives, swimming and fishing, of birds and snakes
and bears, incidents of the road and excursions
into the woods and on the lake, and notices of
the tragic accidents of the neighborhood.   It has
some importance as illustrating the external circumstances of the place, a very rural place indeed, and suggesting that among these country
people Hawthorne found the secret of that fellowship — all he ever had — with the rough and

unlearned, on a footing of democratic equality, with the ease and naturalness of a man. Here at Raymond in his youth, where his personal superiority was too much a matter of course to be noticed, he must have learned this freemasonry with young and old at the same time that he held apart from all in his own life. For the rest, he has told himself in his undoubted words how he swam and hunted, shot hen-hawks and partridges, caught trout, and tracked bear in the snow, and ran wild, yet not wholly free of the call-whistle of his master-passion: "I ran quite wild," he wrote a quarter-century later, "and would, I doubt not, have willingly run wild till this time, fishing all day long, or shooting with an old fowling-piece; but reading a good deal, too, on rainy days, especially in Shakespeare and 'The Pilgrim's Progress,' and any poetry or light books within my reach. These were delightful days. . . . I would skate all alone on Sebago Lake, with the deep shadows of the icy hills on either hand. When I found myself far from home, and weary with the exhaustion of skating, I would sometimes take refuge in a log cabin where half a tree would be burning on the broad hearth. I would sit in the ample chimney, and look at the stars through the great aperture through which the flames went roaring up. Ah, how well I recall the summer days, also, when with my gun I roamed at will through the woods of Maine!" In these memories, it is evident,

many years, younger and older, are diffused in
one recollection. For him, here rather than by
his native sea were those open places of freedom
that boyhood loves, and with them he associated
the beginnings of his spirit, — the dark as well as
the bright; near his end he told Fields, as his
mind wandered back to these days, "I lived in
Maine like a bird of the air, so perfect was the
freedom I enjoyed. But it was there I first got
my cursed habits of solitude." The tone of these
reminiscences is verified by his letters, when he
went back to Salem; in the first months he writes
of "very hard fits of homesickness;" a year later
he breaks out, — "Oh, that I had the wings of a
dove, that I might fly hence and be at rest! How
often do I long for my gun, and wish that I could
again savageize with you! But I shall never again
run wild in Raymond, and I shall never be so
happy as when I did;" and, after another year's
interval, "I have preferred and still prefer Raymond to Salem, through every change of fortune."
There can be no doubt where his heart placed the
home of his boyhood; nor is it, perhaps, fanciful
to observe that in his books the love of nature he
displays is rather for the woods than the sea,
though he was never content to live long away
from the salt air.

It was plainly the need of schooling that took
him from his mother's home at Raymond and
brought him back to Salem by the summer of
1819, when he was just fifteen years old. Even

in the winter interval he seems to have gone for
a few weeks to the house of the Rev. Caleb Brad-
ley, Stroudwater, Westbrook, in the same county
as Raymond, to be tutored. He remained in Salem with his uncles for the next two years, and
was prepared for college, partly, at least, by Benjamin Oliver, a lawyer, at the expense of his uncle
Robert, and during a portion of this time he
earned some money by writing in the office of his
uncle William; but he was occupied chiefly with
his studies, reading, and early compositions. At
the beginning of this period, in his first autumn
letters, he mentions having lately read "Waverley," "The Mysteries of Udolpho," "The Adventures of Ferdinand Count Fathom," "Roderick
Random," and a volume of "The Arabian Nights;"
and he has learned the easy rhyming of first verses,
and stuffs his letters with specimens of his skill,
clever stanzas, well written, modulated in the ca-
dences of the time, with melancholy seriousness
and such play of sad fancy as youthful poets use.
He laid little store by his faculty for verse, and
yet he had practiced it from an early childish age
and had a fair mastery of its simple forms; and
once or twice in mature life he indulged himself
in writing and even in publishing serious poems.
In these years, however, verses were only a part
of the ferment of his literary talent, nor have any
of them individuality. He practiced prose, too,
and in the next summer, 1820, issued four numbers of a boy's paper, "The Spectator," bearing

weekly date from August 21 to September 18, and
apparently he had made an earlier experiment,
without date, in such adolescent journalism; it was
printed with a pen on small note-paper, and contained such serious matter as belongs to themes
at school on "Solitude" and "Industry," with the
usual addresses to subscribers and the liveliness
natural to family news-columns. The composition
is smooth and the manner entertaining, and there
is abundance of good spirits and fun of a boyish
sort. The paper shows the literary spirit and taste
in its very earliest bud; but no precocity of talent
distinguished it, though doubtless the thought of
authorship fed on its tender leaves. Such experiments belong to the life of growing boys where
education is common and literary facility is thought
to be a distinction and sign of promise in the
young; and Hawthorne did not in these ways differ
from the normal boy who was destined for college. Nothing more than these trifles is to be
gleaned of his intellectual life at that time, but
two or three letters pleasantly illustrate his bro-
therly feeling, his spirits, and his uncertainties in
regard to the future, at the same time that they
display his absorption in the author's craft; and
they conclude the narrative of these early days
before college. The first was written in October,
1820, just after the last issue of "The Spectator,"
to his younger sister Louisa, and shows incidentally that these literary pleasures were a family
diversion: —

DEAR SISTER, — I am very angry with you for not sending me some of your poetry, which I consider a great piece of ingratitude. You will not see one line of mine until you return the confidence which I have placed in you. I have bought the "Lord of the Isles," and intend either to send or to bring it to you. I like it as well as any of Scott's other poems. I have read Hogg's "Tales," "Caleb Williams," "St. Leon," and "Mandeville." I admire Godwin's novels, and intend to read them all. I shall read the "Abbot," by the author of "Waverley," as soon as I can hire it. I have read all Scott's novels except that. I wish I had not, that I might have the pleasure of reading them again. Next to these I like "Caleb Williams." I have almost given up writing poetry. No man can be a Poet and a bookkeeper at the same time. I do find this place most "dismal," and have taken to chewing tobacco with all my might, which, I think, raises my spirits. Say nothing of it in your letters, nor of the "Lord of the Isles." . . . I do not think I shall ever go to college. I can scarcely bear the thought of living upon Uncle Robert for four years longer. How happy I should be to be able to say, "I am Lord of myself!" You may cut off this part of my letter, and show the other to Uncle Richard. Do write me some letters in skimmed milk. I must conclude, as I am in a "monstrous hurry"!

Your affectionate brother,

NATH. HATHORNE.

P. S. The most beautiful poetry I think I ever saw begins: —

> "She's gone to dwell in Heaven, my lassie,
> She's gone to dwell in Heaven:
> Ye 're ow're pure quo' a voice aboon
> For dwalling out of Heaven."

It is not the words, but the thoughts. I hope you have read it, as I know you would admire it.

A passage from a second letter, six months later, March 13, 1821, to his mother, reveals the character of his relationship with her: —

I don't read so much now as I did, because I am more taken up in studying. I am quite reconciled to going to college, since I am to spend the vacations with you. Yet four years of the best part of my life is a great deal to throw away. I have not yet concluded what profession I shall have. The being a minister is of course out of the question. I should not think that even you could desire me to choose so dull a way of life. Oh, no, mother, I was not born to vegetate forever in one place, and to live and die as calm and tranquil as — a puddle of water. As to lawyers, there are so many of them already that one half of them (upon a moderate calculation) are in a state of actual starvation. A physician, then, seems to be "Hobson's choice;" but yet I should not like to live by the diseases and infirmities of my fellow-creatures. And it would weigh very heavily on my conscience, in the course of my practice, if I should chance to send any unlucky patient "ad inferum," which being interpreted is, "to the realms below." Oh that I was rich enough to live without a profession! What do you think of my becoming an author, and relying for support upon my pen? Indeed, I think the illegibility of my handwriting is very author-like. How proud you would feel to see my works praised by the reviewers, as equal to the proudest productions of the scribbling sons of John Bull! But authors are always poor devils, and therefore Satan may take them. I am in the same predicament as the honest gentleman in "Espriella's Letters:" —

"I am an Englishman, and naked I stand here,
    A-musing in my mind what garment I shall wear."

But as the mail closes soon, I must stop the career of my pen. I will only inform you that I now write no poetry, or anything else. I hope that either Elizabeth or you will write to me next week. I remain

Your affectionate son,
NATHL. HATHORNE.

Do not show this letter.

A third letter, June 19, 1821, also to his mother, on the eve of his departure for college, is interesting for the solicitude it exhibits for her happiness in the solitary life she had come to live.

"I hope, dear mother, that you will not be tempted by my entreaties to return to Salem to

live. You can never have so much comfort here
as you now enjoy. You are now undisputed mis-
tress of your own house. . . . If you remove to
Salem, I shall have no mother to return to during
the college vacations, and the expense will be too
great for me to come to Salem. If you remain at
Raymond, think how delightfully the time will
pass, with all your children round you, shut out
from the world, and nothing to disturb us. It
will be a second Garden of Eden.

> ' Lo, what an entertaining sight
> Are kindred who agree ! '

Elizabeth is as anxious for you to stay as myself.
She says she is contented to remain here for a
short time, but greatly prefers Raymond as a permanent place of residence. The reason for my
saying so much on this subject is that Mrs. Dike
and Miss Manning are very earnest for you to return to Salem, and I am afraid they will commis-
sion uncle Robert to persuade you to it. But,
mother, if you wish to live in peace, I conjure
you not to consent to it. Grandmother, I think,
is rather in favor of your staying."

A few weeks later, in the summer of 1821, being then seventeen years old, Hawthorne left Salem
for Bowdoin College, in Brunswick, Maine, by
the mail stage from Boston eastward, and before
reaching his destination picked up by the way a
Sophomore, Franklin Pierce, afterwards President
of the United States, and two classmates of his
own, Jonathan Cilley, who went to Congress and

was the victim of the well-remembered political
duel with Graves, and Alfred Mason; he made
friends with these new companions, and Mason
became his room-mate for two years. Bowdoin
was a small college, graduating at that time about
thirty students at its annual Commencement; its
professors were kindly and cultivated men, and its
curriculum the simple academic course of those
days. Hawthorne's class, immortalized fifty years
later by Longfellow's grave and tender anniver-
sary lines, "Morituri Salutamus," was destined
to unusual distinction in after life. Longfellow,
its scholastic star, was a boy of fourteen, favored
by the regard of the professors, and belonging to
the more studious and steady set of fellows, who
gathered in the Peucinian Society. Hawthorne
joined the rival organization, the Athenæum, a
more free and boisterous group of lower standing
in their studies, described as the more democratic
in their feelings. He is remembered as "a slender lad, having a massive head, with dark, brilliant, and most expressive eyes, heavy eyebrows,
and a profusion of dark hair." He carried his
head on one side, which gave a singularity to his
figure, and he had generally a countrified appearance; but he took his place among his mates without much observation. He was reticent in speech
and reserved in manner, and he was averse to intimacy; he had, nevertheless, a full share in col-
legiate life and showed no signs of withdrawal
from the common arena. He did not indulge in

sports, saving some rough-and-tumble play, nor did he ride horseback or drive, nor apparently did he care for that side of youthful life at all, though he was willing to fight on occasion, and joined the military company of which Pierce was captain. His athleticism seems to have been confined to his form. He played cards for small stakes, being a member of the Androscoggin Loo Club, and he took his part in the convivial drinking of the set where he made one, winning the repute of possessing a strong head. These indulgences were almost too trifling to deserve mention, for the scale of life at Bowdoin was of the most inexpensive order, and though there was light gambling and occasional jollification, bad habits were practically impossible in these directions. He was certainly not ashamed of his doings, for on being detected in one of these scrapes, at the end of his Freshman year, anticipating a letter of the President, he wrote to his mother, May 30, 1822, an account of the affair: —

MY DEAR MOTHER, — I hope you have safely arrived in Salem. I have nothing particular to inform you of, except that all the card-players in college have been found out, and my unfortunate self among the number. One has been dismissed from college, two suspended, and the rest, with myself, have been fined fifty cents each. I believe the President intends to write to the friends of all the delinquents. Should that be the case, you

must show the letter to nobody. If I am again
detected, I shall have the honor of being suspended; when the President asked what we played
for, I thought it proper to inform him it was fifty
cents, although it happened to be a quart of wine;
but if I had told him of that, he would probably
have fined me for having a blow. There was no
untruth in the case, as the wine cost fifty cents.
I have not played at all this term. I have not
drank any kind of spirits or wine this term, and
shall not till the last week.

He takes up the subject again in a letter to one
of his sisters, August 5, 1822: —

"To quiet your suspicions, I can assure you
that I am neither ' dead, absconded, or anything
worse.' I have involved myself in no ' foolish
scrape,' as you say all my friends suppose ; but
ever since my misfortune I have been as steady as
a sign-post, and as sober as a deacon, have been
in no ' blows ' this term, nor drank any kind of
' wine or strong drink.' So that your comparison
of me to the ' prodigious son ' will hold good in
nothing, except that I shall probably return penniless, for I have had no money this six weeks.
. . . The President's message is not so severe as
I expected. I perceive that he thinks I have been
led away by the wicked ones, in which, however,
he is greatly mistaken. I was full as willing to
play as the person he suspects of having enticed
me, and would have been influenced by no one.

I have a great mind to commence playing again, merely to show him that I scorn to be seduced by another into anything wrong."

The last week of the term and the close of the Senior year appear to have been the seasons of conviviality, and Hawthorne's life of this sort ended with his being an officer of the Navy Club, an impromptu association of those of his classmates, fourteen out of thirty-eight, who for one reason or another were not to have a Commencement part on graduation. The Club met at the college tavern, Miss Ward's, near the campus, for weekly suppers and every night during Commencement week; this entertainment was for these youths the happy climax of their academic life together.

In his studies Hawthorne must have followed his own will very freely. He refused to declaim, and no power could make him do so, and for this reason he was denied the honor of a Commencement part, which he had won, being number eighteen by rank in his class; he was nervously shy about declaiming, owing, it is said, to his having been laughed at on his first attempt as a school-boy at Salem; but he either delivered or read a Latin theme at a Junior exhibition. He also paid scant attention to mathematics and metaphysics, and had no pride as to failing in recitation in those branches; but he distinguished himself as a Latin scholar and in English. His most fruitful hours, as so often happens, were those spent in the little library of the Athenæum Society, a collection, as he writes home, of eight hundred books, among which he especially mentions Rees's Cyclopædia — such was the wealth of a boy of genius in those days — but among the eight hundred books it is certain that the bulk of English literature was contained. He practiced writing somewhat, though he had given up poetry; and he played a prank by sending to a Boston paper a fabricated account of one of those destroying insects which visit that region from time to time, with notes on ways of exterminating it, — all for the benefit of his uncle, who took the paper; but no other trace of his composition remains except a memory of his elder sister's that he wrote to her of "progress on my novel." His way of life intellectually had not changed since his schoolboy days, for it is noticeable that then he never mentioned his studies, but only the books he read; so now he read the books for pleasure, and let his studies subsist as best they could in the realm of duty. He was poor, and even in the modest simplicity of this country college, where his expenses could hardly have been three hundred dollars a year, was evidently embarrassed with homely difficulties; the state of his clothes seems to have been on his mind a good deal. But he was self-respecting, patient, and grateful; he formed the good habit of hating debt; and he went on his way little burdened except by doubtful hopes.

Though he was familiar with his classmates and contemporaries at college, and firm and fast

friends with a few, like Pierce and Cilley, forming
with them the ties that last through all things, he
had but one confidant, Horatio Bridge, afterwards
of the United States Navy. Hawthorne roomed at
first with Alfred Mason, in Maine Hall, and being
burned out in their Freshman year, they found
temporary quarters elsewhere, but when the Hall
was rebuilt returned to it and occupied room number nineteen for the Sophomore year. The two
chums, however, did not become intimate, beyond
pleasant companionship, and they belonged to different societies; and the last two years Hawthorne
roomed alone in a private house, Mrs. Dunning's,
where both he and Bridge also boarded. It is
from the latter, who remained through life one of
Hawthorne's most serviceable friends, that the account of his college days mainly comes. He especially remembered, besides such matters of fact
as have been recounted, their walks and rambles
together in the pine woods that stretched about
the college unbroken for miles, and by the river
with its rafts of spring logs, and over to the little
bay sent up by a far-reaching arm of the sea; and
he recalled the confidences of Hawthorne in speaking of his hopes of being a writer, in repeating to
him verses as they leaned in the moonlight over
the railing of the bridge below the falls, listening
to the moving waters, and in allowing him some
inward glimpses of his solitary life in the brooding time of youth. Bridge was a fellow of infinite
cheer, and praised him, and clapped him, and

urged him on, and gave him the best companionship in the world for that time of life, if not for all times, — the companionship of being believed in by a friend. Hawthorne did not forget it, and in due time paid the tribute of grateful remembrance in the preface to the volume he dedicated to Bridge, where he recalled his college days and his friend's part in them.

"If anybody is responsible for my being at this day an author, it is yourself. I know not whence your faith came, but while we were lads together at a country college, gathering blueberries in study hours under those tall, academic pines, or watching the great logs as they tumbled along the current of the Androscoggin, or shooting pigeons or gray squirrels in the woods, or bat-fowling in the summer twilight, or catching trout in that shadowy little stream which, I suppose, is still wandering riverward through the forest, though you and I will never cast a line in it again; two idle lads, in short (as we need not fear to acknowledge now), doing a hundred things that the Faculty never heard of, or else it would have been the worse for us — still, it was your prognostic of your friend's destiny that he was to be a writer of fiction."

The picture is a vignette of the time, and being in the open, too, pleasantly ends the tale of college. On separating, it is pleasant to notice, the friends exchanged keepsakes.

The four years had lapsed quietly and quickly

by, and Hawthorne, who now adopted the fanciful spelling of the name after his personal whim, was man grown. There had been trying circumstances in these early days, but he had met them hardily and lightly, as a matter of course; he had practically educated himself by the help of books, and had also discharged his duties as they seemed to the eyes of others; he could go home feeling that he had satisfied his friends. He seems to have feared that he might have satisfied them too well; and, some commendation having preceded him, he endeavored to put them right by a letter to his sister, July 14, 1825: —

"The family had before conceived much too high an opinion of my talents, and had probably formed expectations which I shall never realize. I have thought much upon the subject, and have finally come to the conclusion that I shall never make a distinguished figure in the world, and all I hope or wish is to plod along with the multitude. I do not say this for the purpose of drawing any flattery from you, but merely to set mother and the rest of you right upon a point where your partiality has led you astray. I did hope that uncle Robert's opinion of me was nearer to the truth, as his deportment toward me never expressed a very high estimation of my abilities."

This has the ring of sincerity, like all his home letters, and it is true that so far there had been nothing precocious, brilliant, or extraordinary in him to testify of genius, — he was only one of hundreds of New England boys bred on literature under the shelter of academic culture; and yet there may have been in his heart something left unspoken, another mood equally sincere in its turn, for the heart is a fickle prophet. As Mr. Lathrop suggests in that study of his father-in-law which is so subtly appreciative of those vital suggestions apt to escape record and analysis, another part of the truth may lie in the words of "Fanshawe" where Hawthorne expresses the feelings of his hero in a like situation with himself at the end of college days: —

"He called up the years that, even at his early age, he had spent in solitary study, — in conversation with the dead, — while he had scorned to mingle with the living world, or to be actuated by any of its motives. Fanshawe had hitherto deemed himself unconnected with the world, unconcerned in its feelings, and uninfluenced by it in any of his pursuits. In this respect he probably deceived himself. If his inmost heart could have been laid open, there would have been discovered that dream of undying fame, which, dream as it is, is more powerful than a thousand realities."

II.

THE CHAMBER UNDER THE EAVES.

In the summer of 1825 Hawthorne returned to Salem, going back to the old house on Herbert Street, — the home of his childhood, where his mother, disregarding his boyish dissuasions, had again taken up her abode three years before. He occupied a room on the second floor in the southwest sunshine under the eaves, looking out on the business of the wharf-streets; and in it he spent the next twelve years, a period which remained in his memory as an unbroken tract of time preserving a peculiar character. The way of his life knew little variation from the beginning to the end. He lived in an intellectual solitude deepened by the fact that it was only an inner cell of an outward seclusion almost as complete, for the house had the habits of a hermitage. His mother, after nearly a score of years of widowhood, still maintained her separation even from her home world; she is said to have seen none of her husband's relatives and few of her own, and a visitor must have been a venturesome person. The custom of living apart spread through the household. The elder sister, Elizabeth, who was of a strong

and active mind capable of understanding and
sympathizing with her brother, and the younger
sister, Louisa, who was more like other people,
stayed in their rooms. The meals of the family, even, which usually go on when everything
else fails in the common life of house-mates,
had an uncertain and variable element in their
conduct, as was not unnatural where the mother
never came to the table. The recluse habits of all
doubtless increased with indulgence, and after a
while Hawthorne himself, who was plainly the centre of interest there, fell into the common ways of
isolation. "He had little communication," writes
Mr. Lathrop, "with even the members of his family.
Frequently his meals were brought and left at his
locked door, and it was not often that the four inmates of the old Herbert Street mansion met in
family circle. He never read his stories aloud to
his mother and sisters, as might be imagined from
the picture which Mr. Fields draws of the young
author reciting his new productions to his listening family; though, when they met, he sometimes
read older literature to them. It was the custom
in this household for the several members to remain very much by themselves; the three ladies
were perhaps nearly as rigorous recluses as himself; and, speaking of the isolation which reigned
among them, Hawthorne once said, ' We do not
even *live* at our house! ' " He seldom went out by
day, unless for long excursions in the country; an
early sea bath on summer mornings and a dark

walk after supper, longer in the warm weather, shorter in the winter season, were habitual, and a bowl of thick chocolate with bread crumbed into it, or a plate of fruit, on his return prepared him for the night's work. Study in the morning, composition in the afternoon, and reading in the evening, are described as his routine, but it is unlikely that any such regularity ruled where times and seasons were so much at his own command. He had no visitors and made no friends; hardly twenty persons in the town, he thought, were aware of his existence; but he brought home hundreds of volumes from the Salem Athenæum, and knew the paths of the woods and pastures and the way along the beaches and rocky points, and he had the stuff of his fantasy with which to occupy himself when nature and books failed to satisfy him. At first there must have been great pleasure in being at home, for he had not really lived a home life since he was fifteen years old, and he was fond of home; and, too, in the young ambition to become a writer and his efforts to achieve success, if not fame, in fiction, and in the first motions of his creative genius, there was enough to fill his mind, to provide him with active interest and occupation, and to abate the sense of loneliness in his daily circumstances; but as youth passed and manhood came, and yet fortune lagged with her gifts, this existence became insufficient for him, — it grew burdensome as it showed barren, and depression set in upon him like a chill and obscure fog over the marshes where he walked. This, however, year dragging after year, was a slow process; and the kind of life he led, its gray and deadening monotone, sympathetic though it was with his temperament, was seen by him better in retrospect than in its own time.

It is singular that Hawthorne should have undertaken to live by his pen, or been allowed to do so by his friends, as a practical way of life, but he was indulged at home, the young lord of the family. "We were in those days," says Elizabeth, "almost absolutely obedient to him." Occasionally he thought of going into his uncle's counting-room and so obtaining a business and place in the world, but he never took this step. He probably drifted, more or less, into authorship, partly through a dilatory reluctance to do anything else, and partly led on by the hope of a success with some one of his tales which would justify him.

The first attempts he made in the craft are involved in some obscurity. He may have merely carried over from college days what he then had in hand. At all events his sister Elizabeth, from whom the information comes in respect to these details, remembered a little collection which he had prepared for publication with the title "Seven Tales of my Native Land," and she says that she read it in the summer of 1825; in that case these stories must have been written at college, but her memory may have erred. She gives the names of

two of them as "Alice Doane" and "Susan Grey,"
and adds that he told her, while the volume was
still in the stage of being offered to publishers,
that he would first "write a story which would
make a smaller book, and get it published immediately if possible, before the arrangements for
bringing out the ' Tales ' were completed." This
was presumably "Fanshawe," which may also have
been the novel she recollected his writing to her
about while at college.

"Fanshawe "[1] was published in 1828 by Marsh
and Capen, at Boston, without the author's name
but at his expense, one hundred dollars being the
sum paid; it failed, and Hawthorne looked on it
with so much subsequent displeasure that he called
in all the copies he could find and destroyed them,
and thus nearly succeeded in sinking the book in
oblivion, but the few copies which survived secured
its republication after his death. The novel is
brief, with a melodramatic plot, well-marked scenes,
and strongly contrasted character; the style flows
on pleasantly; but the book is without distinction.
Like many a just graduated collegian, Hawthorne
had recourse to his academic experience in lieu of
anything else, and in the setting of the story and
some of its delineation of character Longfellow
recognized the strong suggestion of Bowdoin days;
in the same way the hero, Fanshawe, borrowed
something from Hawthorne's own temperament.

[1] *Fanshawe.* A Tale. Boston: Marsh & Capen, 362 Washington St. Press of Putnam and Hunt, 1828. 12mo. Pp. 141

The figure of the villain, too, adumbrates, though faintly, the type which engaged Hawthorne's mind in later years. "Fanshawe" as a whole in all its scenes, whether in the house of the old President, the tavern, the hut, or the outdoor encounters of the lovers and rivals, is strongly reminiscent of Scott, the management being entirely in his manner; its low-life tragedy, its romantic scenery, and its bookish humor, as well as the characterization in general, are also from Scott; in fact, notwithstanding what Hawthorne had taken from his own observation and feelings, this provincial sketch, for it is no more, is a Scott story, done with a young man's clever mastery of the manner, but weak internally in plot, character, and dramatic reality. It is as destitute of any brilliant markings of his genius as his undergraduate life itself had been, and is important only as showing the serious care with which he undertook the task of authorship. It is the only relic, except the shadowy "Seven Tales," of his literary work in the first three years after leaving college. The "Tales" he is said to have burned; no better publisher appearing, a young Salem printer, Ferdinand Andrews, undertook to bring them out, but as he delayed the matter through lack of capital, Hawthorne, growing impatient and exasperated, recalled the manuscript and destroyed it.

The example of Scott was, perhaps, the potent influence in fixing Hawthorne's attention on a definite object, and incited him to seek in the history of his own country, and especially in the colonial tradition of New England, which was so near at hand, the field of fiction. He stored his mind, certainly, with the story of his own people during the two centuries since the settlement, and prepared himself to describe its stirring events and striking characters under the veil of imaginative history. The nature of his reading shows that this was a conscious aim; and, besides, it was an opinion, loudly proclaimed and widely shared in that decade, that American writers should look to their own country for their themes; Cooper was doing so in fiction, and Longfellow felt this predilection in his choice of subject for verse. Salem was a true centre of the old times; and a young imagination in that town and neighborhood, already disposed to writing prose romance, would feel the charm of historical association and naturally catch impulse from the past, especially if, as in the case of Hawthorne, the history of his ancestors was inwoven with its good and evil. It is not surprising therefore that, as Hawthorne had begun, though unsuccessfully, with tales of his native land, he should continue to work the vein; and, to adopt what seems to be a reasonable inference, he now gathered from his materials a new series which he knew as "Provincial Tales," in which it remains doubtful how much of the old survived, for the burnt manuscripts of youth have something of the phœnix in their ashes.

The first trace of these is "The Young Pro-

vincial," an anonymous piece,[1] ascribed to him on
internal evidence and contributed to "The Token,"
an annual published at Boston, for its issue of
1830. The story relates the adventures of a
youthful Revolutionary soldier who had handed
down to his descendants a "grandfather's gun; "
it tells of Bunker Hill, of imprisonment at
Halifax and of escape, and it may be from Hawthorne's pen. It must have been written early in
1829, if not before, and it is noticed in the review
of "The Token " in Willis's Boston periodical,
"The American Monthly Magazine " for September, 1829, where it is described as a "pleasing
story, told quite inartificially," and is illustrated
by a brief extract. It may not be irrelevant to

[1] It is unquestionable that Hawthorne contributed to annuals
and periodicals anonymous tales and sketches that he never
claimed, as he states in the preface to *Twice-Told Tales* and
in a letter to Fields in which he beseeches him not to revive them.
The identification of such work, however, is beset with much
temptation to find a tale genuine, if it can be plausibly so represented, and in few cases can the proof be conclusive. Mr. F. B.
Sanborn presents the fullest list, all from *The Token*, which he accepts as genuine, as follows : *The Adventures of a Raindrop*, 1828,
The Young Provincial, 1830, *The Haunted Quack* and *The New
England Village*, 1831, *My Wife's Novel*, 1832, *The Bald Eagle*,
1833, *The Modern Job*, or *The Philosopher's Stone*, 1834. The
correspondence with Goodrich does not indicate that Hawthorne
contributed to *The Token* before the issue for 1831. *The Young
Provincial* seems to be the same sort of a tale as *The Downer's
Banner*, as has been intimated above: yet it would, perhaps, be
more readily accepted, together with *The Haunted Quack* and
The Modern Job. The latest edition of Hawthorne includes all
of these tales, given above, except the first and last, but its
editor does not vouch for their authenticity.

observe that a similar "provincial tale" appeared
in this number of the magazine, "The Downer's
Banner," and if it was not by the same youthful
author, it shows that the same kind of subject
had singularly interested two writers in that neighborhood. It is, however, only in "The Token"
that Hawthorne can be further traced.

The editor of this annual, which was intended
as a literary gift-book for Christmas, was S. G.
Goodrich, famous as "Peter Parley" in after days,
and to him belongs the honor of being Hawthorne's
first literary friend, and he always remained a
faithful one. He was a promoter of publishers'
enterprises, in that part of the field of literature
which is distinctly pervaded with business; and in
it he was successful, as the millions of the Peter
Parley books abundantly attest. At this time he
was sincerely interested, it must be believed, in
furthering the interests of American writers and
artists, according to his lights and means, and
Griswold, who was a good judge, said of him, "It
is questionable whether any other person has done
as much to improve the style of the book manufac-
ture or to promote the arts of engraving." With
such ambitions he had begun, in 1828, the issue
of the annual, which is now best remembered, and
which in its own day longest survived the changes
of public taste. The nature of these volumes, of
which there were many in different publishing
centres, is well described by a writer in Willis's
"Magazine" for 1829: "A few years ago, an ele-

gant taste, joined, perhaps, to a love of 'filthy
lucre,' induced some English publishers to give to
the world the first specimens of those souvenirs and
'Forget Me Nots' which are now so common
through our country. How beautiful they were at
their first appearance, the eagerness with which
they were read will testify. How rapid was their
increase, may be seen by referring to the counters
of every book-store. America, ready and willing
as she ever is to acknowledge the excellence, and
imitate the example of the parent country in every
good thing, has imitated and improved upon the
plan. We can now boast of a species of literature, which is conducted almost wholly by young
men, and which has merited the affection, because
it has developed the power of our native genius.
Those who have made their first essays in literature, through the medium of the pages of a Souvenir, will gain confidence in proportion as they
have tested their own strength. The American
annuals do not profess to be the works of the most
finished or most accomplished writers of this country. They should not be taken as specimens of
what our literature is, but as indications of what
it may one day be. They are not the matured
fruits, but the bright promise and blossoming of
genius; and thus far they have been an honor to
the taste and talent of American writers, and
monuments of the swift progress of our artists
towards excellence in their profession.''

Such was the contemporary view of the annuals,

and it is justified, perhaps, by the fact that Long-fellow, for example, was then contributing to the "Atlantic Souvenir" of Philadelphia, the first of the brood, and that Hawthorne found in "The Token" the principal opportunity to obtain a hearing for himself in his first productive years.

Mr. Goodrich, in his "Recollections," states that he sought out Hawthorne. "I had seen," he says, "some anonymous publications which seemed to me to indicate extraordinary powers. I inquired of the publishers as to the writer, and through them a correspondence ensued between me and 'N. Hawthorne.' This name I considered a disguise, and it was not till after many letters had passed, that I met the author, and found it to be a true title, representing a very substantial personage." This correspondence began, as nearly as can be judged, in 1829, and in the course of it Hawthorne had already sent to Goodrich "The Young Provincial," if that is to be accepted as by him, and also "Roger Malvin's Burial," and, apparently later than this last, at least three other tales, "The Gentle Boy," "My Uncle Molineaux," and "Alice Doane." He had presented these as specimens of the "Provincial Tales," for which he desired a publisher. Goodrich acknowledges these, January 19, 1830, from Hartford, Connecticut, where he lived, and promises in the note to endeavor to find a publisher for the book when he returns to Boston in April. He adds, "Had 'Fanshawe' been in the hands of more extensive

dealers, I do believe it would have paid you a
profit;" from which it may be inferred that "Fanshawe" was the anonymous work which had attracted Goodrich's attention.   He praises the
tales, and offers thirty-five dollars for "The Gentle Boy" to be used in "The Token."   The first
letter from Hawthorne, in respect to the matter,
which has come to light, is on May 6, 1830, and
is given in Derby's "Fifty Years."

"I send you the two pieces for ' The Token.'
They were ready some days ago, but I kept them
in expectation of hearing from you.   I have com-
plied with your wishes in regard to brevity.   You
can insert them (if you think them worthy a place
in your publication) as by the author of ' Provincial Tales,' — such being the title I propose giving my volume.   I can conceive no objection to
your designating them in this manner, even if my
tales should not be published as soon as ' The
Token,' or, indeed, if they never see the light at
all.   An unpublished book is not more obscure
than many that creep into the world, and your
readers will suppose that the ' Provincial Tales '
are among the latter."   The "two pieces" to
which he refers were clearly not members of the
series he proposed to publish in the book, and
perhaps they should be identified as "Sights from
a Steeple," certainly, and for the other either
"The New England Village" or "The Haunted
Quack," both which, besides the first, were published in "The Token" for 1831, and have been

ascribed to Hawthorne on internal evidence of the same sort as that on which "The Young Provincial" has been accepted.

Goodrich did not find a publisher for the "Provincial Tales," and Hawthorne allowed him to use such as he desired for "The Token" for 1832. The publication of this annual, it should be observed, was prepared for early in the preceding year, and the tales which it contained must be regarded as at least a year old when issued. Thus, in respect to the issue for 1832, just mentioned, Goodrich writes May 31, 1831: "I have made a very liberal use of the privilege you gave me as to the insertion of your pieces in 'The Token.' I have already inserted four of them; namely, 'The Wives of the Dead,' 'Roger Malvin's Burial,' 'Major Molineaux,' and 'The Gentle Boy;'" and he adds that they are as good if not better than anything else he gets; and in a later note, written on the publication of the volume, in October, he says, "I am gratified to find that all whose opinion I have heard agree with me as to the merit of the various pieces from your pen." In this issue, besides the four mentioned, the story "My Wife's Novel" has also been attributed to Hawthorne.

The project of the "Provincial Tales" had by this time been abandoned, temporarily at least, and the author's mind turned to other kinds of writing. He had already opened new veins in attempting to sketch contemporary scenes, either after the fashion of the pleasant meditative essay, such as "Sights from a Steeple," or else in the way of humorous description. The scenes he looked down on, in fancy, in this first paper, were the roof-tops and streets and horizon of Salem; but he had wandered in other parts of his native land also, though not widely, and he used these journeys in his compositions. It is noticeable that Hawthorne always used all his material, consumed it, and made stories, essays, and novels of it, except the slag. It was his characteristic from youth. There is the same dubiousness about these journeys, his earliest ventures in the world, as about his first attempts in the field of authorship. He himself says, in the autobiographical notes he furnished to Stoddard, that he left Salem "once a year or thereabouts," for a few weeks; and in his sketches there are traces of these excursions, as at Martha's Vineyard, for example; but their times and localities are verifiable only to a slight degree. It is stated that the fact that his uncles, the Mannings, were interested in stage-lines gave him some privileges as a traveler, or perhaps this only gave occasion for a journey now and then, in which he joined his uncles on some convenient business; thus, it was in company with his uncle Samuel, that he was in New Hampshire in 1831, and visited the Shaker community at Canterbury. Another known journey was in 1830, and took him through Connecticut; and it is said, probably on conjecture, that it was at this time that he went

on, by the canal, to Niagara, and visited Ticonderoga on his return. If his writings, in which he
described these places, are to be taken literally,
he even embarked for Detroit; but information in
respect to the whole Niagara excursion is of the
scantiest. All that is known is that in some way,
during his long stay at Salem in these years, he
made himself acquainted with portions of Connecticut, Vermont, New York, and New Hampshire,
to add to his knowledge of Massachusetts and
Maine; within this rather limited circle his wanderings were confined; and the period when he
went about with most freedom and vivacity of impression was the summer of 1830 and, perhaps,
the next year or two.

These experiences gave him the suggestion and
in part the scene of his next compositions, "The
Canterbury Pilgrims" and "The Seven Vagabonds," the one a New Hampshire, the other a
Connecticut tale, and in Connecticut, too, is laid
"The Bald Eagle," a humorous sketch of a reception of Lafayette which failed to come off, attributed to Hawthorne on the same grounds as the
other doubtful pieces of these years; these three
appeared in "The Token" for 1833, "The Seven
Vagabonds" as by the author of "The Gentle
Boy," the others anonymously, and, in addition,
that issue also contained the historical sketch,
"Sir William Pepperell," described as by the author of "Sights from a Steeple." If "The Haunted
Quack," which had already appeared in 1831, be

regarded as Hawthorne's, the journey by the canal which it records must have taken place as early as 1829, in order for the manuscript to have been ready in time for publication. The particular times and stories, however, are of less importance; nor are these provincial travels noteworthy except for the fact that Hawthorne found in them, whenever or wherever they occurred, suggestions for his pen.

The idea which was the germ of his next conception for a book arose out of this country rambling before the days of railroads. At the end of "The Seven Vagabonds," he represented himself as taking up the character of an itinerant story-teller on the impulse of the moment. To this he now returned, and proposed to write a series of tales on the thread of the adventures of this vagrant, and call it "The Story-Teller." The work, such as he here conceived it,.exists only as a fragment, "Passages from a Relinquished Work," though he doubtless used elsewhere the stories he intended to incorporate into it. In the young man as he is sketched in the opening passage there is, notwithstanding the affectation of levity, a touch of Hawthorne's own position: —

"I was a youth of gay and happy temperament, with an incorrigible levity of spirit, of no vicious propensities, sensible enough, but wayward and fanciful. What a character was this, to be brought in contact ·with the stern old Pilgrim spirit of my guardian! We were at variance on a thousand points; but our chief and final dispute arose from the pertinacity with which he insisted on my adopting a particular profession; while I, being heir to a moderate competence, had avowed my purpose of keeping aloof from the regular business of life.   This would have been a dangerous resolution, anywhere in the world; it was fatal, in New England.   There is a grossness in the conceptions of my countrymen; they will not be convinced that any good thing may consist with what they call idleness; they can anticipate nothing but evil of a young man who neither studies physic, law, nor gospel, nor opens a store, nor takes to farming, but manifests an incomprehensible disposition to be satisfied with what his father left him.   The principle is excellent, in its general influence, but most miserable in its effect on the few that violate it.   I had a quick sensitiveness to public opinion, and felt as if it ranked me with the tavern-haunters and town-paupers, — with the drunken poet, who hawked his own Fourth of July odes, and the broken soldier who had been good for nothing since the last war. The consequence of all this was a piece of light-hearted desperation."

The youth then takes up the character of the writer of "The Seven Vagabonds," saying, "The idea of becoming a wandering story-teller had been suggested, a year or two before, by an encounter with several merry vagabonds in a showman's wagon, where they and I had sheltered ourselves, during a summer shower;" and he announces that he determined to follow that life, the account of which he proceeds to give with this preliminary word of explanation: —

"The following pages will contain a picture of my vagrant life, intermixed with specimens, generally brief and slight, of that great mass of fiction to which I gave existence, and which has vanished like cloud-shapes. Besides the occasions when I sought a pecuniary reward, I was accustomed to exercise my narrative faculty, wherever chance had collected a little audience, idle enough to listen. These rehearsals were useful in testing the strong points of my stories; and, indeed, the flow of fancy soon came upon me so abundantly, that its indulgence was its own reward; though the hope of praise, also, became a powerful incitement. Since I shall never feel the warm gush of new thought, as I did then, let me beseech the reader to believe, that my tales were not always so cold as he may find them now. With each specimen will be given a sketch of the circumstances in which the story was told. Thus my air-drawn pictures will be set in frames, perhaps more valuable than the pictures themselves, since they will be embossed with groups of characteristic figures, amid the lake and mountain scenery, the villages and fertile fields, of our native land. But I write the book for the sake of its moral, which many a dreaming youth may profit by, though it is the experience of a wandering story-teller."

He makes the acquaintance of another itinerant, a preacher, Eliakim Abbott, drawn after the fashion of that crude grotesque which is found in Hawthorne's early work, and is not without a reminiscence of Scott in the literary handling; and the two become fellows of the road, the one with a sermon, the other with a story, and their fortune with their audiences is related.   The only adventure of note, however, is the appearance of the Story-Teller as an attraction of a traveling theatrical company, by special engagement, announced by posters, which also bear on a pasted slip of paper a notice of Eliakim Abbott's religious meeting. On this occasion he recited with great applause the tale of "Mr. Higginbotham's Catastrophe." With this the fragment ends.

It is plain that Hawthorne intended by this scheme to unite with his stories sketches of country life and scenes as he had noticed their features in his wayside travels, and use the latter as the background for his imaginative and fanciful work. These were the two sides of his literary faculty, so far as he had tried his hand, and he would have the benefit of both in one work, which would thereby gain variety and unity.   The success of the experiment cannot be thought striking, and it is doubtful how far he carried the actual composition of the intervening scenes.   He confided the plan to Goodrich, who did not encourage it, so far as can be judged, but took the opening chapters to the editors of "The New England Magazine" on Hawthorne's behalf. This periodical, which had three years before absorbed Willis's "Magazine," had been conducted on somewhat grave and serious lines, as a kind of Boston cousin, as it were, of the "North American," and was now in a state of change. Mr. Buckingham relinquished the editorship, and the magazine went into the hands of Dr. Samuel G. Howe and John O. Sargent. It was at this favorable moment that Goodrich appeared with Hawthorne's manuscript; the piece was accepted; and it was published, half in the first and half in the second number issued by the new editors, in November and December, 1834. The connection proved a fortunate one for Hawthorne, and "The New England Magazine"[1] now became equally with "The Token" a constant medium for the publication of his writings of all sorts. Park Benjamin, who was soon associated with Howe and Sargent in the editorship, took sole charge in March, 1835, and was from the first, and always remained, a firm admirer of the new author's genius. To him, next to

[1] In the Riverside edition of Hawthorne's works a paper, *Hints to Young Ambition*, which appeared in *The New England Magazine*, 1832, signed "H.," is included. The piece is one of several, with the same signature, and there can be little hesitation in rejecting it, as Goodrich would hardly have needed to introduce Hawthorne to a magazine to which he already contributed. The other pieces are not in his vein, and "H." is a common signature in the periodicals of the time. At all events, Hawthorne would have gone further afield for a pseudonym than the initial of his own name, which he is not known ever to have used.

Goodrich, Hawthorne owed his introduction to such readers as he then had.

If Hawthorne made any effort to break a way for himself in reaching the public, it has not been traced, except that one letter exists, January 27, 1832, in which he offers his pen to the "Atlantic Souvenir" of Philadelphia; but that annual was bought out by Goodrich the same year and merged with "The Token," so that Hawthorne's venture only brought him back to the old stand. In 1833 his connection with Goodrich appears to have been temporarily broken, as "The Token" for 1834, which appeared that fall, contains nothing by him. For 1835 he contributed to it "The Haunted Mind" and "The Mermaid, A Revery," now known as "The Village Uncle," anonymously, and "Alice Doane's Appeal" as by the author of "The Gentle Boy." In "Youth's Keepsake" for the same year appeared "Little Annie's Ramble." These stories were published in the fall of 1834, before the venture of "The Story-Teller." Early in 1835 he furnished for the next year's "Token," 1836, "The Wedding Knell" and "The Minister's Black Veil" as by the author of "Sights from a Steeple," and "The May-pole of Merry Mount" as by the author of "The Gentle Boy." What there was left in his hands must have gone almost as a block to "The New England Magazine," and perhaps his stock of unused papers was thus exhausted. To complete the record, he published in this magazine "The Gray Champion" as by the author of "The Gentle Boy," in January; "Old News" anonymously, in February, March, and May; "My Visit to Niagara," in February; "Young Goodman Brown," in April; "Wakefield," in May; "The Ambitious Guest," in June, and in the same month, anonymously in both instances, "Graves and Goblins" and "A Rill from the Town Pump;" "The Old Maid in the Winding Sheet," now known as "The White Old Maid," in July; "The Vision of the Fountain," in August; "The Devil in Manuscript" as by "Ashley A. Royce," in November; "Sketches from Memory" as by "A Pedestrian," in November and December. All these pieces, except as stated above, are given as by the author of "The Gray Champion." It may fairly be thought that he had emptied his desk of its accumulations, though a few tales may have been reserved for Goodrich.

Hawthorne had now been before the public with increasing frequency for five years, but he had made little impression, and his success as an author must have remained as doubtful to him as at the start. Goodrich, in the passage already quoted from his "Recollections," went on to describe him during this early time of their acquaintance, and shows how slight was his progress in winning attention: —

"At this period he was unsettled as to his views; he had tried his hand in literature, and considered himself to have met with a fatal rebuff from the reading world. His mind vacillated between various projects, verging, I think, toward a mercantile profession. I combated his despondence, and assured him of triumph if he would persevere in a literary career. He wrote numerous articles which appeared in ' The Token;' occasionally an astute critic seemed to see through them, and to discover the soul that was in them; but in general they passed without notice. Such articles as ' Sights from a Steeple,' ' Sketches beneath an Umbrella,' ' The Wives of the Dead,' ' The Prophetic Pictures,' now universally acknowledged to be productions of extraordinary depth, meaning, and power, extorted hardly a word of either praise or blame, while columns were given to pieces since totally forgotten. I felt annoyed, almost angry, indeed, at this. I wrote several articles in the papers, directing attention to these productions, and finding no echo to my views, I recollect to have asked John Pickering to read some of them, and give me his opinion of them. He did as I requested; his answer was that they displayed a wonderful beauty of style, with a kind of double vision, a sort of second sight, which revealed, beyond the outward forms of life and being, a sort of Spirit World."

Park Benjamin, in a notice of "The Token" for 1836 published in "The New England Magazine," October, 1835, gave a single line to the author, speaking of him as "the most pleasing writer of fanciful prose, except Irving, in the country;" and in November of the same year, in

a review of the same work, Chorley, the critic of
the London "Athenæum," commended his tales
and gave extracts from them. This was the first
substantial praise of a nature to encourage the
author.

In Hawthorne's own eyes the stories and
sketches had become a source of depression, and
the difficulties he had met with in getting out a
book had especially irritated him. It might be
thought, perhaps, that he had destroyed a good
deal of his work, to judge by his own words, but
this seems unlikely, although he may have rewrit-
ten some of the earlier pieces. The tale of "The
Devil in Manuscript" is taken to be the autobiographical parable, at least, commemorating the
burning of the "Seven Tales of my Native Land;"
but it was written some years later, and reflects
his general experience as a discouraged story-
teller, and it contains touches of bitterness more
marked than occur elsewhere. Its personal character is emphasized by the hero's name, "Oberon," a familiar signature Hawthorne used in his
letters to his old college friend, Bridge. The
following passages are distinctly autobiographical, and afford the most vivid view of the young
author's inner life: —

"You cannot conceive what an effect the composition of these tales has had on me. I have become ambitious of a bubble, and careless of solid
reputation. I am surrounding myself with shadows, which bewilder me, by aping the realities of

life. They have drawn me aside from the beaten path of the world, and led me into a strange sort of solitude, — a solitude in the midst of men, — where nobody wishes for what I do, nor thinks nor feels as I do. The tales have done all this. When they are ashes, perhaps I shall be as I was before they had existence. Moreover, the sacrifice is less than you may suppose, since nobody will publish them. . . .

"But the devil of the business is this. These people have put me so out of conceit with the tales, that I loathe the very thought of them, and actually experience a physical sickness of the stomach, whenever I glance at them on the table. I tell you there is a demon in them! I anticipate a wild enjoyment in seeing them in the blaze; such as I should feel in taking vengeance on an enemy, or destroying something noxious. . . .

"But how many recollections throng upon me, as I turn over these leaves! This scene came into my fancy as I walked along a hilly road, on a starlight October evening; in the pure and bracing air, I became all soul, and felt as if I could climb the sky, and run a race along the Milky Way. Here is another tale, in which I wrapt myself during a dark and dreary night-ride in the month of March, till the rattling of the wheels and the voices of my companions seemed like faint sounds of a dream, and my visions a bright reality. That scribbled page describes shadows which I summoned to my bedside at midnight:

they would not depart when I bade them; the gray dawn came, and found me wide awake and feverish, the victim of my own enchantments! . . .

"Sometimes my ideas were like precious stones under the earth, requiring toil to dig them up, and care to polish and brighten them; but often a delicious stream of thought would gush out upon the page at once, like water sparkling up suddenly in the desert; and when it had passed, I gnawed my pen hopelessly, or blundered on with cold and miserable toil, as if there were a wall of ice between me and my subject."

"Do you now perceive a corresponding difference," inquired I, "between the passages which you wrote so coldly, and those fervid flashes of the mind?"

"No," said Oberon, tossing the manuscripts on the table. "I find no traces of the golden pen with which I wrote in characters of fire. My treasure of fairy coin is changed to worthless dross. My picture, painted in what seemed the loveliest hues, presents nothing but a faded and indistinguishable surface. I have been eloquent and poetical and humorous in a dream, — and behold! it is all nonsense, now that I am awake. . . .

"I will burn them! Not a scorched syllable shall escape! Would you have me a damned author? — To undergo sneers, taunts, abuse, and cold neglect, and faint praise, bestowed, for pity's sake, against the giver's conscience! A hissing and a laughing-stock to my own traitorous thoughts! An outlaw from the protection of the grave, — one whose ashes every careless foot might spurn, unhonored in life, and remembered scornfully in death! Am I to bear all this, when yonder fire will insure me from the whole? No! There go the tales! May my hand wither when it would write another!"

These extracts set forth the mixed emotions of young authorship in a life-like manner. They have the stamp of personal experience. A supplement to them is found in one of his more obscure pieces, "The Journal of a Solitary Man," in which Hawthorne bids farewell to that eidolon of himself which he had embodied as "Oberon." He describes the character as an imaginary friend, from whose journals he gives extracts; but the veil thrown over his own personality is transparent.

"Merely skimming the surface of life, I know nothing, by my own experience, of its deep and warm realities. I have achieved none of those objects which the instinct of mankind especially prompts them to pursue, and the accomplishment of which must therefore beget a native satisfaction. The truly wise, after all their speculations, will be led into the common path, and, in homage to the human nature that pervades them, will gather gold, and till the earth, and set out trees, and build a house. But I have scorned such wisdom. I have rejected, also, the settled, sober, careful gladness of a man by his own fireside, with those around him whose welfare is committed to his trust, and all their guidance to his fond authority. Without influence among serious affairs, my footsteps were not imprinted on the earth, but lost in air; and I shall leave no son to inherit my share of life, with a better sense of its privileges and duties, when his father should vanish like a bubble; so that few mortals, even the humblest and the weakest, have been such ineffectual shadows in the world, or die so utterly as I must. Even a young man's bliss has not been mine. With a thousand vagrant fantasies, I have never truly loved, and perhaps shall be doomed to loneliness throughout the eternal future, because, here on earth, my soul has never married itself to the soul of woman.

"Such are the repinings of one who feels, too late, that the sympathies of his nature have avenged themselves upon him. They have prostrated, with a joyless life and the prospect of a reluctant death, my selfish purpose to keep aloof from mortal disquietudes, and be a pleasant idler among care-stricken and laborious men. I have other regrets, too, savoring more of my old spirit. The time has been when I meant to visit every region of the earth, except the poles and Central Africa. I had a strange longing to see the Pyramids. To Persia and Arabia, and all the gorgeous East, I owed a pilgrimage for the sake of their magic tales. And England, the land of my ancestors! Once I had fancied that my sleep would not be quiet in the grave unless I should return, as it were, to my home of past ages, and see the very cities, and castles, and battle-fields of history, and stand within the holy gloom of its cathedrals, and kneel at the shrines of its immortal poets, there asserting myself their hereditary countryman. This feeling lay among the deepest in my heart.   Yet, with this homesickness for the fatherland, and all these plans of remote travel, — which I yet believe that my peculiar instinct impelled me to form, and upbraided me for not accomplishing, — the utmost limit of my wanderings has been little more than six hundred miles from my native village. Thus, in whatever way I consider my life, or what must be termed such, I cannot feel as if I had lived at all.

"I am possessed, also, with the thought that I have never yet discovered the real secret of my powers; that there has been a mighty treasure within my reach, a mine of gold beneath my feet, worthless because I have never known how to seek for it; and for want of perhaps one fortunate idea, I am to die

'Unwept, unhonored, and unsung.'"

"Oberon" is represented as in the position of the "Story-Teller," and leaves home because of some fancied oppression; he visits Niagara, of which he gives some scenes as well as other anecdotes of his pedestrian journey, but he falls ill and determines to return home to die. As he approaches his birthplace he pleases himself with the fancy that there is some youth there whom he can teach by the lesson of his life, and he moralizes in a vein in which self-criticism may be read between the lines: —

"He shall be taught by my life, and by my death, that the world is a sad one for him who shrinks from its sober duties. My experience shall warn him to adopt some great and serious aim, such as manhood will cling to, that he may not feel himself, too late, a cumberer of this over-laden earth, but a man among men. I will be-seech him not to follow an eccentric path, nor, by stepping aside from the highway of human affairs, to relinquish his claim upon human sympathy. And often, as a text of deep and varied meaning, I will remind him that he is an American."

Finally he describes the power he has obtained by the use of his imagination, in the view of life: —

"I have already a spiritual sense of human nature, and see deeply into the hearts of mankind, discovering what is hidden from the wisest. The loves of young men and virgins are known to me, before the first kiss, before the whispered word, with the birth of the first sigh. My glance com-prehends the crowd, and penetrates the breast of the solitary man. I think better of the world than formerly, more generously of its virtues, more mercifully of its faults, with a higher esti-mate of its present happiness, and brighter hopes of its destiny."

These passages from "The Devil in Manuscript" and "The Journal of a Solitary Man" may fairly be taken as a contemporary general account of Hawthorne's secret life in the years before his own "Note-Books" begin. The latter afford rather a view of his existence, from day to day. The earliest of them which has survived opens in the summer of 1835, and while containing scraps of information that he had jotted down as in a commonplace book, and also brief memoranda of ideas for tales and sketches, it also keeps record of his observations in his walks and drives, and thus pictures his outward life. He lived at Salem still, in the habits of seclusion that had always obtained in the house, and saw little of mankind. Society, if he sought it at all, was found for him among common people at the tavern or by the wayside, and was of the sort that he enjoyed on his summer journeys. But solitude was his normal state. This was indulged in his own room; or else he took a morning or afternoon to wander out to the near Salem beaches and points, or to the pleasant lanes of Danvers or across the river to the upland or seashore of Beverly. He occasionally drove a dozen miles or more to Ipswich, Nahant, or Andover. What he saw, however, was only rustic life of the countryside, or the natural views of wood and sky and sea, with the nearer objects to attract particular attention, of which he has left so many minute descriptions. His observation at such times, though without the naturalist's preoccupation, — rather with the poet's or novelist's, — was as keen and detailed as Thoreau's. These Note-Books, however, do not open his familiar life except as a record of changing seasons and of detached thoughts to be worked up in fiction. Many of his later tales are found here in the germ, in 1835 and for the year or two after; but the diary is not so much a confidant as it afterward became.

The time had now come when he must make some further step in establishing himself in some means of livelihood. He never showed much power of initiative, and at every stage was materially aided by his friends in obtaining employment and position. In this instance it was Goodrich again who gave him opportunity. It was not a great chance, but it was doubtless all Goodrich had to offer. He procured for him the editorship of a small publication which undertook to disseminate popular information, called "The American Magazine of Useful and Entertaining Knowledge," and published by the Bewick Company, at Boston, with which Goodrich had some connection through his interests in engraving. His salary was to be five hundred dollars, and he entered on his duties about the beginning of 1836. The change was welcomed by his friends, or such of them as were still near enough to him to know of his affairs; and from this time his college mates, Pierce, Cilley, and especially Bridge, interested themselves in his fortunes. Bridge, writing from Havana, February 20, 1836, congratulated him, as did also Pierce from Washington, on the intelligence concerning his "late engagement in active and responsible business," and particularly on his having got "out of Salem," which he credits with "a peculiar dulness;" and in later letters he continues to hearten him, subscribes for his magazine, reads and praises it, in the most cordial and cheering way. But the event did not justify these hopes and prognostications of a better fortune. The magazine was, after all, the merest hack-work. Hawthorne, with the aid of his sister Elizabeth, wrote most of it, compiling the matter from books or utilizing his own notes of travel. In it appeared, of such pieces as have found a place in his works, "An Ontario Steamboat," "The Duston Family," "Nature of Sleep," "Bells," besides much that has been suffered to repose in its scarce pages. The material, though conscientiously dealt with according to the measure of time at his disposal, is the slightest in interest, and the least re-worked from the raw state, of any of his writings. He had, however, little temptation to do more for the magazine than its limited scope required. He found great difficulty in collecting his salary, and for this he blames Goodrich, who had made promises of pay which he kept very imperfectly. Hawthorne states that of forty-five dollars he was to receive on coming to Boston he got only a small part, and on June 3, 1836, he received a notice, in answer to a dunning letter, that the Bewick Company had

made an assignment, and he would have to wait
until the settlement. Shortly after this he gave
up the editorship, and returned to Salem. The
incident was unfortunate, as in the course of it he
developed a great deal of irritation toward Goodrich, who was his best friend in practical ways,
and broke off communication with him. This,
however, did not last long; and Goodrich offered
him the job of compiling a "Peter Parley" book,
for one hundred dollars. He wrote this, also with
the aid of his sister Elizabeth, and gave her the
money.   The volume was "Peter Parley's Universal History on the basis of Geography,"[1] and
was published in 1837, and had a very large sale,
amounting finally, it is said, to more than a mil-
lion copies.

In the mean time, Hawthorne had found cause
of complaint also in his relations with " The New
England Magazine." This periodical had come
to an end in 1835, and at the close of that year
was merged in "The American Monthly Magazine" of New York, whither Park Benjamin, its
editor, went. It paid, according to its own statement, only one dollar a page for contributions,
but it appears to have been in arrears with Hawthorne at the time of the change. Bridge states
that when Hawthorne, in consequence, stopped

---

[1] *Peter Parley's Universal History on the basis of Geography.*
For the Use of Families. Illustrated by Maps and Engravings.
Boston: American Stationers' Company.   John B. Russell, 1837.
12mo, cloth. 2 vols., pp. 380, 374.

writing for it, the editor "begged for a mass of
manuscript in his possession, as yet unpublished,
and it was scornfully bestowed. 'Thus,' wrote
Hawthorne, ' has this man, who would be considered a Mæcenas, taken from a penniless writer
material incomparably better than any his own
brain can supply.'" In this Hawthorne, if cor-
rectly reported, was scarcely just. Park Benjamin,
who had a violent quarrel with Goodrich, ex-
empted Hawthorne from any adverse criticism,
even when writing a short notice of "The Token,"
and always spoke well of him. The manuscripts
he carried to New York could have been but few
and slight, unless they were burned in the fire
which destroyed the archives of the "American
Monthly Magazine" not long afterwards. At all
events, the only paper by Hawthorne in that magazine appears to have been "Old Ticonderoga," a
note of travel, published in February, 1836, unless "The Journal of a Solitary Man," which did
not appear till July, 1837, be added as one of the
left-over manuscripts, and also a paper, never yet
attributed to him but which seems clearly from
his pen, "A Visit to the Clerk of the Weather,"
anonymously published in May, 1836. Whatever
the coolness was between Hawthorne and Benjamin, it was overcome by the end of the year, and
the quarrel was made up. In 1836, too, he kept
his temper with Goodrich sufficiently to allow
him to contribute to "The Token" of 1837, published in the preceding fall, a group of tales, eight

in number: "Monsieur du Miroir," as by the author of "Sights from a Steeple;" "Mrs. Bullfrog," as by the author of "The Wives of the Dead;" "Sunday at Home" and "The Man of Adamant," both as by the author of "The Gentle Boy," "David Swan, A Fantasy," "Fancy's Show Box, A Morality," and "The Prophetic Pictures," all anonymously; and "The Great Carbuncle," as by the author of "The Wedding Knell." These papers constituted one third of the volume, and for them he was paid a dollar a page, or one hundred and eight dollars, which may be regarded therefore as the normal price he received from Goodrich. Two of these tales are on subjects set down in his "Note-Book" of 1835; the others are perhaps earlier in conception. These tales were his substantial work for the year.

They gave occasion for what appears to have been the first public mention of Nathaniel Hawthorne as the author who had hitherto disguised himself under so many descriptions. It is not surprising that his name was unknown, for he had sedulously suppressed it. His sister, referring to these years, said, "He kept his very existence a secret so far as possible." He had never signed an article in the twelve years since leaving college. He had preferred to become known in "the author of Waverley" style, but the charm did not work. In "The Token" he was, in the main, the author of "Sights from a Steeple" or "The Gentle Boy;" in "The New England Magazine" he was the author of "The Gray Champion." But now his anonymity was to be dissipated in a friendly if rude way. It was, doubtless, Park Benjamin, in New York, who wrote thus of these last tales in " The Token," in " The American Monthly Magazine" for October, 1836: —

"The author of ' Sights from a Steeple,' of ' The Gentle Boy,' and of ' The Wedding Knell,' we believe to be one and the same individual. The assertion may sound very bold, yet we hesitate not to call this author second to no man in this country, except Washington Irving. We refer simply to romance writing; and trust no wise man of Gotham will talk of Dewey, and Channing, and Everett, and Verplanck. Yes, to us the style of NATHANIEL HAWTHORNE is more pleasing, more fascinating, than any one's except their dear Geoffry Crayon! This mention of the real name of our author may be reprobated by him. His modesty is the best proof of his true excellence. How different does such a man appear to us from one who anxiously writes his name on every public post! We have read a sufficient number of his pieces to make the reputation of a dozen of our Yankee scribblers; and yet how few have heard the name above written! He does not even cover himself with the same anonymous shield at all times; but liberally gives the praise, which, concentrated on one, would be great, to several unknowns. If Mr. Hawthorne would but collect his various tales and essays into one volume, we can assure him that their success would be brilliant — certainly in England, perhaps in this country."

It was in this way that the world began to hear of Mr. Nathaniel Hawthorne, of Salem; but it was still long before the public knew him. Meanwhile, at the very moment of the disclosure, he was in the lowest ebb of discouragement, in spirits, that he ever knew. It is to this time that his gloomiest memories attached themselves. He had tried to enter the world, he had even tried to earn a living, and had failed. Cilley, his old college mate, was just elected to Congress from Maine, Pierce was just elected Senator from New Hampshire, and Longfellow had found the ways of literature as smooth as the primrose path to the everlasting bonfire. Hawthorne was of a noble disposition, and glad of the fortunes that came to these of his circle in boyhood at Bowdoin; but it was not in human nature to be oblivious of the difference in his own lot. To this mood must be referred the dream he described afterwards as one that recurred through life: —

"For a long, long while I have been occasionally visited with a singular dream; and I have an impression that I have dreamed it ever since I have been in England. It is, that I am still at college, — or, sometimes, even at school, — and there is a sense that I have been there unconscionably long, and have quite failed to make such progress as my contemporaries have done; and I

seem to meet some of them with a feeling of shame
and depression that broods over me as I think of
it, even when awake.   This dream, recurring all
through these twenty or thirty years, must be one
of the effects of that heavy seclusion in which I
shut myself up for twelve years after leaving college, when everybody moved onward, and left me
behind."

Under another picture, he describes this same
state in the preface to "The Snow Image," dedicated to Bridge: —

"I sat down by the wayside of life, like a man
under enchantment, and a shrubbery sprung up
around me, and the bushes grew to be saplings,
and the saplings became trees, until no exit appeared possible, through the entangling depths of
my obscurity.   And there, perhaps, I should be
sitting at this moment, with the moss on the im-
prisoning tree-trunks, and the yellow leaves of
more than a score of autumns piled above me, if
it had not been for you.   For it was through your
interposition — and that, moreover, unknown to
himself — that your early friend was brought before the public, somewhat more prominently than
heretofore, in the first volume of ' Twice-Told
Tales.' "

Bridge had been, in fact, his only confidant
from boyish days.   To him he showed the misery
of "hope deferred" that then was in his heart,
and to him allowed himself to speak in words that
went beyond his steady sense of the situation,

though representing moments of low courage. "I'm a doomed man," he wrote to him, "and over I must go."

It was under the impulse of the sight of this deep discouragement in Hawthorne, in 1836, that this cheerful and sanguine friend made up his mind to find out why Hawthorne could not get a volume of tales published. He applied to Goodrich for information, and received an answer, October 20, 1836, in which it was stated that if a guarantee of two hundred and fifty dollars were furnished by Bridge, an edition of one thousand copies, costing four hundred and fifty dollars and paying Hawthorne a royalty of ten per cent, would be issued. Goodrich was not himself a publisher, at that time, and he elsewhere says that he had previously attempted to have the Stationers' Company, which now undertook the volume on Bridge's guarantee, publish it, but without success; he adds that he relinquished his own rights to Hawthorne, who had sold the tales to him so far as they had appeared in "The Token," and that he also joined in the bond given by Bridge; but in these remarks he seems to be taking credit to himself, for the tales were valueless to him and his property in them was of a sort not often claimed by an editor, while Bridge took the real risk. This transaction was unknown to Hawthorne at the time, and Bridge felt obliged to warn him not to be too grateful to Goodrich. A glance at the other letters of this month shows that Bridge was almost alarmed by Hawthorne's depression, and endeavoring in thoughtful ways to reassure him, as well as to bring him forward in public. "I have just received your last," he writes, October 22, 1836, "and do not like its tone at all. There is a kind of desperate coolness about it that seems dangerous. I fear you are too good a subject for suicide, and that some day you will end your mortal woes on your own responsibility." The prospect of the book, even, was not wholly an undoubted blessing to Hawthorne, now he had come to its realization, and in December, on Christmas Day, the work being then in proofs, Bridge writes to him again: —

"Whether your book will sell extensively may be doubtful; but that is of small importance in the first one you publish. At all events, keep up your spirits till the result is ascertained; and, my word for it, there is more honor and emolument in store for you, from your writings, than you imagine. The bane of your life has been self-distrust. This has kept you back for many years; which, if you had improved by publishing, would long ago have given you what you must now wait a short time for. It may be for the best, but I doubt it.

"I have been trying to think what you are so miserable for. Although you have not much property, you have good health and powers of writing, which have made, and can still make, you independent.

"Suppose you get ' but $300 per annum for your writings. You can, with economy, live upon that, though it would be a tight squeeze. You have no family dependent upon you, and why should you ' borrow trouble ' ?

"This is taking the worst view of your case that it can possibly bear. It seems to me that you never look at the bright side with any hope or confidence. It is not the philosophy to make one happy.

"I expect, next summer, to be full of money, a part of which shall be heartily at your service, if it comes."

Before the new volume went to press Hawthorne had made a connection, apparently on the editor's initiative, with S. Gaylord Clark's "Knickerbocker Magazine," and contributed to it, in the January number, "The Fountain of Youth," now known as "Dr. Heidegger's Experiment; " and in the opening months of the year he was engaged in preparing his usual group of articles for the next "Token." Goodrich had also offered to him a new "Peter Parley" book, on the manners and customs of all nations, for three hundred dollars, but this Hawthorne seems to have declined.

"Twice-Told Tales "[1] appeared, under the au-

---

[1] *Twice-Told Tales.* By Nathaniel Hawthorne.   Boston : American Stationers' Co.   John B. Russell, 1837.   12mo, cloth. Pp. 334.   It contained the following tales : The Gray Champion, Sunday at Home, The Wedding Knell, The Minister's Black

thor's name, from the press of the Boston American Stationers' Co., early in March, 1837. It contained eighteen pieces only, out of the thirty-six undoubtedly by Hawthorne published up to this time, to neglect all others which have been ascribed to him during this period; and it must reflect his own judgment of what was best in his work. Far as it was from being a complete collection, it was large and varied enough to afford an adequate experiment of the public taste, and it included all those articles, whether tale or essay, which had made him known in the circle of his readers. The reception of the volume was, he thought, cool, but it sold somewhat from the first, and within two months six or seven hundred copies had been disposed of. Goodrich states that it "was deemed a failure for more than a year, when a breeze seemed to rise and fill its sails, and with it the author was carried on to fame and fortune." Bridge was much pleased with the success of his venture, and when he met Goodrich, in April, some of his good feeling overflowed upon him: "I like him very much better than before," he wrote. "He told me that the book was successful. It seemed that he was inclined to take too much credit to himself for your present standing,

Veil, The May-Pole of Merry Mount, The Gentle Boy, Mr. Higginbotham's Catastrophe, Little Annie's Ramble, Wakefield, A Rill from the Town Pump, The Great Carbuncle, The Prophetic Pictures, David Swan, Sights from a Steeple, The Hollow of the Three Hills, The Vision of the Fountain, Fancy's Show Box, Dr. Heidegger's Experiment.

on the ground of having early discovered and brought you forward. But, on the whole, I like him much." Hawthorne's view of Goodrich is contained in a letter written to his sister-in-law, Elizabeth Peabody, twenty years later: —

"As regards Goodrich's accounts of the relations between him and me, it is funny enough to see him taking the airs of a patron; but I do not mind it in the least, nor feel the slightest inclination to defend myself or be defended. I should as soon think of controverting his statement about my personal appearance (of which he draws no very lovely picture) as about anything else that he says. So pray do not take up the cudgels on my behalf; especially as I perceive that your recollections are rather inaccurate. For instance, it was Park Benjamin, not Goodrich, who cut up the 'Storyteller.' As for Goodrich, I have rather a kindly feeling towards him, and he himself is a not unkindly man, in spite of his propensity to feed and fatten himself on better brains than his own. Only let him do that, and he will really sometimes put himself to some trouble to do a good-natured act. His quarrel with me was, that I broke away from him before he had quite finished his meal, and while a portion of my brain was left; and I have not the slightest doubt that he really felt himself wronged by my so doing. Really, I half think so too. He was born to do what he did, as maggots to feed on rich cheese."

There is something too little generous in this.

The record shows beyond any cavil that Goodrich was the first and most constant friend of Hawthorne in the way of helping him to get his work before the public; he was also interested in him, thoughtful for him, and gave him hack work to do, which, though it be a lowly is a true service, however unwelcome the task may be in itself; and he used such influence as he had in introducing Hawthorne to other employers and to publishers. During these twelve years it may fairly be said that Goodrich was the only person, not a relative, who cared for Hawthorne's genius or did anything for him until Park Benjamin appeared as a second in the periodical world and Horatio Bridge came to the rescue as a business friend. It is true that Goodrich did not succeed in exploiting his author; but he paid him the market price and gave him his chance, and after all those days were not for Goodrich what our days have since become for men of his calibre. Advertisement was not then the tenth Muse.

If the papers were "cool," as Hawthorne thought, there was a word of comfort here and there in the periodicals. "The American Monthly Magazine," recalling its announcement of Hawthorne as the author of these tales in the preceding fall, took occasion in a notice of "The Token" for 1838 to flatter itself that the new volume was due to its own suggestion; and the writer, who is presumably Park Benjamin, renews his old praise. A later notice of the book itself, ascribed by Mr. Lathrop to Charles Fenno Hoffman, appeared in March, 1838, and, while somewhat ineffective and sentimental, discovers at the end the right new word to say: "His pathos we would call New England pathos, if we were not afraid it would excite a smile; it is the pathos of an American, of a New Englander. It is redolent of the images, objects, thoughts, and feelings that spring up in that soil and nowhere else." It was, however, to Longfellow that both Bridge and Hawthorne looked to help his old college mate's book with the criticism that would have the accent of good taste and literary authority, and would carry weight in those higher social circles where fame was lost and won, at least as was then believed. Hawthorne sent him the volume as soon as it was issued, with a note regretting that they were not better acquainted at college and expressing his gladness in Longfellow's success as a writer, author of "Outre-Mer," and also in obtaining his Harvard professorship; and some three months later he followed this with a letter, so characteristic and valuable autobiographically that it cannot be passed over, and interesting also as beginning that easy and amiable friendliness which continued between them unbroken thereafter: —

"Not to burden you with my correspondence, I have delayed a rejoinder to your very kind and cordial letter, until now. It gratifies me that you have occasionally felt an interest in my situation; but your quotation from Jean Paul about the 'lark's nest' makes me smile. You would have been much nearer the truth if you had pictured me as dwelling in an owl's nest; for mine is about as dismal, and like the owl I seldom venture abroad till after dusk. By some witchcraft or other — for I really cannot assign any reasonable why and wherefore — I have been carried apart from the main current of life, and find it impossible to get back again. Since we last met, which you remember was in Sawtell's room, where you read a farewell poem to the relics of the class, — ever since that time I have secluded myself from society; and yet I never meant any such thing, nor dreamed what sort of life I was going to lead. I have made a captive of myself, and put me into a dungeon, and now I cannot find the key to let myself out, — and if the door were open, I should be almost afraid to come out. You tell me that you have met with troubles and changes. I know not what these may have been, but I can assure you that trouble is the next best thing to enjoyment, and that there is no fate in this world so horrible as to have no share in either its joys or sorrows. For the last ten years, I have not lived, but only dreamed of living. It may be true that there have been some unsubstantial pleasures here in the shade, which I might have missed in the sunshine, but you cannot conceive how utterly devoid of satisfaction all my retrospects are. I have laid up no treasure of pleasant remembrances against old age; but there is some comfort in thinking that future years can hardly fail to be more varied and therefore more tolerable than the past.

"You give me more credit than I deserve, in supposing that I have led a studious life. I have indeed turned over a good many books, but in so desultory a way that it cannot be called study, nor has it left me the fruits of study. As to my literary efforts, I do not think much of them, neither is it worth while to be ashamed of them. They would have been better, I trust, if written under more favorable circumstances. I have had no external excitement, — no consciousness that the public would like what I wrote, nor much hope nor a passionate desire that they should do so. Nevertheless, having nothing else to be ambitious of, I have been considerably interested in literature; and if my writings had made any decided impression, I should have been stimulated to greater exertions; but there has been no warmth of approbation, so that I have always written with benumbed fingers. I have another great difficulty in the lack of materials; for I have seen so little of the world that I have nothing but thin air to concoct my stories of, and it is not easy to give a lifelike semblance to such shadowy stuff. Sometimes through a peep-hole I have caught a glimpse of the real world, and the two or three articles in which I have portrayed these glimpses please me better than the others.

"I have now, or shall soon have, a sharper spur to exertion, which I lacked at an earlier period; for I see little prospect but that I shall have to scribble for a living. But this troubles me much less than you would suppose. I can turn my pen to all sorts of drudgery, such as children's books, etc., and by and by I shall get some editorship that will answer my purpose. Frank Pierce, who was with us at college, offered me his influence to obtain an office in the Exploring Expedition ; but I believe that he was mistaken in supposing that a vacancy existed. If such a post were attainable, I should certainly accept it; for, though fixed so long to one spot, I have always had a desire to run round the world. . . . I intend in a week or two to come out of my owl's nest, and not return till late in the summer, — employing the interval in making a tour somewhere in New England. You who have the dust of distant countries on your ' sandal-shòon ' cannot imagine how much enjoyment I shall have in this little excursion."

Longfellow's notice of "Twice-Told Tales" appeared in the July number of "The North American Review," and gave perhaps more pleasure to Hawthorne than he had hoped for; and in acknowledging it he mentions, with a home-touch that carries more gratitude than a score of golden phrases, the happiness that "my mother, my two sisters, and my old maiden aunt " have had in it. The notice itself is elegant, kindly, warm even, with the old-fashioned academic distinction of man-

ner, through which the young poet's picturesque
fancy keeps playing, like a flutter of light; it
gives one a strange sense of old-world youthfulness
to read it now. Its characteristic passages, apart
from this glamour, are its praise of the lucid style
and of the home-bred quality, "the nationality"
of the Tales: "The author has chosen his themes
among the traditions of New England, the dusty
legends of 'the good old colony times when we lived
under a king.' This is the right material for
story." But, notwithstanding the good-will of
Hawthorne's few friends, and this handsome treatment by that one of them who had the greatest
opportunity to applaud him, his place was not yet
won.

Meanwhile, his political friends had not been
idle. The problem of a livelihood, of an active
share in the world's business, which Hawthorne
now sincerely desired, was not likely to be much
advanced by the publication of this volume. In
any case, it would seem that Hawthorne's friends
were agreed that what he needed was to be got into
an entirely different set of surroundings, to have
a change of scene. It was, perhaps, with some
such idea that Pierce suggested to him to join the
South Sea Exploring Expedition, then being
planned by Reynolds, as historian. There is
something humorous, unconscious though it was,
in sending Hawthorne from the monotony and
loneliness of Salem to seek society in the polar
regions, though no hint of it appears in the corre-

spondence. The scheme appealed to Hawthorne, however, and he was desirous to go; but though his friends were active in his interest, and brought the Maine and New Hampshire delegations to support his candidacy, success was doubtful, and, the expedition being temporarily abandoned, the plan came to nothing. On its failure Hawthorne went to visit Bridge at his home in Augusta, Maine, and passed the month of July with him very happily, as he tells at large in his Note-Books of that period.

On his return to Salem at midsummer he could hardly have flattered himself on any perceptible change in his position. He fell into the old life of rambling about the country and writing new tales; and, except that he was in communication with his old friends, Bridge, Pierce, and Cilley, and occasionally saw them in Boston, he was as much isolated and without prospects as ever. The connection he had established with "The Knickerbocker Magazine" he had kept up by contributing to it "A Bell's Biography" as by the author of "Twice-Told Tales," in March, and he now published, in the September issue, "Edward Fane's Rosebud" anonymously. The publication of the book had attracted to him the notice of the new "Democratic Review," edited by John O'Sullivan, a young fellow of enterprise, spirits, and an Irish charm, who had solicited Hawthorne to contribute to it, early in April. In reply to this application, presumably, "A Toll Gatherer's Day," as by the

author of "Twice-Told Tales," appeared in the
October number.   The stories which Hawthorne
had prepared in the spring for "The Token" of
1838 now came out in the fall of 1837, five in
number: two of them, "Peter Goldthwaite's Treasure" and "The Shaker Bridal" as by the author
of the "Twice-Told Tales," and three anonymously, "Night Scenes under an Umbrella,"
"Endicott and the Red Cross," and "Sylph Eth-
eredge."   He still persistently neglected to put his
own name to his work.   There was a reason for
his anonymity in "The Token," but elsewhere he
continued his old custom, and was to be known
habitually only under the style "The Author of
'Twice-Told Tales,'" which he adopted henceforth.   To this time belong some further traces
of a more varied mixing with society in Salem
than he had hitherto shown.   He attended the
meetings of a club at Miss Burley's, where the
transcendental group appears to have gathered, and
among them Jones Very.   The most singular episode of the time, however, is one that would hardly
be credited, had it not been mentioned by those
who should have known the truth.   It is said that
Hawthorne's sympathies were so engaged by a lady
who confided to him the injurious treatment she
alleged she had suffered from an acquaintance that
he challenged the man to a duel; he went to
Washington for the purpose, and was only withdrawn from the affair, under the advice of Cilley
and Pierce, by the discovery that he had been

practiced upon by the lady, who had been led on by a spirit of mischief or malice to deceive him, there being no basis for the affair. A dark turn is given to the incident by the suggestion that it was the citing of this example of Hawthorne's to his friend Cilley which persuaded the latter to enter on the duel with Graves, in which he lost his life not long after these events. Bridge, however, denies that this was the case, and he should have known. Just when this incident occurred is not stated; but Hawthorne's solitude in Salem must have been less complete than has been represented in order for it to occur at all; and it must be believed that he had at all times associates, whom he met in one way and another, both men and women, however small the circle.

The period of twelve years which he used to refer to as the time of his isolation in Salem had now come to an end; but he remained in the old house for some time longer, though with a difference in his mood and life. The habit of seclusion and the sense of separation from the world had been somewhat broken up by the rally that his college friends, led by Bridge, had made for him and the feeling of renewed companionship with them, as well as by his appearance before the public in his own right as the author of "Twice-Told Tales;" the old state of affairs, however, was not ended by these things, but by a more vital matter. There can be no doubt that in his own mind the acquaintance and growing intimacy which now sprang up between himself and Sophia Peabody coincided with the disappearance of the solitary depression of these years, — for him the twelve years ended when he first saw this small, graceful, intensely alive invalid, dressed in a simple white wrapper, who had come down from her room to meet him in the family parlor. She might seem, indeed, like himself, rather a "visitant" than an inhabitant of this planet, and their courtship not unlike one of his own stories of half immaterial lovers who go hand in hand, with sentiments for sentences and great heedlessness of mortal matters, to an idyllic union of hearts. He rose, on her entrance, to greet her, and looked at her with great intentness; and it immediately occurred to her sister that he would fall in love with her.

The narrative of this love-making has been very fully told, and in the most lifelike way, since the characters have been allowed to speak for themselves in their diaries and letters. It is a story so touched with delicacies, and with such shades of humor, too, as to defy any re-telling; even to outline it seems crude, because the effect lies all in the details of trifles, phrases, and spontaneous things. The Peabody family was of a type that flourished in that period, as good as was ever produced on this soil, with the most sterling qualities, and blending an intellectual culture of transcendental kinship with practical and hospitable duties. The home, which was one of very moderate means, was characterized by a moral high-mindedness pervading its life, and by those literary and artistic tastes then spreading in the community, which, though it is easy to smile at them in a vein of latter-day superiority, were everywhere the signs of a nascent intellectual life among our people. In this case, the fruits are the best comment on the home, for of the three daughters, the eldest, Elizabeth, passed a much honored and long life as a teacher in Boston, the friend of every good cause; the second, Mary, became the wife of Horace Mann; and the third, Sophia, the wife of Hawthorne. The Peabodys had been neighbors of the Hawthornes in much earlier years, and the elder children had been little playmates together; but the family had removed from Salem, and came back again in 1828. It was not, however, till 1837, on the publication of "Twice-Told Tales," that Elizabeth Peabody recognized in the author the same person she had known as a child. She took steps to renew the acquaintance with his sisters, and so to meet him again, till by many little attentions, notes, books, walks, flowers, and whatever she could invent, she succeeded in establishing an interchange of social civility between the two houses. She affords, in her recollections, the best glimpse of Hawthorne's mother. "Madame Hawthorne," she says, "always looked as if she had walked out of an old picture, with her antique costume, and a face of lovely sensibility and great brightness — for she did not *seem* at all a victim of morbid sensibility, notwithstanding her all but

Hindoo self-devotion to the manes of her husband. She was a woman of fine understanding and very cultivated mind. But she had very sensitive nerves." Elizabeth, Hawthorne's sister, was strong-minded but abnormally retired, jealous of her brother, and not much disposed to have him stolen out of the house. Louisa was more companionable, and with his mother would sit with Hawthorne after tea; and there was an old maiden aunt flitting about in the little garden, apparently as recluse as the rest. With these feminine members of the household Elizabeth Peabody made friends, and though a year elapsed in the process, she then had her reward in receiving Hawthorne and his sisters, who one evening came to call. She ran upstairs to her sister, exclaiming, "Oh, Sophia, you must get up and dress and come down! The Hawthornes are here, and you never saw anything so splendid as he is, — he is handsomer than Lord Byron!" But Sophia did not come down, and it was only on the second call that the two met as has been described.

Sophia Peabody was at this time twenty-six years old, having been born in 1811, and had been an invalid through her girlhood; she was afflicted with an acute nervous headache which lasted uninterruptedly, says her son, from her twelfth to her thirty-first year, though the pain was not so severe, her sister remarks, but that she could sometimes read. She had received her education at home, mainly from her sister, who kept a school in the house, and in spite of her ill-health had many and varied acquisitions. She read Latin, Greek, and Hebrew, and was somewhat familiar with history. Passages in her journal show the character and range of her reading, which was of that strangely mixed sort that belonged to the notion of culture in those days; thus, for instance, in her twentieth year, she records having read on one day De Gérando, Fénelon, St. Luke and Isaiah, Young, Addison, and four comedies of Shakspere, besides doing some sewing. She was a good French and Italian scholar. Filled with intellectual enthusiasm and ambition as she was, her sensibilities seem rather to have been roused by natural beauty, effects of sky and weather and color, and her active powers took the direction of art; she sketched, painted, and modeled in clay. In 1832 she had gone to Cuba with her mother for three years, and received some benefit from the climate. She had especially practiced horseback-riding there, of which she was fond. No permanent improvement, however, had followed, on her return to Salem in 1835. When Hawthorne came to know her, she was living a half-invalid life, taking her meals in her own room, which she had fitted up with artistic prettiness, and yet suffering the full transcendental tide of culture and emotion. Perhaps no single passage can better illustrate her mind and feelings than a description of Emerson's call in the spring of 1838, which she writes to her sister, whom, at an earlier time, he had taught Greek: —

"We had an exquisite visit from Waldo. It was the warbling of the Attic bird. The gleam of his *diffused* smile; the musical thunder of his voice; his repose, so full of the essence of life; his simplicity — just think of all these, and of my privilege in seeing and hearing him. He enjoyed everything we showed him so much! He talked so divinely to Raphael's Madonna del Pesce! I vainly imagined I was very quiet all the while, preserving a very demure exterior, and supposed I was sharing his oceanic calm. But the next day I was aware that I had been in a very intense state. I told Mary, that night after he had gone, that I felt like a *gem;* that was the only way I could express it. I don't know what Mary hoped to get from him, but *I* was sure of drinking in that which would make me paint Cuban skies better than even my recollections could have made me, were they as vivid as the rays of the sun in that sunniest of climates. He made me feel as Eliza Dwight did once, when she looked uncommonly beautiful and animated. I felt as if her beauty was all about the room, and that I was in it, and therefore beautiful too. It seemed just so with Waldo's soul-beauty."

She had been in communication with others of the leading spirits of that day besides Emerson. Dr. Channing and Allston sent her messages, kindly and flattering, about her drawings and painting. She had copied some of Allston's pictures. Her studio was the centre of her life; and

there her friends "glided in," to use her phrase,
with roses and columbines, little girls came to
take peeps at its wonders, and from it came the
sunshine of the house. Here, to give some further
trifling indications, she described herself, after a
visit of Hawthorne, as feeling "quite lark-like, or
like John of Bologna's Mercury; " or she indulged
one of her "dearest visions," which was "to get
well enough to go into prisons and tell felons I
have sympathy for them, especially women; " or,
when Hawthorne called, lamented that she should
have to smooth her hair, and dress, "while he was
being wasted downstairs." She felt his attractive power from the first, and was happy in his
attentions, in the walks they took, in their visits
to Miss Burley's weekly meetings, in the picture
of Ilbrahim, "The Gentle Boy," which she made
for him, in her story, "Edward Randolph's Portrait," which he wrote for her, in the columbines
and tulips that strewed the way of love-making,
and, in brief, in the thousand trifles of the old
story. Hawthorne, on his part, was equally attracted in his different ways, and responded to
the vivacity and ebullience of this intense feminine nature disclosed to him in the live woman
who had met him, as if coming out of a vision, on
life's road. The spring budded and flowered into
summer, and when he took his habitual journey
into the world, — this time into Berkshire and Vermont, from July 23 to September 24, — meaning,
as he told her, to cut himself wholly away from

every one, so that even his mother should not know his whereabouts, it is not unlikely that he was desirous of this solitude to think it all over.

They became engaged at the close of the year, though the matter was kept a profound secret, there being apparently some apprehension that his mother would not approve of it. His sister Elizabeth, was, perhaps, not very cordial about it, also, but there was, as it proved, no occasion for anxiety. It might well have seemed imprudent for Hawthorne, whose worldly success had been slight, to marry an invalid wife. Fortune, however, was not wholly unkind, and George Bancroft, whose attention had been called to Hawthorne's needs, gave him an appointment at the Boston Custom House as weigher and gauger, at a salary of twelve hundred dollars. It was this opportunity, possibly, which emboldened Hawthorne to take the final step; and marriage would be hoped for, should this experiment of entering on a fixed employment prove successful.

During the progress of this courtship, to complete the chronicle of Hawthorne's literary publications, he had written the carrier's address, "Time's Portraiture," for "The Salem Gazette," January 2, 1838, the home paper which had made him known to his fellow-townsmen by reprinting "The Fountain of Youth," in the preceding March; and for the same paper he wrote the address for the following year, January 1, 1839, "The Sister Years." He had also contributed to

"The American Monthly Magazine," for January, 1838, an article under his own name on his friend, Thomas Green Fessenden, a Maine politician who had recently died; and to the same periodical, for March, "The Three-fold Destiny" under the old pseudonym of Ashley Allen Royce. It was, however, "The Democratic Review" which served as the principal channel of publication. It contained successively "Footprints on the Beach," January; "Snowflakes," February; "Howe's Masquerade," May; "Edward Randolph's Portrait," July; "Lady Eleanore's Mantle," "Chippings with a Chisel," and a sketch of Jonathan Cilley, his friend who had just been shot by Graves in a duel, all in September; and these tales he signed as by The Author of "Twice-Told Tales." The Province House series was concluded by "Old Esther Dudley," in this same periodical, April, 1839, and to this he affixed his own name for the first time. "The Lily's Quest" had appeared, January 19, 1839, in "The Southern Rose," published at Charleston, South Carolina. Here the first stage of his literary career ended.

He was now to leave that chamber under the eaves, in which these years, lengthened to fourteen now, had been spent, but not without a farewell. Here he had written, in 1835, "In this dismal chamber fame was won." A dismal sort of fame he thought it then. It was on returning to it in 1840 that he penned the well-known passage: —

" Here I sit in my old, accustomed chamber,

where I used to sit in days gone by. . . . Here I have written many tales, — many that have been burned to ashes, many that doubtless deserved the same fate. This claims to be called a haunted chamber, for thousands upon thousands of visions have appeared to me in it; and some few of them have become visible to the world. If ever I should have a biographer, he ought to make great mention of this chamber in my memoirs, because so much of my lonely youth was wasted here, and here my mind and character were formed; and here I have been glad and hopeful, and here I have been despondent. And here I sat a long, long time, waiting patiently for the world to know me, and sometimes wondering why it did not know me sooner, or whether it would ever know me at all, — at least, till I were in my grave. And sometimes it seemed as if I were already in the grave, with only life enough to be chilled and benumbed. But oftener I was happy, — at least, as happy as I then knew how to be, or was aware of the possibility of being. By and by, the world found me out in my lonely chamber, and called me forth, — not, indeed, with a loud roar of acclamation, but rather with a still, small voice, — and forth I went, but found nothing in the world that I thought preferable to my old solitude till now. . . . And now I begin to understand why I was imprisoned so many years in this lonely chamber, and why I could never break through the viewless bolts and bars; for if I had sooner made my escape into the world, I should have grown hard and rough, and been covered with earthly dust, and my heart might have become callous by rude encounters with the multitude. . . . But living in solitude till the fullness of time was come, I still kept the dew of my youth and the freshness of my heart. . . . I used to think I could imagine all passions, all feelings, and states of the heart and mind; but how little did I know! . . . Indeed, we are but shadows; we are not endowed with real life, and all that seems most real about us is but the thinnest substance of a dream, — till the heart be touched. That touch creates us, — then we begin to be, — thereby we are beings of reality and inheritors of eternity."

This sentiment always continued to play about this room, and whenever he returned to it he was apt to set down some word of memory. In one passage he even describes it as a shrine of literary pilgrimage, and mentions, with that well-known touch, half fantastic, half grotesque, its various articles of furniture, — the washstand, the mahogany-framed glass, the pine table, the flag-bottomed chair, the old chest of drawers, the closet, the worn-out shoe-brush, imagining the thoughts of the pilgrim on beholding these relics. It was the type for him of the old life of loneliness, of disappointment, of household gloom; but it was also the place where he had spent those "tranquil and not unhappy years," of which he afterwards said these early tales were the memorials; and, however the room might darken in comparison with the happiness of his married life, his last thought in regard to it was that contained in a letter written late in life: "I am disposed to thank God for the gloom and chill of my early life, in the hope that my share of adversity came then, when I bore it alone."

III.

EARLY in January, 1839, Hawthorne took up his new duties as weigher and gauger in the Boston Custom House. He wrote very cheerfully to Longfellow that he had no reason to doubt his capacity to fulfill his duties, since he had not yet learned what they were, and he indulges his humor in fancying imaginary little essays which he will write in the unoccupied time he pleasantly anticipates will be his lot. He was glad to have a material task to do, something with the stubbornness of fact in its resistance, a practical duty such as belongs in the ordinary lives of men. This desire to come out of his old way of existence, with its preoccupation with the imaginary world, had become a strong and rooted feeling, a fixed idea. "If I could only make tables," he said, "I should feel myself more of a man." In the bustle of the wharves he felt himself in touch with the world's business, and he took hold of his work with interest and vigor as well as with that conscientious fidelity which belonged to his character. Bancroft, a few months later, told Emerson that he was "the most efficient and best of the Custom House officers," and Mr. Lathrop says that he "used to make it a point in all weathers to get to the wharf at the earliest possible hour," so that the laborers, who were employed by the hour, might not lose their time. The life he led is fully described in his own journals, with all its details of shipping business, of the sailors and laborers and their tasks, of the salt, salt fish, oil, iron, molasses, and other inelegant merchandise, and the day's work in its various aspects of character, things, and weather. Hawthorne's powers of observation, which he had previously exercised in the taverns of New England and along his native roadside and beaches, were now fully occupied and newly animated with the novelty of the scene and his part in it. He made these careful notes almost by instinct, but after all, they were of curiously little use to him; it would seem rather that they gave his mind occupation in the intervals of his imaginative creation; they were a resource to him like the recreation of a walk; they represent the vacant and idle times of his genius; and for this reason his observations, which are in the main a kind of admirable reporting, afford a well-nigh complete setting for his life, and constitute an external autobiography. He is hardly to be truly seen apart from them.

At the end of six months he had begun to feel the wearisome drag upon his spirits which was to be expected from toilsome days. Practical life as a sort of vacation was welcome, but as it became the continuing business of his time, and that other world of the artistic faculty was now, in turn, known only by visiting glimpses, the look of the facts changed. "I do not mean to imply," he writes, "that I am unhappy or discontented, for this is not the case. My life only is a burden in the same way that it is to every toilsome man; and mine is a healthy weariness, such as needs only a night's sleep to remove it. But from henceforth forever I shall be entitled to call the sons of toil my brethren, and shall know how to sympathize with them, seeing that I likewise have risen at the dawn, and borne the fervor of the midday sun, nor turned my heavy footsteps homeward till eventide." At first, no doubt, the outdoor occupation and the having to do with sea and harbor life, for which he had an hereditary affection, were important elements in his happiness; and the association with rough and hardy men, whose contact with life was primitive and had the genuineness and health of such occupations, was the kind of human companionship which he felt most naturally and pleasurably. But the wearing in of the facts upon him is seen in the way in which the blackness of coal and the whiteness of salt begin to color the page, until it would seem as if he handled and saw no other objects, and also in the comfort that the cold sea-wind, and freshening waves, and the horizon of cloud and green are to him. At the end of a year the signs of weariness come out clear in a well-known passage of the "Note-Books," as a condensed picture of these two years of life: —

"I have been measuring coal all day, on board of a black little British schooner, in a dismal dock at the north end of the city. Most of the time I paced the deck to keep myself warm; for the wind (northeast, I believe) blew up through the dock, as if it had been the pipe of a pair of bellows. The vessel lying deep between two wharves, there was no more delightful prospect, on the right hand and on the left, than the posts and timbers, half immersed in the water, and covered with ice, which the rising and falling of successive tides had left upon them, so that they looked like immense icicles. Across the water, however, not more than half a mile off, appeared the Bunker Hill monument; and, what interested me considerably more, a church-steeple, with the dial of a clock upon it, whereby I was enabled to measure the march of the weary hours. Sometimes I descended into the dirty little cabin of the schooner, and warmed myself by a red-hot stove, among biscuit-barrels, pots and kettles, sea-chests, and innumerable lumber of all sorts, — my olfactories, meanwhile, being greatly refreshed by the odor of a pipe, which the captain or some one of his crew was smoking. But at last came the sunset, with delicate clouds, and a purple light upon the islands; and I blessed it, because it was the signal of my release."

He soon began to "pray that in one year more I may find some way of escaping from this unblest Custom House; for it is a very grievous thralldom;" and beginning now to write again, he feels as if "the noblest part of man had been left out of my composition or had decayed out of it since my nature was given to my own keeping." Yet he tries to be just to his experience, and adds what he thought the good of it had been: —

"It is only once in a while that the image and desire of a better and happier life makes me feel the iron of my chain; for, after all, a human spirit may find no insufficiency of food fit for it, even in the Custom House. And, with such materials as these, I do think and feel and learn things that are worth knowing, and which I should not know unless I had learned them there, so that the present portion of my life shall not be quite left out of the sum of my real existence. . . . It is good for me, on many accounts, that my life has had this passage in it. I know much more than I did a year ago. I have a stronger sense of power to act as a man among men. I have gained worldly wisdom, and wisdom also that is not altogether of this world. And, when I quit this earthly cavern, where I am now buried, nothing will cling to me that ought to be left behind."

The rebellion, nevertheless, continued, and as the spring came on the Custom House is a "darksome dungeon," where he "murders the joyful young day," quenching the sunshine; when he shall be free again, he thinks, he will enjoy all things anew like a child of five, and "go forth and stand in a summer shower, and all the worldly dust that has collected on me shall be washed away at once, and my heart will be like a bank of fresh flowers for the weary to rest upon." He goes to the Common, to the highest point, where he could "see miles and miles into the country. Blessed be God for this green tract, and the view which it affords, whereby we poor citizens may be put in mind, sometimes, that all his earth is not composed of blocks of brick houses, and of stone or wooden pavements. Blessed be God for the sky, too, though the smoke of the city may somewhat change its aspect, — but still it is better than if each street were covered over with a roof. There were a good many people walking the mall, — mechanics apparently, and shopkeepers' clerks, with their wives; and boys were rolling on the grass, and I would have liked to lie down and roll too."

He looks out over the waters. "The footsteps of May can be traced upon the islands in the harbor, and I have been watching the tints of green upon them gradually deepening, till now they are almost as beautiful as they ever can be." He is convinced that "Christian's burden consisted of coal," and he takes comfort in salt: "Salt is white and pure — there is something holy in salt." Yet this tone was not constant, and from time to time he shows something of his first appreciation and enjoyment of the element of labor and reality in the experience. Almost at the end of his life on the wharf, after more than two years of it, he exemplifies his later feeling perhaps most justly: —

"I have been busy all day, from early breakfast-time till late in the afternoon; and old Father Time has gone onward somewhat less heavily than is his wont when I am imprisoned within the walls of the Custom House. It has been a brisk, breezy day, an effervescent atmosphere, and I have enjoyed it in all its freshness, — breathing air which had not been breathed in advance by the hundred thousand pairs of lungs which have common and invisible property in the atmosphere of this great city. My breath had never belonged to anybody but me. It came fresh from the wilderness of ocean. . . . It was exhilarating to see the vessels, how they bounded over the waves, while a sheet of foam broke out around them. I found a good deal of enjoyment, too, in the busy scene around me; for several vessels were disgorging themselves (what an unseemly figure is this, — 'disgorge,' quotha, as if the vessel were sick) on the wharf, and everybody seemed to be working with might and main. It pleased me to think that I also had a part to act in the material and tangible business of this life, and that a portion of all this industry could not have gone on without my presence. Nevertheless, I must not pride myself too much on my activity and utilitarianism. I shall, doubtless, soon bewail myself at being compelled to earn my bread by taking some little share in the toils of mortal men."

The truth was that Hawthorne led a life apart in his own genius, and this life of the spirit rose out of his daily and habitual existence, or flowed through it like a hidden stream, and did not mingle with the tide of the hours as they passed. He felt the need of a fuller, earthly, practical life, a real life, as he would have called it by contrast with the impalpable things of his genius, and sought it in outward employments; but in these, when his spirit awoke, he felt himself a captive, and defrauded of that higher life of the soul; and after the day's work or the year's labor was over, he could not be content with the fact that it had been, and had served its purpose, and was gone, but he still was compelled to ask how it had served this higher life, in what ways it had fed the spirit which should be master of all the days of one's life, and he found no satisfactory answer except the crude one that possibly his experience and observation might be useful, though doubtfully, as material for the books that were to be. After all he was not content with practical life as an end; it was a means only, such was the necessity of his constitution; he felt its interference with his creative faculty and he was far from being convinced that he had gained anything from it which would be fruitful when he should find time and strength to write again. The leisure he had fondly anticipated was only a dream. He had to work too hard.

During these two years, from January, 1839, to April, 1841, the other part of Hawthorne's life lay in his companionship with Sophia Peabody.

At first, communication was mostly by letters; but the Peabodys removed from Salem to Boston in 1840, and after that the two lovers — for they were lovers in the most simple sense — met constantly. The memorials of the time, touching as they are in their intimacy of feeling, have that essential privacy which best bespeaks a noble nature. The exchanges of confidences, the little gifts, such as the two pictures which she sent him and which he always held so preciously in his affection, the trifles of lovers' talk, like his confession that he always washed his hands before reading her letters, the quiet, firm advice, the consolations, the happy praise he renders her, — all these belong to the love-story, if it must needs be told. But, besides this, Hawthorne felt toward this love of his married life in a peculiar way not often so purely disclosed; there were touches of solemnity in it, something not of this world; there was that sense of what can be described only as sacredness, which he intimates and in part reveals as a thing never absent from his heart, whether with her or away from her. Love had come to him, not in his youth, but after the years of solitude had ripened both heart and imagination, — a man's love; it filled his whole nature, and with it went a feeling of glad release from the past, of the coming of a freeing power bringing new life, which gave something of heavenly gratitude to his bosom. How deep, serious, truly sacred, his love was, can be read in all the lines of his writing that even remotely allude to it; and at this time he gave expression to it with a sincerity so unconscious that in reading his letters — and there are many of them, though happily he destroyed his wife's — one looks straight into his heart. It is strange, he thinks, that "such a flower as our affection should have blossomed amid snow and wintry winds ; " and in all ways this love had the singularity that deep natures feel in their own experiences. "I never till now," writes Hawthorne, "had a friend who could give me repose; all have disturbed me, and whether for pleasure or pain, it was still disturbance. But peace overflows from your heart into mine." So one might weave the chain of lovers' phrases, linking the old words over; but here, at least, it will be enough to let one or two separate passages stand for his abiding mood. In June, 1840, he writes to her when she is at Concord : —

"My heart thirsts and languishes to be there, away from the hot sun, and the coal-dust, and the steaming docks, and the thick-pated, stubborn, contentious men, with whom I brawl from morning till night, and all the weary toil that quite engrosses me, and yet occupies only a small part of my being, which I did not know existed before I became a measurer. I do think I should sink down quite disheartened and inanimate if you were not happy, and gathering from earth and sky enjoyment for both of us; but this makes me feel that my real, innermost soul is apart from all these unlovely circumstances, and that it has not ceased to exist, as I might sometimes suspect, but is nourished and kept alive through you. You know not what comfort I have in thinking of you amid those beautiful scenes and amid those sympathizing hearts. If you are well and happy, if your step is light and joyous there, and your cheek is becoming rosier, and if your heart makes pleasant music, then is it not better for you to stay there a little longer? And if better for you, is it not so for me likewise? Now, I do not press you to stay, but leave it all to your wisdom; and if you feel it is now time to come home, then let it be so."

Similarly, in the fall of the same year, from Boston, and again from Salem, he sums in memory what this new life had been to him now for nearly two years: —

"Sometimes, during my solitary life in our old Salem house, it seemed to me as if I had only life enough to know that I was not alive; for I had no wife then to keep my heart warm. But, at length, you were revealed to me, in the shadow of a seclusion as deep as my own. I drew nearer and nearer to you, and opened my heart to you, and you came to me, and will remain forever, keeping my heart warm and renewing my life with your own. You only have taught me that I have a heart, — you only have thrown a light, deep downward and upward, into my soul. You only have revealed me to myself; for without your aid my best knowledge of myself would have been merely to know my own shadow, — to watch it flickering on the wall, and mistake its fantasies for my own real actions. . . .

"Whenever I return to Salem, I feel how dark my life would be without the light that you shed upon it, — how cold, without the warmth of your love. Sitting in this chamber, where my youth wasted itself in vain, I can partly estimate the change that has been wrought. It seems as if the better part of me had been born since then. I had walked those many years in darkness, and might so have walked through life, with only a dreamy notion that there was any light in the universe, if you had not kissed my eyelids and given me to see. You, dearest, have always been positively happy. Not so I, — I have only not been miserable."

To turn to other matters, the preoccupation of Hawthorne's mind with his business, together with the distraction of his courtship, proved unfavorable to imaginative work. It may be, too, that the impulse to create had been somewhat exhausted by the rapid production of his later tales in the year or two preceding. Only one original story appeared in this period of labor and love, "John Inglefield's Thanksgiving," which was published in the "Democratic Review" for March, 1840, as by the Rev. A. A. Royce. An interesting edition of "The Gentle Boy,"[1] under Haw-

---

[1] *The Gentle Boy.* A Thrice Told Tale. By Nathaniel Haw-

thorne's name, had been issued in 1839 at his own
expense; it contained the original sketch of Ibra-
him, by Sophia Peabody, engraved by J. Andrews,
and was evidently intended only as a kind of
lover's gift to her, to whom it was dedicated. He
gave his attention now to writing some children's
books, partly under the influence of his old "Peter
Parley" instruction and experience, and partly,
no doubt, under the encouragement and advice of
Elizabeth Peabody, who was interested in such
literature. The Peabodys, on removing to Boston, had opened a shop, a library and book-store
and homœopathic drug-store, all in one, of which
she was the head, and with her name Hawthorne
associated his new ventures. He had contem-
plated writing children's books, as a probable
means of profit, before he received his appointment in the Custom House, as he said in his letter
to Longfellow; and he merely stuck to the plan
under the new conditions. The result was three
volumes of historical tales for young people, drawn
from New England in the colonial and revolutionary times, under different titles, but making one
series: "Grandfather's Chair,"[1] "Famous Old

thorne. With an Original Illustration. Boston: Weeks, Jordan
& Co., 121 Washington Street. New York & London: Wiley &
Putnam. 1839. 4to. Pp. 20.

[1] *Grandfather's Chair*. A History for Youth. By Nathaniel
Hawthorne, author of Twice-Told Tales. Boston: E. P. Peabody.
New York: Wiley & Putnam. 1841. 32mo. Pp. vii, 140.
The preface is dated Boston, November, 1840.

People," [1] and "Liberty Tree." [2]   They appeared
in rapid succession in 1841, and were successful.
But notwithstanding the high character of these
little books as entertainment for children, it will
hardly be thought that literature had profited
much by the devotion of genius to coal and salt
and the oversight of day laborers.

In the spring of 1841, immediately after the
change of administration in March, Hawthorne
lost his place in the Custom House, and he at once
betook himself to Brook Farm, in Roxbury, a
suburb of Boston, or, to give its full name, "The
Brook Farm Institute of Agriculture and Education." The place, the celebrities who gathered
there in their youth, and their way of life, have
all been many times described, so that there is no
occasion to renew a detailed account, especially as
Hawthorne's interest in the scheme was purely
incidental. He must have had his plans already
made in preparation for a change in his life. The
shop of the Peabodys in Boston was a centre of
transcendentalism, "The Dial" being published
there; and Hawthorne's attention may have been
drawn to the movement for a practical application

---

[1] *Famous Old People.* Being the Second Epoch of Grand-
father's Chair. By Nathaniel Hawthorne, author of Twice-
Told Tales. Boston : E. P. Peabody, 13 West St. 1841. 32mo.
Pp. vii, 158. The preface is dated December 30, 1840.

[2] *Liberty Tree.* With the Last Words of Grandfather's Chair.
By Nathaniel Hawthorne, author of Twice-Told Tales. Boston :
E. P. Peabody, 13 West St. 1841. 32mo. Pp. vii, 160. The
preface is dated Boston, February 27, 1841.

of the new social ideas by this circumstance, and he may well have made the acquaintance of Ripley, the chief projector, through these family friends. It is to be remembered, too, that he had been interested previously in the community idea, in the case of the Shakers, and had twice written tales on motives suggested by their life. But an experiment in the regeneration of society by a group of radicals would hardly have given him much practical concern, had it not fallen in with some peculiarities of his private position. Something, it is true, is to be allowed for the infection of the time, which would touch a morally speculative mind such as Hawthorne's to some degree; he would have observed these dreamers, breaking out new paths in the hardened old world of custom and inheritance, and would have followed the fortunes of the dream in its effects on individual lives, for it would appeal to the moral imagination and to his general sentiment about human life; but to become one of the promoters would require, in a man so wary, so hard-headed and cool as he naturally was in one half of his brain at least, a certain pressure of fact upon him. No man was less of a reformer than Hawthorne; he was constitutionally phlegmatic about society, a party man in politics, and an ironical critic of all "come-outers," as these people were then popularly named; and, in this instance, which is the only apparently freakish action of his life, he was certainly swayed by what he supposed to be his own interest. He was merely prospecting for a home in which to settle. He was anxious to be married; he was thirty-seven years old, and Sophia was thirty, and the engagement had already lasted two years and more. In this new community hopes were held out that there would be cottages for families, and the whole business of supporting a family was to be simplified and made easier by the joint arrangements of the community, in an economical sense; moreover, that blessed union of manual toil with intellectual labor was a prime part of the enterprise, and something akin to this Hawthorne still very much desired in his own mind. To have some material work to do, to sustain a practical relation with men and their general life, to have daily contact with matter of fact as a means of escape from the old life of shadows, were still very definite and prized ends with him. He was fairly possessed with this idea for some years. It may fairly be believed that he had no ulterior purpose or belief in the affair, but merely for his personal convenience desired on the one hand to solve the old problem of living in the world while not of it, and to provide a house for his wife to come to. He was willing to try the new scheme, nothing else seeming so feasible at the time to accomplish his immediate purpose; and he put into it all his savings, one thousand dollars, but with the idea of withdrawing this capital in case he was dissatisfied with the results, and should return to the ordinary ways of the world.

Hawthorne arrived at the farm among the first of the new settlers, in an April snowstorm, on the twelfth of the month, and began at once to make the acquaintance of the barnyard. He was entirely destitute of agricultural talents, original or acquired, a green hand in every sense of the word, with that muscular willingness to learn which exhibits itself by unusual destructive capacity upon implements of toil and the docility of patient farm animals. He had physical strength, and after attempting to chop, hay, and milk, he was given a dung-fork and set to work at a pile of manure. He writes about these details with a softening of the raw facts by elegancies of language, and much gentle fun, but from the start he shows a playfulness of disposition in regard to the whole affair, like a great boy on a vacation, as if the sense of it all being, so far as he was concerned, a surprising joke on a novel scale were in his mind and attitude all the time; and it is this humor, interlacing on the page like sunshine, that makes the life of his narrative. Occasionally there is the touch of true enjoyment out of doors, as when, under the clear blue sky on the hillside, it seemed as if he "were at work in the sky itself," and he notices the wild flowers coming into the chill world; but, as before at the wharf, so now at his farming, doubts assail his mind whether this manual labor is a satisfactory solution of his difficulties in adjusting himself to the world and opening communication with his fellow-men. The

disillusion, if there really had ever been any true
hope on his part, was effected even more quickly
than before.   Six weeks of manuring had brought
him to enthusiastic thankfulness that it was near
done: —

"That abominable gold-mine!   Thank God, we
anticipate getting rid of its treasures in the course
of two or three days!   Of all hateful places that
is the worst, and I shall never comfort myself for
having spent so many days of blessed sunshine
there.   It is my opinion that a man's soul may be
buried and perish under a dung-heap, or in a fur-
row of the field, just as well as under a pile of
money."

Ten weeks more finished the matter.   "Joyful
thought! in a little more than a fortnight I shall
be free from my bondage, . . . free to enjoy
Nature, — free to think and feel! . . . Even my
Custom House experience was not such a thraldom
and weariness; my mind and heart were free.   Oh,
labor is the curse of the world, and nobody can
meddle with it without becoming proportionably
brutified!   Is it a praiseworthy matter that I have
spent five golden months in providing food for
cows and horses?   It is not so."

Shortly after this outburst he made a visit to
his home at Salem, where he had been much
missed.   The few letters that his sister Louisa
wrote to him after he first went to the farm afford
the pleasantest, and almost the only glimpse of
his place in the family.   His experiment was

plainly not welcome to them; his mother "groaned over it;" but, apart from that, in which there may have been some family pride, though there was also real personal solicitude, it is noticeable how his sister counts the weeks he has been gone, and expresses their vehement desires for his return, and shows the thoughtfulness of the family for him in many ways. "Mother apostrophizes your picture because you do not come home," she writes, after "nine weeks" of absence, — "a great deal too long." In that secluded home he must indeed have been missed, and doubtless it seemed to them day by day more certain that he had really gone out from them into another world of his own. When he was in Salem in September, however, he no sooner crossed the threshold than he felt the old deserted life fall on him again like an evil spirit. "How immediately and irrecoverably," he writes to Sophia, "should I relapse into the way of life in which I spent my youth! If it were not for you, this present world would see no more of me forever. The sunshine would never fall on me, no more than on a ghost. Once in a while people might discern my figure gliding stealthily through the dim evening, — that would be all. I should be only a shadow of the night; it is you that give me reality, and make all things real for me. If, in the interval since I quitted this lonely old chamber, I had found no woman (and you were the only possible one) to impart reality and significance to life, I should have come back hither ere now, with a feeling that all was a dream and a mockery."

Brook Farm seems to him now only another dream, and he gives his final judgment on that matter: —

"Really I should judge it to be twenty years since I left Brook Farm; and I take this to be one proof that my life there was an unnatural and unsuitable, and therefore an unreal one. It already looks like a dream behind me. The real Me was never an associate of the community; there has been a spectral Appearance there, sounding the horn at daybreak, and milking the cows, and hoeing potatoes, and raking hay, toiling in the sun, and doing me the honor to assume my name. But this spectre was not myself. Nevertheless, it is somewhat remarkable that my hands have, during the past summer, grown very brown and rough, insomuch that many people persist in believing that I, after all, was the aforesaid spectral horn-sounder, cow-milker, potato-hoer, and hay-raker. But such people do not know a reality from a shadow. Enough of nonsense."

Nevertheless he went back for a while, not now as a farmhand, but apparently as a boarder, though he was made a trustee of the association and chairman of the committee on finance. He took, from this time, little part in the working life of the community. He had made up his mind that there was to be no home for him there, though "weary, weary, thrice weary of waiting so many ages."

He turns his mind to other plans of book-making, but does not have the seclusion he had found necessary for composition, and rather mournfully writes that he "must observe, and think, and feel, and content myself with catching glimpses of things which may be wrought out hereafter." He did observe with his habitual closeness the people who came and went, and the life of the inmates, sitting himself apart a good deal with a book before his face. He made friends with a few, a very few, of whom George Bradford and Frank Farley remained to him in later times; but he was, as always, averse to literary society, and came nearer to men of a different type in his human intercourse. Sophia, who had seen him there amid the fraternity, described his relationship to the others accurately, one of "courtesy and conformableness and geniality;" but, she tells him, the expression of his countenance was "that of a witness and hearer rather than of comradeship." In the fall weather he spent much of his time rambling about, and the scarlet color of the pastures, the warmth of the autumn woods, and the fading of the blue-fringed gentian, last blossom of the year, made up the texture of his notable life, just as similar things had earlier done by the Salem shore. In the spring he left the community, and made ready to go to Concord, where a place had been found for him to settle.

In the production of literature, life at Brook Farm had proved as barren as the years on Long

Wharf. He had contributed one story, "A Virtuoso's Collection," to "The Boston Miscellany" for May, 1842, and had added one more to his little books, "Biographical Stories [1] for Children." The volume was added to the "Grandfather's Chair" series, which was brought out in a new edition in 1842. To the same year belongs the enlarged edition of "Twice-Told Tales," [2] in two volumes, in which the number of stories was doubled, but the collection still left out many titles which were afterwards gathered.

Hawthorne had now been practically idle, so far as his genius was concerned, for three years, and had experimented to his heart's contènt in other

---

[1] *Biographical Stories for Children.* Benjamin West, Sir Isaac Newton, Samuel Johnson, Oliver Cromwell, Benjamin Franklin, Queen Christina. By Nathaniel Hawthorne. Author of Historical Tales for Youth, Twice-Told Tales, etc. Boston: Tappan and Dennet, 114 Washington St. 1842. 18mo. Pp. v, 161. "Historical Tales for Youth" was made up by binding the three Grandfather's Chair books in the 18mo second edition, 1842, together with this volume, and issued as four volumes in two, so labeled on the back.

[2] *Twice-Told Tales.* By Nathaniel Hawthorne. Boston: James Munroe and Company. 1842. 2 vols. 12mo. Pp. 331, 356. The first volume contained the same tales as the former edition, with The Toll-Gatherer's Day added. The second volume contained the following: Howe's Masquerade, Edward Randolph's Portrait, Lady Eleanore's Mantle, Old Esther Dudley, The Haunted Mind, The Village Uncle, The Ambitious Guest, The Sister Years, Snowflakes, The Seven Vagabonds, The White Old Maid, Peter Goldthwaite's Treasure, Chippings with a Chisel, The Shaker Bridal, Night Sketches, Endicott and the Red Cross, The Lily's Quest, Footprints on the Sea-Shore, Edward Fane's Rosebud, The Threefold Destiny.

modes of life. He had decided on immediate marriage. Sophia had recovered from her invalidism, and the lifelong headache she had experienced disappeared. It remained only to inform Madam Hawthorne of the engagement which had been so long concealed. He felt some trepidation, since, he says, "almost every agitating circumstance of her life had cost her a fit of illness." But his fears were groundless; she came out of her chamber to meet him as soon as he arrived, looking better and more cheerful than usual, and full of kindness. "Foolish me," he writes happily to Sophia, "to doubt that my mother's love could be wise, like all other genuine love! . . . It seems that our mother had seen how things were a long time ago; at first her heart was troubled, because she knew that much of outward as well as inward fitness was requisite to secure our peace; but gradually and quietly God has taught her that all is good, and so we shall have her fullest blessing and concurrence. My sisters, too, begin to sympathize as they ought, and all is well. God be praised! I thank Him on my knees, and pray Him to make me worthy of the happiness you bring me." The quiet marriage took place on July 9, 1842, at the home of the Peabodys in Boston, and Hawthorne and his wife went to Concord to reside at the Old Manse.

IV.

THE OLD MANSE.

THE life upon which the Hawthornes now entered for a period of three years and more was one of village quiet and country happiness. Concord was a characteristic town of eastern Massachusetts, with woodland, pasture, and hill lying unevenly in a diversified landscape, and in the midst the little river winding its slow way along by the famous bridge. The neighbors were few, and for the most part were members of the literary group of residents or visitors which gave Concord its later distinction. Yet even here, amid this rural peace and in so restricted a society, life at the Old Manse had a still deeper seclusion, as of a place of retreat and inviolable privacy; there was an atmosphere of solitude about it, wrapping it round, a sense of life with nature, and only slight and distant contact with the world, the privacy of a house that is snow-bound, lasting on as if by enchantment through July heats as well as February drifts. Hawthorne enjoyed this freedom in the place that first seemed to him like real home; and he and his wife pleased their fancy with thinking of it as a native paradise, with themselves as the new Adam and Eve, a thought which he had held in prospect before marriage and now clung to with a curious tenacity, pursuing it through many changes of idea; and, on the level of fact, he used to write that he had never lived so like a boy since he really was a boy in the old days in Maine.

The situation of the house lent itself to his tastes and inclinations. It was set back from the street, toward which an avenue of trees led out, and in the rear was the apple orchard with the river on its edge. He could look from his windows on the life of the road, with its occasional passers-by, for it was seldom that any one turned up the avenue to call; and he could go down to the stream to bathe and fish in summer, and to skate in winter on the black ice. He would wander out over the fields and into the woods with Ellery Channing, and go boating with Thoreau, both of whom were companions he liked to be with; or if he met Margaret Fuller in the paths of Sleepy Hollow, he could spend an hour or two in such half transcendental, half-sentimental talk as he records from such a chance encounter. Emerson came, also, to talk and walk with a man who was so firm-set in his own ways, being attracted to him by the subtleties of personality, for he never could read Hawthorne's tales then or afterwards, so profound was the opposition of their genius. If visitors stayed at the manse, it would be George Bradford, whom Hawthorne respected in the highest degree which his appreciation of others ever reached, or

Frank Farley, the half-crazy Brook Farmer, whom he gave himself to in a more self-sacrificing way to aid and comfort in his bewildered and imperfect state; or else Hillard would arrive, with much cheerfulness and news from Longfellow or others of the Cambridge men. But Hawthorne still kept the social world at a distance from his private and intimate self; these men, though he maintained kindly intercourse with them, never penetrated the shell of his true reserve; the contact was but superficial; and though they were good for company, he was often glad when they were gone and he was again alone with nature and his dreams, and the ways and things of household life.

In doors, and out doors, too, the new life was full of happiness. The gentle felicity of the literary recluse breathes through the description he gave of the place and time and habits of existence in the Manse, which he wrote out for his readers in the pleasantest of his autobiographical papers; and as for details to supply a more complete picture, — are they not written at large in the family letters? His wife worshiped him, and named him all the names of classic mythology and history, — Endymion, Epaminondas, Apollo, — glorying in his physical kinghood, as she saw it, when he glided skating in the rose-colored air of twilight, and also in the divine qualities of his spirit in doors, where he, on occasion — and the occasion grew more and more frequent — would wash the dishes, do the chores, cook the meals even, reliev-

ing her of every care of this kind in servant matters. He read to her in the evenings Macaulay,
all of Shakspere, the Sermon on the Mount for
Sunday, and generally the old books over, Thomson's "Castle," Spenser's faeryland, and the rest.
She rejoiced in him and all that was his; and she
painted and modeled a good deal and worked out
her artistic instincts very happily for herself,
and much to her husband's sympathetic pleasure.
Una, the first child, was born March 3, 1844, and
with this new revelation life went on in deeper
and sweeter ways of feeling, thought, and service.
The home is easily to be seen now, though it was
then so private a place, — a home essentially not
of an uncommon New England type, where refined
qualities and noble behavior flourished close to
the soil of homely duties and the daily happiness
of natural lives under whatever hardships; a home
of friendly ties, of high thoughts within, and of
poverty bravely borne.

There is no other word for it. Into this paradise of the Manse at Concord, set in the very heart
of outer and inward peace so complete, poverty
had come. Hawthorne had never had any super-
fluity in the things that give comfort and ease to
life even on a small scale. The years at Salem
had been marked by strict economies always, it is
plain; there was no more than enough in that
house, and thence arose in part its proud instinct
of isolation; and Bridge, it may be recalled, had
cheered up Hawthorne's doubting spirits on one

occasion by telling him that the three hundred dollars he earned, at the age of thirty, was sufficient to support him. On such a scale, he would not have called himself poor. But he was poor now, with that frank meaning that the word has to a man willing to do without, who cannot pay his small debts; in fact the smallness of the debt gives its edge to the misery. Hawthorne's whole New England nature rebelled against it; for there is nothing so deep-grained in the old New England character as the dislike to be "dependent," as the word is used. Hawthorne had gone through his training, too, in boyhood; he had never contracted debts till he had the money to pay them; and now he had miscalculated the "honesty" — as he doubtless named it in his thoughts — of other men. He had expected to draw out the thousand dollars invested at Brook Farm, and he supposed he would get it, especially if he really needed it, so unbusiness-like were his ideas; but as a matter of fact, he had lost that money in the speculation as much as if he had risked it in any other way. There was more to justify his irritation in the fact that "The Democratic Review," which had begun by paying five dollars a page, and had dropped to twenty dollars an article independent of length, had practically failed. He could not get paid for his work, and so he could not pay the small bills of household expenses. They were insignificant, in one sense, but the fact that they were not paid was independent of the amount. Emerson told him, so his wife writes, "to whistle for it, . . . everybody was in debt, . . . all worse than he was." There had been hardship almost from the first, as appears from Hawthorne's anger at Mr. Upham for telling tales in Salem of their "poverty and misery," on which his most significant comment, perhaps, is, "We never have been quite paupers." This was in March, 1843, and it is not unlikely that the modest ways of the house, and possibly that disregard for regular meals in which Hawthorne had long been experienced, may have given an impression of greater economy than there was need of; but, for all Hawthorne's natural disclaimer, the family plainly spent as little as possible, and he found the kitchen garden, whose fortunes he follows with such interest, gave him food as well as exercise. The "Paradisaical dinner," on Christmas Day, 1843, "of preserved quince and apple, dates, and bread and cheese, and milk," though of course its simplicity was only due to the cook's absence in Boston, indicates other difficulties of housekeeping, as also do a hundred half-amusing details of the household life. But the time of trouble came in dead earnest in the course of 1845, and in the fall of that year extremity is seen nigh at hand when Mrs. Hawthorne writes to her mother: "He and Una are my perpetual Paradise, and I besieged heaven with prayers that we might not find it our duty to separate, whatever privations we must outwardly suffer in consequence of remaining together."

The way out of all this trouble was found for Hawthorne by the same friends who had formerly rescued him in the time of his bitter discouragement before his engagement. In the spring of 1845, Bridge and Frank Pierce appeared on the scene, and finding Hawthorne at his daily task of chopping wood in the shed, they had a meeting of the old college-boy sort that brightens the page with one of those human scenes that, occurring seldom in Hawthorne's life, have such realistic effect.

"Mr. Bridge caught a glimpse of him, and began a sort of waltz towards him. Mr. Pierce followed; and when they reappeared, Mr. Pierce's arm was encircling my husband's old blue frock. How his friends do love him! Mr. Bridge was perfectly wild with spirits. He danced and gesticulated and opened his round eyes like an owl. . . . My husband says Mr. Pierce's affection for and reliance upon him are perhaps greater than any other person's. He called him ' Nathaniel,' and spoke to him and looked at him with peculiar tenderness."

The friends agreed that something should be done for Hawthorne through political influence, and in the course of the succeeding months there was much discussion of one and another office without immediate result; and meanwhile Hawthorne prepared to remove to Salem again, where he would so arrange matters that his mother and sisters should live in the same house with him. He had occasionally visited them during his married life, and on one of these short stays at home an incident occurred that should be recorded, not only for its singularity, but for its glimpse of his mother in a new light.

"For the first time since my husband can remember, he dined with his mother! This is only one of the miracles which the baby is to perform. Her grandmother held her on her lap till one of us should finish dining, and then ate her own meal. She thinks Una is a beauty, and, I believe, is not at all disappointed in her. Her grandmother also says she has the most perfect form she ever saw in a baby."

It was a year later than this anecdote that the family was reunited in Salem, but before following Hawthorne in his return to his native, though never very well loved town, his literary work in these years at Concord should be looked at.

When Hawthorne came to live at the Old Manse it was some time since he had produced any imaginative work, or, indeed, written anything except the stories for children in "Grandfather's Chair," which hardly rise above the class of hack work. Since leaving Salem in January, 1840, he had published but one paper that is remembered in his better writings, and that, "A Virtuoso's Collection," was of a peculiar character, being no more than a play of fancy, a curiosity of literary invention. After the lapse of two years and a half, duing which his imagination was uncreative, it might have been anticipated that, under the new conditions of tranquillity and private happiness, in the favorable surroundings of the Manse, he would have shown unusual fruitfulness; but such was not the case.   In the additional three years and a half that had now passed since he settled at Concord, he gave to the world only eighteen papers. They did not begin until 1843, and were distributed, for the most part, evenly over the next two years. "Little Daffydowndilly" appeared in "The Boys' and Girls' Magazine" in 1843.   Lowell's periodical, "The Pioneer," which lived only through the first three months of that year, contained "The Hall of Fantasy," in the February, and "The Birthmark," in the March number.   " The Democratic Review," which was still edited by O'Sullivan, a warm friend though editorially impecunious, received the remaining tales and sketches with a few exceptions.   It published them as follows: in 1843, "The New Adam and Eve," February; "Egotism, or The Bosom Serpent," March; "The Procession of Life," April; "The Celestial Railroad," May; "Buds and Bird Voices," June; "Fire Worship," December; in 1844, "The Christmas Banquet," January; "The Intelligence Office," March; "The Artist of the Beautiful," June; "A Select Party," July; "Rappaccini's Daughter," December; in 1845, "P.'s Correspondence," April.   "Earth's Holocaust" had appeared in "Graham's Magazine," March, 1844, apparently on Griswold's invitation; and two tales, "Drowne's Wooden Image," and "The Old Apple Dealer," were published, if at all, in some unknown place. All of these appeared under the author's own name, except that he once relapsed into his old habit by sending forth "Rappaccini's Daughter" as a part of the writings of Aubépine, a former pseudonym. "The Celestial Railroad" [1] was published separately as a pamphlet. He had edited for "The Democratic Review" also the "Papers of an old Dartmoor Prisoner;" and, in 1845, he assisted his friend Bridge to appear as an author by arranging and revising his "Journal of an African Cruiser." [2] This amount of literary work, taken altogther, is not considerable, and it is noticeable that in the last year, 1845, he seems to have practically ceased writing. He may have been a slow, and possibly an infrequent writer; such, in fact, is the inference to be drawn also from his earlier years, when he does not seem to have been a rapid producer except at the time of the issue of "Twice-Told Tales," when he had the strongest spur of ambition and most felt the need of succeeding. He had written, in all, about ninety tales and sketches

[1] *The Celestial Railroad.* By Nathaniel Hawthorne. Boston: published by Wilder & Co., No. 46 Washington Street. 1843. 32mo, paper. Pp. 32.

[2] *Journal of an African Cruiser.* Comprising Sketches of the Canaries, The Cape de Verdes, Liberia, Madeira, Sierra Leone, and Other Places of Interest on the West Coast of Africa. By an Officer of the U. S. Navy. Edited by Nathaniel Hawthorne. New York & London: Wiley and Putnam. 1845. 12mo. Pp. 179.

in twenty years, so far as is known, of which thirty-nine had been collected in the "Twice-Told Tales." He now took all his new tales and, adding to them five others from his earlier uncollected stock, wrote the introductory sketch of his Concord life, and issued them as "Mosses from an Old Manse"[1] in Wiley and Putnam's Library of American Books, New York. The work appeared in the earlier part of 1846. Later he was to gather up the yet uncollected papers of the first period, and add the very few tales afterwards written; but, in fact, Hawthorne's activity as a writer of tales practically ended with his leaving Concord. His work of that kind was done; and some idea of what he had accomplished, some analysis of his temperament and art as disclosed in these tales that were the only enduring fruits of the score of years since he left college and began the literary life, may now fairly be built on the total result.

These hundred tales and sketches of Hawthorne, broadly speaking, embody the literary results of his life, especially from his thirtieth to his fortieth year, and represent all its activities. In comparison with his later romances on the larger scale of

[1] *Mosses from an Old Manse.* By Nathaniel Hawthorne. In two parts. New York: Wiley and Putnam. 1846. 12mo. Pp. 211. The volume, the two parts bound as one, contained The Old Manse, The Birthmark, A Select Party, Young Goodman Brown, Rappaccini's Daughter, Mrs. Bullfrog, Fire Worship, Buds and Bird Voices, Monsieur du Miroir, The Hall of Fantasy, The Celestial Railroad, The Procession of Life.

life, they are studies, the 'prentice work of his
learning hand, and they disclose successively the
varieties and modes of his growth, which was
one of slow and almost imperceptible gradations,
until his method was fully formed, perhaps un-
consciously, and became the artistic mould of his
genius.   In his first attempts there was little, if
anything, more than in the instinctive motions of a
bird's wings, — the disposition for flight.   He had
the faculty of literary expression, which had been
nourished within and outwardly shaped in manner
by constant contact with the English classic authors, and especially with good prose, clear, simple,
and direct, from which melodious cadence had not
yet been eliminated.   He was touched, also, by
some vague literary ambition, not well defined,
but predisposed to fiction; and he had a physically
indolent habit, which kept him disengaged from
practical affairs and led him more and more into
meditative ways.   He did not have any inspiration
from within, any enthusiasm of sympathy or purpose, any life of his own, seeking expression; nor
did he find easily a definite subject outside himself
to observe, describe, and animate.   He turned,
in his early tales, to the local traditions and memories of his native place, and his stories were no
more than sketched history, provincial in atmosphere; nor did his genius show even faintly in
them any of its characteristic lines.   Scott, undoubtedly, was the author who had most affected
his mental habit, and with this exception, notwith-

standing what some critics have alleged of his so-
called "American predecessors," Charles Brockden
Brown and the author of "Peter Rugg," there is
no trace of any other literary influence upon him
either in this preparatory time or later in life; but
something of Scott is to be found permanently in
his creative work, — in the figure-grouping, the
high speeches, the oddities of character humor-
ously treated, and especially in the use of set
scenes individually elaborated to give the high
lights and to advance the story. But Scott's
method was at first inadequately applied, nor is
there any sign that the young author yet appreciated the artistic capabilities of the material he
was using.

Hawthorne's instinct was always right in the
preferences he showed among his works, of which
he was an excellent critic. It was not merely by
accident that he was first known as the author of
"Sights from a Steeple," though accident may
have had its share in the matter; and he long
continued to use this signature. This little essay
is very carefully written, and displays in remarkable perfection one quality that became so characteristic of his work that he has no rival in it except
Poe; it has that harmony of tone which is known
as keeping, a unity of design and development so
pervasive that the heavens above and the earth
below are seen from the little steeple as from a
centre, and nature and life seem to revolve around
the eye at that altitude with complete breadth as

well as smallness of proportion. It is the simplest
of trifles, as a composition; and, like much of
Hawthorne's writing, has a curious accent of the
school reader, as if it were meant for that, so well
is it adjusted to ready comprehension, so mild is
its interest, so matter-of-fact yet playful in fancy
is its substance, and so immediate is its village
charm. He was proud of it as a piece of writing,
and justly enough, for though it may seem like
one of the books of Lilliput, it perfectly accomplishes its little life. The type once struck out
in this clear way, Hawthorne returned to it again
and again, and always with the same happiness in
execution and the same delight in the thing itself.
In such a frame he would set the miniature of a
day, as in "The Toll-Gatherer's Day," or "Footprints on the Sea-Shore," or "Sunday at Home;"
or he would enclose a portrait, of Dutch faithfulness in detail, and suggestive also of the school in
other ways, as in "The Old Apple Dealer," or
with greater breadth of life, in "The Village
Uncle." "A Rill from the Town Pump" and
"Main Street" belong to the same kind of writing; and most akin to it, at least, are such mingled nature and home pieces as "Snowflakes,"
"Buds and Bird Voices," and "Fire Worship."
These titles cover the whole period of the tales,
but there is no change in the manner or quality,
— they are all of one kind.

To make sketches so slight as these interesting,
much more to embalm them in literature, requires

some magical touch either in the hand of the author or the heart of the reader. They are the thistledown of literature, creatures of a contemplative idleness as pure as childhood's own, the sun's impartial photography on the film of a rambler's eye; yet in these few pages are condensed some thousands, probably, of Hawthorne's days. The life they depict has been called barren, and the literary product has been described as thin. "What triviality, what monotony, what emptiness!" the critics exclaim. It is, indeed, provincial; rusticity is its element. Hawthorne, however, did not choose it, as a topic, for that reason, with a conscious intention to exploit it. He could not have been aware, he could not have half known even, how provincial it was, for he had never gone out of this countryside in which he was bred, or become acquainted with a different world; even on his journeys in stage-coaches he had not got free of it. The sketches made no artificial appeal; they have the true flavor of the soil, and are written for those who sprang from it and dwelt upon it and would be buried in it. This is the charm that still clings to them, and indeed pervades them like an aromatic odor in East Indian wood. They are true transcripts of life, though vanished now from its place at least in that region, which then enjoyed the seclusion of a nest of villages uninvaded by railroads, and was nearer perhaps to Calcutta and Sumatra and the Gold Coast than to New York. He was not so solitary and alone in

this life, after all. That part of New England was
not far from being a Forest of Arden, when Emerson might be met any day with a pail berrying
in the pastures, or Margaret Fuller reclining by
a brook, or Hawthorne on a high rock throwing
stones at his own shadow in the water. There
was a Thoreau — there still is — in every New
England village, usually inglorious. The lone
fisherman of the Isaak Walton type had become,
in the New World, the wood-walker, the flower-
hunter, the bird-fancier, the berry-picker, and
many another variety of the modern ruralist.
Hawthorne might easily have found a companion
or two of similar wandering habits and half her-
mit-like intellectual life, though seldom so fortunate as to be able to give themselves entirely up
to vagrancy of mind, like himself. Thoreau is,
perhaps, the type, on the nature side; and Hawthorne was to the village what Thoreau was to the
wild wood.

The truth of these sketches is their prime quality, for Hawthorne wrote them with the familiar
affection and home-attachment of one who had
fleeted the golden time of his youth amid these
scenes of common day, and prolonged it far into
manhood, and should never quite lose its glow of
mere existence, its kindliness for humble things,
its generous leisure for the perishable beauty of
nature dotted here and there with human life. It
is a countrified scene that is disclosed, but this
truth which characterizes it, this fidelity of fact

and sentiment and mood, suggests new and deeper values, — a charm, a health, even a power comes to the surface as one gazes, the power of peace in quiet places; and even a cultivated man, if he be not callous with culture, may feel its attractiveness, a sense that the tide of life grows full in the still coves as well as on all the sounding beaches of the world; and an existence in which the smell of peat-smoke is an event, and the sight of some children paddling in the water is a day's memory, and the mere drawing in of the salt sea wind is life itself, may seem as important in its simplicity as the varied impressions of a day in the season. This was Hawthorne's life; was it after all so valueless? He was well aware that even the native moralist, though unenlightened, would call him to account for wasting his time; and he made his apology after having obeyed his mood: —

"Setting forth at my last ramble on a September morning, I bound myself with a hermit's vow to interchange no thoughts with man or woman, to share no social pleasure, but to derive all that day's enjoyment from shore and sea and sky, — from my soul's communion with these, and from fantasies and recollections, or anticipated realities. Surely here is enough to feed a human spirit for a single day. Farewell, then, busy world! Till your evening lights shall shine along the street, — till they gleam upon my sea-flushed face as I tread homeward, — free me from your ties, and let me be a peaceful outlaw.

". . . But grudge me not the day that has been spent in seclusion, which yet was not solitude, since the great sea has been my companion, and the little sea-birds my friends, and the wind has told me his secrets, and airy shapes have flitted around me in my hermitage. Such companionship works an effect upon a man's character, as if he had been admitted to the society of creatures that are not mortal. And when, at noontide, I tread the crowded streets, the influence of this day will still be felt; so that I shall walk among men kindly and as a brother, with affection and sympathy, but yet shall not melt into the indistinguishable mass of humankind. I shall think my own thoughts, and feel my own emotions, and possess my individuality unviolated."

The apology seems adapted to the comprehension of the native moralist, it must be confessed, and is only an afterthought; for Hawthorne enjoyed his out-door life for its own sake, with little reference to its ameliorating influence on his social behavior. It is his own life, nothing more or less, that he thus describes, in the surroundings that heaven vouchsafed to him for better or worse in the Salem streets, in the Danvers lanes, by the coves of Marblehead, and along the western river uplands or the winding seashore of Beverly beside the islands. If he went far afield to Nantucket, he returned with " Chippings with a Chisel;" if he took an umbrella for a walk in the rain at home, he brought back " Night Sketches."

Such was his place.   His own delight in this existence is noticeable, for it fitted his nature; in
none of his works is the pleasure of the author in
writing them so marked a trait, and in none does
one come nearer to his natural self.   They are
complete and intimate revelations of the life of
his senses, the sounds and sights and happenings
of daily life.   They pleased the readers he had
at that time in New England, because they were
a faithful reproduction of the commonplace, played
upon by sentiment and slightly moralized, but
quite in the tone of the community; and all men
like to see themselves and their ways reflected in
the mirror of words.   They continue to yield the
same mild pleasure now, perhaps rather by virtue
of a reminiscent charm, for this life still exists
on the horizons of memory as a part of the days
gone by.   They belong with the literature of the
old red schoolhouse, the moss-covered bucket,
and the barefoot boy, — they are of a past that was
countrified and old-fashioned, and are its best
record; and even in the style, the mode of conception, they have the look of antiquated things.
Their nearness to the school has been adverted
to; the cognate piece, "A Bell's Biography," has
the completeness of a boy's composition; there is
a touch of nonage in them all, intellectually.   In
this, too, they are true to the time.   Things provincial seen by a provincial mind and set forth
by a provincial art, — such are these delicately
minute sketches; and unless one takes them so,

he misses their excellence, their virtue, the vitality they have. Life in the provinces, however, is also a divine gift, and its values have seldom been better portrayed, its breadth, its narrowness, its shadings through sunshine and nightfall, its sentiment, its miscellaneousness, its weariness ; but its controlling characteristic is its rural peace, such as one likes to see in a painting on the wall for year-long contemplation, and if this be broken, it is with real tragedy, disasters of the sea, or such an inland story as the drowning of the young woman at Concord so accurately told in the "Note-Books." Hawthorne's personality counts for much, too, in these pieces, as Irving's also does in his sketches. The sense of a kindly temperament, hospitable to all that lives and is in the dusty world, is felt like a touch of nature making us akin to the writer; the classic quality of the prose itself gilds all with sunshine; and one only needs love of the soil to complete the charm.

These records of memory and sentiment, however, belong to Hawthorne's ocular observation, in the main, and to the exterior sphere of his art. It is in the historical tales that his imagination first acts with seeing power; and here, too, the story by which he preferred to be known, "The Gentle Boy," stands out, though its prominence is rather a matter of priority than of distinction, for it is the fruit of his sympathies more than of his imagination. The remembrance of his ancestor's share in the persecution of the Quakers may have suggested the theme, and specially drawn out his own gentleness in the treatment. The singularity of the tale is partly due to the fascination of the child's name, Ilbrahim, which brings before the mind an eastern background, emphasizes his loneliness, and gives a suggestion of Scriptural charm to the narrative. One almost expects to see palm-trees growing up over him. He is, however, not individualized, — he is the universal orphan child; nor does it require any stretch of fancy to see in him the Christchild that St. Christopher bore over the river, for so might that Child have come into this wilderness preaching the eternal lesson. The pathetic story is a fable of piety, in fact, and is somewhat nervelessly handled for reality; the figures seem to glide in their motions, they are not quite set on the earth, they are impalpable except in their emotions. The facts lack firmness, though the feeling is wrought out with truth and refinement and makes an irresistible appeal of pity. It is, however, rather in the second historical tale which Hawthorne chose to stand as his pseudonym of authorship, "The Gray Champion," that he finds the type whose method he afterward repeats while developing it more richly. This tale is a picture, a scene, ending in a tableau; the surrounding stir of life, excitement, and atmosphere is first prepared, then the procession comes down the street, and is arrested, challenged, and thrown back by the venerable figure of the old Puritan who stands alone, like a prophet come back from the dead to deliver the people. The composition, the development, the focusing are in Scott's manner; it is from him that this dramatic presentation of history in a single scene, as here, or by a succession of scenes carrying on a story, is derived; partly pictorial, partly theatrical, always dramatic, this is the method which Hawthorne applied, the art of "The Author of Waverley," who was its great master in English fiction. "Endicott and the Red Cross " is a small study of the same sort; and in that sketch, and elsewhere, it is noticeable that in bearing and language the characters resemble the Covenanters, as Scott fixed the type in literature, more than they recall the real New England Puritans. Hawthorne's interest in colonial history found its most complete early expression in the "Tales of the Province House," in which he for once succeeded in grouping a series in a natural and effective way so as to make a larger whole. "Sir William Howe's Masquerade " is told by a succession of scenes, quite in the manner described, and the suggestion of mystery, the supernatural intention felt in the incident though not explicitly present in the fact, which in this story attends the last descending figure of the line of royal governors, as it also attended the figure of the Gray Champion, is also in Scott's manner, though more subtly effected. In "Edward Randolph's Portrait " the appearance of the picture on the faded canvas is mechanically accounted for, but at the

moment of its discovery this same supernatural
expectancy, as it were, is aroused in the behold-
ers; the incident itself recalls the appearance of
the portrait of old Lord Ravenswood at the
marriage ball of "The Bride of Lammermoor,"
though the analogy may very likely never have
occurred to Hawthorne.   "Old Esther Dudley"
is hardly more than a character portrait, — the
memory of the Province House and all it stood
for preserved in the devotion of the old servant
into whose life it had passed and whose spirit it
occupied like a reliquary of old time.   The best
of these four tales is "Lady Eleanore's Mantle,"
and it is so because in it Hawthorne's genius
passed out of the sphere of history and touched on
that universal moral world where his most original
creation was to lie.   It is necessary here only to
observe that in this tale he has fully seized the
power of the physical object, plainly sensible to
all as matter of fact, to serve as the medium for
moral suggestion often difficult to put into words,
of that sort whose effect is rather in the feelings
than in thought; and this, without turning the
object into an express symbol.   The mantle of
Lady Eleanore is a garment of pride, and also a
garment of death in its dread form of pestilence;
the story continually returns to it, as its physical theme, and the imagination fixes upon it by
a kind of fascination, as through it the double
aspect of Lady Eleanore's isolation is sensibly
clothed, her haughtiness and her contagion, whose

fatal bond is in this mantle, which finally seems not only to express her life but to rule her tragedy. Here one feels a new power, because while Hawthorne still retains the method of narration he had adopted, he has enriched it with an art and genius distinctly his own. In another tale, — which is provincial if not historical, and which was one of his earlier pieces, — "Roger Malvin's Burial," there is also a noticeable beginning in his art, for in this he uses undesigned coincidence to give that impression of a guided accomplishment of fate, which is so dramatically effective to the moral sense. From these few instances it will be observed that Hawthorne reached artistic consciousness, and a mastery of aim and method, slowly and along no one line of development; rather his genius seemingly put forth many tendrils, seeking direction and support and growth, and gradually in these hundred tales he found himself and his art.

History assisted Hawthorne's imagination in its operation by affording that firmness and distinctness of outline which was most needed in his work; it gave body to his creations, but in his most characteristic and original tales this body was not to be one of external fact, but of moral thought. His genius contained a primary element of reflection, of meditation on life, of the abstract; and while his imagination might take its start and find an initial impulse, an occasion, in some concrete object on which it fastened, its course in working itself out was governed by this abstract moral intention. In dealing with life directly, and not through history, the tales which are at the least remove from mere observation are those that were immediately suggested by his journeys and embody these experiences in their background if not in the whole; such are "The Seven Vagabonds" and the two Shaker episodes, "The Canterbury Pilgrims" and "A Shaker Bridal." His experiments in the grotesque style, "Mr. Higginbotham's Catastrophe" and "Mrs. Bullfrog," can be left one side, for they never passed the stage of amateurish weakness, and led to nothing. His meditation on life sometimes centres about an individual, but this is only seeming; his real interest was always in collective life or in the atmosphere round about all lives. To take a simple case, but one typical of his point of view and method, "The Haunted Mind" is a study in the night-atmosphere of the human soul, in a certain state, and is rendered with the vividness of personal experience. "Fancy's Show-Box" is a more individualized variant of the same motive, and yet its substance is the frankly abstract question of responsibility for guilt which is not acted but only entertained; and as in this tale the story is of the sins that hover round the soul waiting to be born, so in "David Swan" the story is of the events that might happen to an unsuspecting man, but pass by innocuous after merely shadowing his sleep like a threat. To this atmosphere of life also belongs the elaborate shadow sketch, "Monsieur de Miroir," a motive often treated in literature and here more lightly handled than one would have anticipated, and hence more ineffectively, for Hawthorne's power did not lie in his playfulness of fancy so much as in its darker workings. Hawthorne let his mind brood over these possibilities of life, these half-vital acts, thoughts, and beings, like fears in an anxious mind, things that have only partial being, but are real enough at times to trouble the mind's eye. A touch of this atmosphere of unreality is found, also, in such a tale as "Wakefield," the story of the man who disappeared from his place in life though he remained in the neighborhood unknown; the main theme is rather the man cut off from life, which Hawthorne so often recurred to, but the element of life's contingency, the nearness of an event that might happen but never does, is what makes the strangeness of this curious study.

In approaching life itself in its individual forms, the slightness of Hawthorne's attempt in the earlier pieces is very marked. A good example of it is "The Wives of the Dead." Two wives, who suppose their husbands have been lost at sea, are told separately at different hours of the night, in the house they occupy together, that the lost has been saved; each believing the other a widow leaves her to sleep. Here are merely two dramatic moments described and opposed, a perfect example of likeness in difference on a small scale, done with great truth to nature; the sketch is finely wrought, and gains by its intense condensation of situation and its brief single mood. Two such moments, in his simpler tales, Hawthorne was accustomed to take, and treat by opposition; the power lies in the contrast. Such, to give examples, are "The White Old Maid," "Edward Fane's Rosebud," and with less distinctness, "The Wedding Knell," where the contrast goes back to lost youth for effect. In the very artificial fable, which has elements of the fairy story in it, "The Three-fold Destiny," there is this simple construction, and it is found also in "The Prophetic Pictures," though that tale is primarily a study in the idea of fate, a subject seldom touched by Hawthorne, the notion of an inevitable destiny foreseen by the painter's intuition and forecast on the canvas, but implicit from the beginning in character. In all these tales scene, situation, and character, as well as the dialogue, are handled with little variation; pictorial and dramatic effects are sought, and the slight plot is developed, by the means usual to Hawthorne's hand. The allegorizing method, it should be observed, though it appears with greater or less influence, is not employed with any exclusiveness, but takes its place with other resources of his art. In "The Great Carbuncle," however, and in "The Man of Adamant," the allegory is predominant and absorbs the tale. Perhaps it is as an offshoot of this allegorizing mood that the tales of pure fancy should be regarded, those masque-like inventions, "A Select Party" and "The Hall of Fantasy," together with "The Intelligence Office" and "A Virtuoso's Collection," also remnants of old-fashioned ingenuity. In such fantasy Hawthorne found a better channel for that play of his mind which had earlier sought expression in the grotesque; oddity of thought he had in plenty, and the sense of oddity was often as far as his humorous faculty reached, for it was perceptive rather than sympathetic.

Of collective life, frankly so treated, Hawthorne wrote frequently, — the group is an important one. The crowd attracted him by its polarity to his own solitude, and it is curious to observe how fond he was of the processional in his work. The simple illustration of this sort is "The Procession of Life;" here he marshals mankind, as with the power of a magician's rod, in hordes. In "The New Adam and Eve" he reviews society in its institutions and its garniture of civilization; and the conception is a happy device by which to obtain the requisite distance and wholeness for a single point of view. "Earth's Holocaust," though superficially different, is a variant of the same theme, presenting the product of life in masses; its inclusion of the indestructibility of the good is noticeable as a philosophical idea such as he rarely introduced in an explicit way. The felicitous allegory of "The Celestial Railroad" satirizes human nature without bitterness; but, while the universality of Bunyan's emblems is strikingly shown by the ease with which they are adapted to the new age of steam, the tale is, as it were, music transposed; the cleverness is Hawthorne's, but Bunyan wrote the piece. These four tales, admirable as they are in breadth, are nevertheless essentially reflective. The imaginative group of the same scope is of a higher rank. In it the general life is set forth with more individuality, though life in the abstract still occupies the foreground. To set aside such a moral parable as "The Lily's Quest," or such an illustration of the power of love to raise a man above himself temporarily as "Drowne's Wooden Image," or such a study of isolation as "The Man of Adamant," in all of which the didacticism is rather nakedly felt, there are two tales that equally exemplify this class, "Dr. Heidegger's Experiment" and "The Christmas Banquet." In the first the ghastliness of the reversal of the course of life backward, as the guests drink the elixir of youth, while it suggests the paltriness of our pleasures, is a powerful lesson in the beneficence of that daily death whereby we resign the past; this rejuvenation violates nature, and so shocks us, and by the very shock we are reconciled with nature, from which we had parted in thought. "The Christmas Banquet" is one of the most artistically conceived of all the tales, though its subject repels us; the wretchedness of life is shown in the persons of numerous guests through a succession of

years, with the effect of a multiplicity of instances;
yet at the end it is found that the worst wretch of
all is the constant guest with the cold, unfeeling
heart, — the climax of misery is not to have lived
at all. The tale is carefully composed, especially
in those points of keeping, balance, and contrast
in which Hawthorne was expert, yet by some mis-
adventure it fails to interpret itself clearly. In
proportion, however, as imagination enters into
these stories under the impulse of the artistic faculty, it will be seen that they lend themselves less
readily to such definite classification as has thus
far been attempted; the various elements of Hawthorne's genius and art draw together and com-
bine, and in the group that remains to be noticed
his originality is most conspicuous, and this requires a more flexible treatment, though without
exception these tales fall under the head of the
general life set forth reflectively in the forms of
concrete imagination.

Probably in no one point is Hawthorne's peculiarity so obviously marked as in the persistency
with which he clings to a physical image, vividly
impressing it upon the mind, like a text which
gathers atmosphere and discloses significance under the special treatment of the preacher. It is
said that he had, artistically, the allegorizing temperament, and he in fact did use all those forms of
imagery — the fable, apologue, parable — which
belong to this mode of presentation; but in his
most effective work the allegory is more subtly

embodied, — it exists in suggestion, and its appeal is as much emotional as didactic. The nucleus of this new mystery is the physical object that he seizes upon and in which his imagination works as if it were clay, recreating it so that it becomes more than pure symbol, as has been illustrated in "Lady Eleanore's Mantle;" and sometimes it is almost vitalized into a life of its own. This power of such an object to become the medium of thought and emotion as well as to convey merely allegorical meaning he gradually discovered; and doubtless he especially valued its function to afford by its crude definiteness a balance to the tenuous and impalpable, the vagueness, refinement, and mystery, to which it is the complement, in his art; he gains reality by its presence for what else, as a whole, might seem too insubstantial, too much a part of that shadow world in which he dreaded to dwell altogether.

Such an object is, at all events, a necessity for him in his greater work. A crude form of it is the snake, in the tale of "The Bosom Serpent," one of those "allegories of the heart" which he apparently meant to write in a series of which he never found the key. The idea is an old one; the man with a snake in his bosom is a hypochondriac, who by centring his thoughts on himself has developed this fancy and is tortured by it. The cure is wrought when he forgets himself in returning to the love of his wife. The almost physical dismissal of the serpent into the fountain, which is neither averred nor denied, like a devil cast out as in old times, is puerile; but Hawthorne was, in other tales, not averse to a naturalistic explanation of his mysteries, as if a basis of matter of fact, however irrelevant essentially, gave more plausibility to their truth. If the snake is "egotism," if it is the torture of self in a man, if its cure is the loss of self in love, then making the snake real and physical is absurdity; medicine and morals are confounded; the scientific fact has nothing to do with the artistic meaning and is a concession to the gross senses of the reader. The story illustrates the method, rather than its successful application; for the physical horror is really greater here than the moral revulsion. In "The Minister's Black Veil" the object is more happily dealt with. It is to be noticed that Hawthorne did not invent these objects, he found them; and, in this case, he has used the tradition of an old Puritan minister of the past age. He uses the veil to typify man's concealment of himself from others, even the nearest; and while it visibly isolates the minister among his fellow-men, it finally unites him with them in a single lot; for to the mind's eye, educated by this image to a new power of seeing, all men wear this veil; humanity is clothed with it in life, and moulders away beneath it in the grave, whither its secrets are carried. The seeming exception is found to be the rule; the horror attaching to the one unseen face is now felt in all faces; the race is veiled, and the bit of crape has fallen like the blackness of night upon all life, for life has become a thing of darkness, a concealment. Here the moral idea is predominant, and in it the symbol issues into its full life.

Hawthorne's art became always, not only more vividly symbolized, but more deeply moralized. The secrecy of men's bosoms was a matter that interested him very much; the idea had a fascination for him. It is the substance of the tale of " Young Goodman Brown," who goes to the witches' Sabbath in the Essex woods and there sees those who have taught him religion, the righteous and the good, men and women, and his own wife, — sees them or their devil-brewed phantasms; he calls on heaven, and finds himself suddenly alone; but when he returns to the village, and looks again on the venerable fathers and mothers of his childhood and his own tender and loving wife, he cannot free his mind from the doubt, — were they what they seemed or had he indeed beheld them there in the woods at their orgy? It is as if for him the veil were lifted, and he alone saw, like omniscience, into the bosoms of all. Suspicion, arising from his own contact with evil, though he escaped, has imparted the look of hypocrisy to all life; this is his bedevilment. Here the place of the physical object is taken by the incident of the woods, and the moral idea is less clearly stated; the story is one of those whose significance is felt to contain mystery which Hawthorne meant to remain in its dark state.

In "The Birthmark" the physical object is again found as the initial point of the tale and the guiding clue of the imagination in working it out. The situation presents the opposition of the love of science to human love, but no conflict is described, because the first is the master passion from the beginning, and, being indulged, leads to the loss of the second in the death of the wife, who perishes in having the birthmark removed. The moral idea, as not unfrequently happens, seems to flake off from the tale, like the moral of the old fable, and is to the effect that imperfection belongs to mortal life, and if it is removed wholly mortality must go with it; and the lesson is of the acceptance of imperfection in what men love, as a permanent condition, and indeed almost as the humanizing feature, of earthly life. It is noticeable that the clergyman, the physician, and the artist are the only specific types that attracted Hawthorne; he held them all romantically, and science he conceived as alchemy. This same predisposition appears in "Rappaccini's Daughter; " she was the experiment of her father in creating a live poison-woman, a vitalized flower, the Dryad as it were of the poison-tree humanized in mortal shape; the physical object is here the flowering tree, with its heavy fragrance; and the plot lies only in the gradual transformation of the young man by continuous and unconscious inoculation until he is drawn into the circle of death to share the woman's isolation as a lover, both being shut

off from their kind by the poison atmosphere that
exhales from them; the catastrophe lies in the
moral idea that for such poison there is no anti-
dote but death, and the lady dies in drinking the
draught that should free her. The fact that Hawthorne, when writing the story, said he did not
know how it would end, is interesting as indicat-
ing that his literary habit was to let the story
tell itself from within according to its impulses,
and not to shape it from without by his own pre-
determined purpose; a pure allegorist, it may be
observed, would have followed naturally the latter
method. This may account for the indefiniteness
and mystery of effect often felt, as well as for
the inartistic didacticism in the concluding sentences, frequently to be observed, where it appears as one or more afterthoughts possibly to
be drawn from the story, but not exhausting its
moral significance. In this case, powerful as the
tale is, the moral intention is left vague, though
except as a parable the invention is meaningless.

In the last story to be instanced, "The Artist of
the Beautiful," the lucidity of the parable is complete. The physical object is the butterfly; on its
wings the tale moves, and perishes in its destruc-
tion. The moral idea lies in the exposition of
achievement as a freeing of the artist's soul so
that his work has become a thing of indifference
to him, let its fortunes be what they will, — it is
the dead chrysalis from which he has escaped;
and the isolation of the artist's life is set forth

pathetically but with no suggestion of evil in it, for though the world has rejected him he lives in his own world in the calm of victory. No tale is so delicately wrought as this; in it the symbolism, which is carried out in minute and precise detail, the moral significance, which is as clear as it is deep, and the presence of a spiritual world in life for which a visible language is found, are all present, in harmonious blending; and it has the added and rare charm of happiness without loss of truth. It is unique; and if one were to choose a single tale, best representing Hawthorne's powers, methods, and successes, technically and temperamentally as well as in imaginative reach and spiritual appeal, it is by this he should be known.

In these six tales in which Hawthorne's originality is most characteristically expressed, the idea of isolation is common to all; like the secrecy of men's bosoms, this solitude in life is a fixed idea in his imagination, an integral part of life as it was viewed by him, and he seldom freed his attention from it even temporarily. On the other hand, sin, conscience, evil, though their realm is felt to be a neighboring province, are not here directly dealt with. His probings in that sphere belong to a later time. These tales, like the others, are studies of life, not of the evil principle by itself as a thing of special interest; they view life as lying under a shadow, it is true, but this shadow is their atmosphere, not their world. The point should be defined, perhaps more explicitly:

the Calvinism of New England, its interest in the
perversion of man's will, his sinful state, and the
mysterious modes of salvation, is not the region
of Hawthorne's imagination, as here disclosed.
It is enough to note this, here, as bearing on his
representative character. The most surprising
thing, however, is that his genius is found to be
so purely objective; he himself emphasized the objectivity of his art. From the beginning, as has
been said, he had no message, no inspiration welling up within him, no inward life of his own that
sought expression. He was not even introspective. He was primarily a moralist, an observer
of life, which he saw as a thing of the outside,
and he was keen in observation, cool, interested.
If there was any mystery in his tales, it was in
the object, not in the author's breast; he makes
no confessions either direct or indirect, — he describes the thing he sees. He maintained that
his tales were perfectly intelligible, and he meant
this to apply not only to style but to theme. It is
best to cite his own testimony. His personal temper is indicated in the fragmentary phrase in the
"Note-Books;" "not that I have any love of mystery, but because I abhor it," he writes; and again
in the oft-quoted passage, he describes perfectly the
way in which his nature coöperated with his art
to give the common ground of human sympathy,
but without anything peculiar to himself being
called into play: —

"A cloudy veil stretches over the abyss of my

nature. I have, however, no love of secrecy and darkness. I am glad to think that God sees through my heart, and, if any angel has power to penetrate into it, he is welcome to know everything that is there. Yes, and so may any mortal who is capable of full sympathy, and therefore worthy to come into my depths. But he must find his own way there. I can neither guide nor enlighten him. It is this involuntary reserve, I suppose, that has given the objectivity to my writings; and when people think that I am pouring myself out in a tale or an essay, I am merely telling what is common to human nature, not what is peculiar to myself. I sympathize with them, not they with me."

In the preface to "Twice-Told Tales," which however was prefixed to a late edition and may be fairly held to cover his view of his tales in general, he directs attention to their objectivity in another form: —

"The sketches are not, it is hardly necessary to say, profound; but it is rather more remarkable that they so seldom, if ever, show any design on the writer's part to make them so. They have none of the abstruseness of idea or obscurity of expression which mark the written communications of a solitary mind with itself. They never need translation. It is, in fact, the style of a man of society. Every sentence, so far as it embodies thought or sensibility, may be understood and felt by anybody who will give himself the trouble to read it, and will take up the book in a proper mood."

A little further on he adds his statement of what the sketches both are and are not: —

"They are not the talk of a secluded man with his own mind and heart (had it been so, they could hardly have failed to be more deeply and permanently valuable), but his attempts, and very imperfectly successful ones, to open an intercourse with the world."

To Hawthorne himself these tales seemed so external; and his analysis, however much may be allowed for modesty in the statement, appears to be true.

Hawthorne left himself out of his work, so far as a man can. Indeed, his own life was neither vigorous nor one of much variety of faculty, outside of his art. He had the indolence of the meditative habit, or of the artistic nature, if one chooses to call it so. He clearly spent a great deal of time doing nothing in particular; he read, observed the world of the passing seasons, made long memoranda of nature and human nature and short notes of ideas for tales and sketches, and had in fact large leisure, except in the years when he was in the Boston Custom House, and he was not without leisure even then. He shows no inclination toward scholarship, but was a desultory reader of English, with some French; he had no intellectual interests, apparently, of a philosophical kind; the aloofness in which he stood from

Longfellow and Emerson, for example, was not shyness of nature wholly, but stood for the real aloofness of his mind from their ways of life, from the things that absorbed them in their poetic and speculative activity; it is but another example, if it is added that he took no interest in public affairs, truly speaking. He was a Democrat, but that does not fully account for his indifference to those philanthropies which his literary friends shared; for, as a party man, he was not zealous. His nature was torpid in all these ways; there was dullness of temperament, indifference to all except the one thing in which he truly lived, his artistic nature; and here he was an observer, using an objective method with as little indebtedness to personal experience as ever artist had. His reserve amounted to suppression; and, in fact, his personal life was not of the sort that must find a voice. He seemed to feel that the "Twice-Told Tales," at least, which he described as "memorials of tranquil and not unhappy years," had contracted some faintness of life from their author's mind, as if a low vital tone characterized them, owing to his incapacity to yield himself with fullness of power even to this reflective or creative art: —

"They have the pale tint of flowers that blossomed in too retired a shade, — the coolness of a meditative habit, which diffuses itself through the feeling and observation of every sketch. Instead of passion there is sentiment; and, even in what

purport to be pictures of actual life, we have allegory, not always so warmly dressed in its habili-
ments of flesh and blood as to be taken into the
reader's mind without a shiver. Whether from
lack of power, or an unconquerable reserve, the
Author's touches have often an effect of tameness;
the merriest man can hardly contrive to laugh at
his broadest humor; the tenderest woman, one
would suppose, will hardly shed warm tears at his
deepest pathos. The book, if you would see anything in it, requires to be read in the clear, brown,
twilight atmosphere in which it was written; if
opened in the sunshine, it is apt to look exceedingly like a volume of blank pages."

This is, of course, the natural overstatement of
an author whose work has gone from him and
seems less vital because he has outlived it; but
nevertheless it contains sound judgment as to the
limitations of his art.

But notwithstanding Hawthorne's objectivity
and reserve, of which he justly makes so much,
and the low vital tone of his work, resulting from
whatever cause, he did not altogether escape from
himself in his art; his shadow followed him into
that world. The "clear brown twilight atmosphere " of which he speaks was an affair of temperament; it exhaled from his personality. That
recurring idea of isolation, the sense of the secrecy
of men's bosoms, the perception of life as always
lying in the shadow that falls on it, proceeded
from predilections of his own, differentiating him

from other men; there may have been no very
perilous stuff in his breast, nothing to confess or
record peculiar to himself in act or experience, no
intensity of self-life, but there was this temperament of the solitary brooder upon life. In that
common fund of human nature which he said
was the basis of sympathy between himself and
the world, there was also some specialization,
which is rightly ascribed to his race qualities. He
took practically no interest in life except as seen
under its moral aspects as a life of the soul; and
this absorption in the moral sphere was due to
his being a child of New England. It was his inheritance from Puritanism. What distinguished
Puritan life and the people who grew up under its
influences was an intense self-consciousness of
life in the soul, — in a word, spirituality of life;
and Hawthorne, as he came to find himself in his
growth, disclosed one form of this spirituality
both reflectively and imaginatively in his writings,
the form that lived in him. The moral world, the
supremacy of the soul's interests, how life fared
in the soul, was his region; he thought about
nothing else. He desired to present what he saw
through the medium of romantic art, but he was
never able to be wholly content with this medium;
he desired to make assurance doubly sure by expressing it in its abstract moral terms also, either
explicitly in an idea which shows through the
story, or else imperfectly in an allegory or symbol
where the moral element should be definitely felt

in its intellectual, its unartistic form. The fact that this abstract element really outvalues the tale and its characters is shown, for example, by the lack of interest one feels in the future of his characters, in what becomes of them at the end of the story; they are lost from the mind, because their function is fulfilled in illustrating an idea; and, that once conveyed, the characters cease to have life,— they disappear, like the man of science or the artist of the beautiful, into the background of the general world; they fade out. It is by this abstract moral element that Hawthorne's art is universalized.

His manner, it must be acknowledged, retains provinciality; in the best of the tales, just as in those sketches of observation in Salem, there is something countrified in the mode of handling, something archaic and stiff in the literary mould, something awkward, cramped, and bare in the way his art works in its main motions, however felicitous in word and fall is the garment of prose as language. There is a lack of urban ease, certainty, and perfection of manner. The limitation, however, stops there. The world in which the artist works is the universal world of man's nature, just as much as is Shakespeare's. He escapes from provincialism here, in the substance, because he was a New Englander, not in spite of that fact; for the spirituality which is the central fact of New England life itself escapes from provincialism, being a pure expression of that

Christianity in which alone true cosmopolitan-
ism is found, of that faith which presents mankind
as one and indivisible. Hence arises in Hawthorne a second distinctly Puritan trait, his democracy. He looks only at the soul; all outward
distinctions of rank and place, fortune, pride,
poverty, disappear as unconcerning things; he
sees all men as in the light of the judgment day.
He does this naturally, too, almost without knowing it, so inbred in him is that preconception of
the Christian soul, whose moral fortune constitutes
alone the significance of life. In these ways the
race element, the New England element, is shown;
from it springs the moral prepossession of his art,
its universal quality, and its democratic substance.
This was the nucleus of inheritance and breeding,
which together with his temperament governs his
art from within, even amid all its personal reserve
and its objectivity. The gradually increasing
power of these elements gave his tales greater intensity and reach, and was to lift his romances to
another level; for what was inchoate and experimental in the tales, in many ways, was to receive
a new and greater development in his later work,
on which his world-wide fame rests. The tales
had not brought him fame; as yet, his audience
was small, and confined to New England. He
had advanced so far as to seem like one talking
to his friends, instead of, as at first, one talking
to himself in a dark place, as he said; but recog-
nition, such as he desired, he had not obtained.

There is certainly some irritation in his repeated
references to the early neglect he felt from the
public, at the time when, as he says, he "was for
a good many years the obscurest man of letters
in America." He thought this lack of appreciation palsied his efforts, so that he did not do what
he might have done, and it may have been the
case; but before the days when he wrote "The
Artist of the Beautiful" he must have learned that
one must serve the Muses for themselves alone.

V.

THE SCARLET LETTER.

AMID the hard conditions of his life at Concord
Hawthorne had decided to place himself again
under the ægis of his political friends to earn his
living as a public officer. He had no confidence
in his literary capacity as a means of livelihood.
He found himself, he says, unable to write more
than a third of the time, and he composed slowly
and with difficulty; he refers more than once to
that hatred of the pen which belongs to a tired
writer, and he was frequently indisposed to composition for long periods; and, in any event, he
thought that what he wrote must appeal necessarily to so small an audience that, should he continue to devote himself exclusively to a literary
career, he must do so as a professional hack-writer
of children's books, translations, newspaper essays, and such miscellaneous drudgery. His habits, formed in his years at Salem, included an element of large leisure, an indulgence of one's self in
times and seasons of mental activity, a certain
lethargy of life; and he had not shown any power
of sustained production in the monotony of daily
work for bread. He felt a dread of such neces-

sity. "God keep me," he writes to Hillard before this time, "from ever being really a writer
for bread!" The only alternative for him was
office-holding.

The election of Polk to the Presidency gave
his friends the opening, and the campaign to secure an appointment was begun. Bridge, then
living in bachelor quarters at Portsmouth Navy
Yard, conceived the rather daring idea of a sailor
house-party with Hawthorne as its centre, for the
purpose of making him acquainted with the political group in whose hands influence lay; and, if
it be remembered that the Hawthornes had not
spent an evening out for years, and still continued
their seclusive life, the proposition may well seem
a bold stroke. The party, however, gathered in
the summer of 1845; Franklin Pierce and his
wife, Senator Atherton and his wife, of New
Hampshire, and Senator Fairfield of Maine, to
mention the notables, were the principal guests,
and there were several others, making a greater
company than Hawthorne had been thrown with
since he lodged at Brook Farm. It was an in-
formal naval picnic, apparently, of two or three
weeks, and Bridge thought that its main object of
popularizing Hawthorne with the Senators was
attained. The point of attack was the Salem
Post Office, but this proved impracticable, and
attention was turned to the Custom House, where
either the surveyorship or the naval office might
be got. Meanwhile Bancroft offered him a clerk-

ship in the Charlestown Navy Yard, which he declined. He was sufficiently sure of success to make him remove from Concord to Salem to reside, and early in October he was established again in the old chamber of his youth, having decided to share his mother's house for the present. He spent his time in writing the introductory sketch of the Old Manse, and in seeing the "Mosses" through the press. The appointment lagged, owing to local complications in the party, but an arrangement was finally made which was agreeable to all concerned, so that Hawthorne took office without enmity from disappointed candidates who would have benefited if he had not appeared upon the scene backed by what must have been locally regarded as outside interference. He received notice of his nomination as surveyor on March 23, 1846, and it was described "as decidedly popular with the party," as well as with men of letters and the community; he soon took charge of the office, those who had made way for him were appointed inspectors under him, and he entered on the enjoyment of a salary of twelve hundred dollars.

It was indeed a singular chance of life that had transformed the recluse romancer of the silent Herbert Street house, where for all the years of early manhood he had lived unnoticed and almost unknown, into the high business official of the Custom House, the lofty neighbor of that humble dwelling, on whose wide granite steps, columned portico, and emblematic eagle, with the flag over all, he must have looked so often with never a thought that there was to be his distinguished place in the world of men; and yet Hawthorne, on coming into this office, seems to have been pleased with a sense of making a part of Salem as his ancestors had done in the old days. He did not love Salem, but genuine truth gives body to those passages of autobiography in which he claims his parentage and kinship and seems writing the obituary of his race there, in connection with his memories of the Custom House. He knew himself a story-teller whom these ancestors would little approve, for all his mask as the surveyor, but in his official place he felt himself a Salemite with some peculiar thoroughness; and, familiar as the passage is, no other words can take the place of his own expression of this sense of rootedness in the soil, which is so close to the secret of his genius: —

"This old town of Salem — my native place, though I have dwelt much away from it, both in boyhood and maturer years — possesses, or did possess, a hold on my affections, the force of which I have never realized during my seasons of actual residence here. Indeed, so far as its physical aspect is concerned, with its flat, unvaried surface, covered chiefly with wooden houses, few or none of which pretend to architectural beauty, — its irregularity, which is neither picturesque nor quaint, but only tame, — its long and lazy street lounging wearisomely through the whole extent of the peninsula, with Gallows Hill and New Guinea at one end, and a view of the almshouse at the other, — such being the features of my native town, it would be quite as reasonable to form a sentimental attachment to a disarranged checker-board. And yet, though invariably happiest else-where, there is within me a feeling for old Salem, which, in lack of a better phrase, I must be con-tent to call affection. The sentiment is probably assignable to the deep and aged roots which my family has struck into the soil. It is now nearly two centuries and a quarter since the original Briton, the earliest emigrant of my name, made his appearance in the wild and forest-bordered settlement, which has since become a city. And here his descendants have been born and died, and have mingled their earthly substance with the soil, until no small portion of it must necessarily be akin to the mortal frame wherewith, for a little while, I walk the streets. In part, therefore, the attachment which I speak of is the mere sensuous sympathy of dust for dust. Few of my country-men can know what it is; nor, as frequent trans-plantation is perhaps better for the stock, need they consider it desirable to know.

"But the sentiment has likewise its moral qual-ity. The figure of that first ancestor, invested by family tradition with a dim and dusky gran-deur, was present to my boyish imagination, as far back as I can remember. It still haunts me, and

induces a sort of home-feeling with the past, which
I scarcely claim in reference to the present phase
of the town.   I seem to have a stronger claim to
a residence here on account of this grave, bearded,
sable-cloaked and steeple-crowned progenitor, —
who came so early, with his Bible and his sword,
and trode the unworn street with such a stately
port, and made so large a figure, as a man of war
and peace, — a stronger claim than for myself,
whose name is seldom heard and my face hardly
known.   He was a soldier, legislator, judge; he
was a ruler in the Church; he had all the Puri-
tanic traits, both good and evil.   He was likewise
a bitter persecutor, as witness the Quakers, who
have remembered him in their histories, and relate
an incident of his hard severity towards a woman
of their sect, which will last longer, it is to be
feared, than any record of his better deeds, although these were many.   His son, too, inherited
the persecuting spirit, and made himself so conspicuous in the martyrdom of the witches, that
their blood may fairly be said to have left a stain
upon him.   So deep a stain, indeed, that his old
dry bones, in the Charter Street burial-ground,
must still retain it, if they have not crumbled
utterly to dust! . . . Let them scorn me as they
will, strong traits of their nature have intertwined
themselves with mine.

"Planted deep, in the town's earliest infancy
and childhood, by these two earnest and energetic
men, the race has ever since subsisted here, —

always, too, in respectability; never, so far as I
have known, disgraced by a single unworthy member; but seldom or never, on the other hand,
after the first two generations, performing any
memorable deed, or so much as putting forward
a claim to public notice. Gradually, they have
sunk almost out of sight, as old houses, here and
there about the streets, get covered halfway to
the eaves by the accumulation of new soil. From
father to son, for above a hundred years, they followed the sea; a gray-headed shipmaster, in each
generation, retiring from the quarter-deck to the
homestead, while a boy of fourteen took the hereditary place before the mast, confronting the
salt spray and the gale, which had blustered
against his sire and grandsire. The boy, also,
in due time, passed from the forecastle to the
cabin, spent a tempestuous manhood, and returned from his world-wanderings, ·to grow old,
and die, and mingle his dust with the natal earth.
This long connection of a family with one spot,
as its place of birth and burial, creates a kindred
between the human being and the locality, quite
independent of any charm in the scenery or moral
circumstances that surround him. It is not love,
but instinct. The new inhabitant — who came
himself from a foreign land, or whose father or
grandfather came — has little claim to be called
a Salemite; he has no conception of the oysterlike
tenacity with which an old settler, over whom his
third century is creeping, clings to the spot where

his successive generations have been imbedded. It is no matter that the place is joyless for him; that he is weary of the old wooden houses, the mud and dust, the dead level of site and sentiment, the chill east wind, and the chillest of social atmospheres, — all these, and whatever faults besides he may see or imagine, are nothing to the purpose. The spell survives, and just as powerfully as if the natal spot were an earthly paradise. So has it been in my case. I felt it almost as a destiny to make Salem my home; so that the mould of features and cast of character which had all along been familiar here — ever, as one representative of the race lay down in his grave, another assuming, as it were, his sentry-march along the main street — might still in my little day be seen and recognized in the old town. . . . On emerging from the Old Manse, it was chiefly this strange, indolent, unjoyous attachment for my native town that brought me to fill a place in Uncle Sam's brick edifice, when I might as well, or better, have gone somewhere else. My doom was on me."

Long as this extract is, it dispenses with pages of critical analysis, and the hundred details requisite to build up such an impression of ancestry from the soil, of the way in which the New England past had entered into the fibre of Hawthorne's nature, of the sort of historic consciousness that was latent, like clairvoyance, in his imagination. Here, too, it serves to give Hawthorne a natural right in his new public place in the community. He did not feel himself a stranger there; the floor of the Custom House was as much home to his feet as a ship's deck. He made, it is said, a good surveyor, as in Boston previously he had been an excellent under officer. His duties were not arduous; they consumed about three hours and a half of his day, leaving him ample leisure. He has himself made of his stay at the Custom House a half humorous story by drawing the characters of his associates and setting forth the general atmosphere of the place with such lifelike drollery as only genius can achieve. He does it with no kindly hand. He was capable of great irritation, at times; and, as was shown on rare occasions, he had outbursts of anger. Dr. Loring describes him as "tempestuous and irresistible when aroused," and tells the anecdote of one dismayed captain who "fled up the wharf and took refuge in the office, inquiring, ' What in God's name have you sent on board my ship as an inspector?' " In writing of his old associates satirically, he was not indulging in any rage of anger, but he would hardly have felt the impulse to give his pen such liberty unless grievances had still rankled in his memory. The scene he sets forth is one of burlesque, done like fiction. "On ascending the steps you would discern," he says, "a row of venerable figures, sitting in old-fashioned chairs, which were tipped on their hind legs back against the wall. Oftentimes they were asleep, but occasionally might be heard talking together, in voices between speech and a snore, and with that lack of energy that distinguishes the occupants of almshouses, and all other human beings who depend for subsistence on charity, on monopolized labor, or anything else but their own independent exertions. These old gentlemen — seated, like Matthew, at the receipt of customs, but not very liable to be summoned thence, like him, for apostolic errands — were Custom House officers." When he comes to the details, in this style, the portrait approaches — if it does not realize — caricature. There was another side, we may be sure, to the lives and characters of these men whom Hawthorne has portrayed as if human nature existed to be the pigment of an artist's brush and should laugh or weep, look silly or solemn, at the whim of his temperament and will. All the time he got on with them very amiably, and if he found some of them in his own silent thoughts rather foolish and superfluous, doubtless it would have been the same in any other group among whom his lot might have been thrown. With others of his associates, whatever he thought of them and their ways, he was friendly and tolerant, if not sociable; it was in connection with these that the gossip circulated of his "loafing about with hard drinkers." Dr. Loring describes them to the life as "a group of men all of whom had remarkable characteristics, not of the best many times, but original, strong, highly-flavored, defiant democrats, with

whom he was officially connected, who made no
appeal to him, but responded to the uncultivated
side of his nature, and to whose defects he was
blind on account of their originality." This picture must be added to that which Hawthorne gave,
and between the two, if some allowance, also, be
made for the unfavorable temper in which he
wrote, it will appear, perhaps, that in the Custom
House he found human nature about as it is always in an office having to do with sea business,
in which naturally a rough, racy, unpolished,
original, sturdy stock took a leading part, and a
place was found for the retired old hulks of the
profession to enjoy a comfortable anchorage.

Hawthorne, in fact, repeated in the Custom
House the experience he had formerly had on the
Boston wharf and at Brook Farm. At first, the
change was a pleasure and a relief to him. He
had once more escaped, if not from the dreamland
of his own solitary fancy, at least from the unreality which the literary life seems always to have had
for him, and which he now associated particularly
with the character of his friendships. The tone
of relief is unmistakable : —

"After my fellowship of toil and impracticable
schemes with the dreamy brethren of Brook Farm;
after living for three years within the subtile influence of an intellect like Emerson's; after those
wild, free days on the Assabeth, indulging fantastic speculations, beside our fire of fallen boughs,
with Ellery Channing; after talking with Thoreau

about pine-trees and Indian relics, in his hermitage at Walden; after growing fastidious by sympathy with the classic refinement of Hillard's
culture; after becoming imbued with poetic sentiment at Longfellow's hearth-stone, — it was
time, at length, that I should exercise other faculties of my nature, and nourish myself with food
for which I had hitherto had little appetite. Even
the old inspector was desirable, as a change of
diet, to a man who had known Alcott. I look
upon it as an evidence, in some measure, of a system naturally well balanced, and lacking no essential part of a thorough organization, that, with
such associates to remember, I could mingle at
once with men of altogether different qualities,
and never murmur at the change."

So he mixed in the new scene, laughed with
the others at the old sea-yarns and jokes, joined
in with his associates on more even terms than
was his habit with the literary friends of Concord,
and was once more a part of this material world.
But it was not long before the old disgust and
restlessness came over him; he felt his imaginative nature deadened; this after all was not his
own life, and the figures that moved in it, the
business they were concerned with, the existence
they led round about him took on the same shabby
color of fact that had formerly spread over the
coal and salt of the wharf, and the manure of
Brook Farm; and that feeling of repulsion from
it all, which came to involve also a half-contempt

for the people and their affairs, grew in him. He describes the torpor that fell upon his faculties; he ceased to write, just as in the earlier time; he could not create, and though he had time enough, and the sea and the woods and the winter moonlight were all there, they did not unlock his magical power as of old. He laments over it, but confesses it; he had temporarily ceased to be a man of letters.

Domestic affairs contributed to withhold him from his pen. The old Herbert Street house had proved an inconvenient domicile for the two families, and they had removed to a dwelling in Chestnut Street. For a while Mrs. Hawthorne had been absent in Boston, and there a boy, Julian, had been born, so that there were two children in the nursery. It was in this room that Hawthorne spent his afternoons, for he had no study, and there for a year his desk stood, says his wife, without having been once opened. They moved again to another house, more easily adapted to the needs of both households, in Mall Street, and here Hawthorne again had a study "high from all noise," and Madame Hawthorne was provided for with a suite wholly separate. She and her two daughters still maintained the lifelong habit of isolation. "Elizabeth," says Mrs. Hawthorne, "is an invisible entity. I have seen her but once in two years; and Louisa never intrudes;" and she adds her satisfaction in knowing that Madame Hawthorne would have the pleasure of her son's and the children's company for the rest of her life. "I am so glad to win her out of that Castle Dismal, and from the mysterious chamber into which no mortal ever peeped till Una was born, and Julian, — for they alone have entered the *penetralia*. Into that chamber the sun never shines. Into these rooms in Mall Street it blazes without stint." Mrs. Hawthorne was very happy in this life with her husband, though they were still retired in their habits. He had, however, become an officer of the Lyceum, and they attended the lectures. They went out very seldom, only on such an occasion as when Emerson was visiting a neighbor, for example. The happiness was all indoors and in their hearts. "No art nor beauty," the wife writes, "can excel my daily life, with such a husband and such children, the exponents of all art and beauty. I really have not even the temptation to go out of my house to find anything better." The husband expresses the same felicity, in his turn, repeatedly, as on one occasion during a visit of Mrs. Hawthorne in Boston. "Oh, Phœbe," he writes to her, "I want thee much. Thou art the only person in the world that ever was necessary to me. Other people have occasionally been more or less agreeable; but I think I was always more at ease alone than in anybody's company, till I knew thee. And now I am only myself when thou art within my reach. Thou art an unspeakably beloved woman."

They still spent their evenings together, mostly

in reading. He never wrote at night, and for a year and a half seems not to have written at all, except some slight unremembered article, it might be, for a Salem newspaper. In November, 1847, he began to compose regularly every afternoon. In the year following he produced "The Snow Image," "The Great Stone Face," "Main Street," and possibly "Ethan Brand," but these, with the exception of the third, which appeared in Elizabeth Peabody's "Æsthetic Papers," 1849, remained unpublished. He had exhausted himself as a writer of short tales and sketches; the kind no longer appealed to him, and he wrote with much difficulty and against the grain. "At length," he writes in a letter of literary business, December 14, 1848, "by main strength I have wrenched and torn an idea out of my miserable brain; or rather, the fragment of an idea, like a tooth ill-drawn, and leaving the roots to torture me." His imagination had, in fact, begun to work upon a larger scale and in a higher world of art, though he apparently did not know the change in scope that he was undergoing, and thought of his new story only as a longer tale; the idea of "The Scarlet Letter," after lying for some years in his brain, was unfolding in the form of a great romance. It was to be his resource when the Custom House failed.

It was on June 8, 1849, that the news of his dismissal from office came. Tyler's Whig administration had come in, and Democratic heads would naturally fall; but Hawthorne, having obtained office, as he conceived it, as a literary man provided for by government, had not expected to be turned out on the change of parties, especially as he was not a partisan or in fact a politician at all. He resented the action, even when it was only threatened, as unjust, and took some steps to secure himself in place by suggesting an appeal to men in Boston, among whom he mentions Rufus Choate, "whose favorable influence," he says, "would make it impossible to remove me, and whose support and sympathy might fairly be obtained on my behalf, — not on the ground that I am a very good writer, but because I gained my position, such as it is, by my literary character, and have done nothing to forfeit that tenure." When he found, however, that he had been removed, ostensibly at least, on the ground of a paper forwarded from Salem and charging him with political partisanship, both as a writer for the newspaper press and in his official capacity, his resentment became a much warmer feeling. The story of a removal from office is usually unedifying, and there is no occasion to go into all the details. It appears that one man, Charles W. Upham, was especially singled out by Hawthorne as the principal mover, and on him he deliberately avenged himself at a later time. The charges Hawthorne met very fully and specifically, and showed that he had indeed rather incurred the reproach of his party for not taking a partisan course than deserved the criticism of his enemies. He was, however, very angry; his wife writes to her father, "The lion was roused in him;" and the numerous letters to his friends show that he was much disturbed, but much more by what he regarded as the attack made secretly upon his character than by the loss of the office. There was a small tempest in the town, in which his friends male and female bore their part, and plans of one kind and another were discussed to secure his retention; but, as usually happens in such cases, the affair soon blew over. In a political scuffle, Hawthorne was a man out of his element.

The most unfortunate thing in the whole incident was the effect it had on Hawthorne's attachment to his native place. It turned his cold love to a bitter feeling that he never overcame; and it also threw upon Salem the reproach of having injured as well as neglected her most famous son. Citizens of both parties joined in the movement by which he was ousted, and no one of influence withstood them; but there was probably no enmity in the matter, and the simple explanation, perhaps, was that the new candidate had more cordial friends in the community on both sides, for Hawthorne was not personally popular with the merchants as a class. He kept them at a distance just as he did men of letters, and could not mix with them on even and frank terms. Dr. Loring, in discussing the subject of Hawthorne's treatment by his fellow townsmen, very justly says that

"Salem did not treat its illustrious son, at all, because he gave it no opportunity." He was, so far as then appeared, an author, forty-five years old, who had written two or three books of short tales and sketches, not yet famous, and he held a not very lucrative public office, which he had secured, not in the usual way, by party service, but by the political influence of his old college mates, who were strangers to the town. He was inoffensive, but he was not liked, and took no pains to make himself one of the community; he was ignored by the citizens of the place because he ignored them, and when his Washington friends lost power, there was no one else interested in keeping him in office, and he had no influence of his own on the spot. In private life he was uncommonly solitary, and he was in no sense a public man. What happened was perfectly natural, and might fairly have been foreseen; for the notion of providing a government post for a man because he was an author, and retaining him in it by a literary tenure, must have seemed very novel to the gentlemen of the Essex district in those days, as it would seem now. But Hawthorne had the sense of superiority, the silent, suppressed pride, the susceptibility of a solitary nature; and whatever might be the public side of the matter, of which he was no very good judge, privately he felt aggrieved and outraged; that irritability toward the general public which has already been remarked upon, just because he was "for some years the most obscure man of letters in America," was condensed, as it were, and discharged upon Salem, which stood as the deaf and blind and hateful embodiment of the unappreciative world that would have none of him, but rather took away the little bread and salt he had contrived to earn for himself, and would not give him room even in a paltry office among the old sea-dogs he has described. "I mean as soon as possible," he writes two months later, "to bid farewell forever to this abominable city."

Apart from the disagreeable circumstances of his removal and the penniless condition in which it left him, there is no reason to think that Hawthorne was anything but happy to leave office. His first thought was of his poverty; before he had laid down the telegram he heard the wolf at the door. He at once wrote the news to Hillard, and after saying that he had paid his old debts but had saved nothing, requests his friendly aid in words through which, brief and straight as they are, one feels the stern grip of the fact as it immediately took hold on him, the poor man's need: —

"If you could do anything in the way of procuring me some stated literary employment, in connection with a newspaper, or as corrector of the press to some printing establishment, etc., it could not come at a better time. Perhaps Epes Sargent, who is a friend of mine, would know of something. I shall not stand upon my dignity;

that must take care of itself. Perhaps there may be some subordinate office connected with the Boston Athenæum. Do not think anything too humble to be mentioned to me. . . . The intelligence has just reached me, and Sophia has not yet heard it. She will bear it like a woman, — that is to say, better than a man."

He went home at once to tell his wife, and as his son tells the story, on his meeting her expression of pleasure at seeing him so soon with the remark that "he had left his head behind him," she exclaimed, "Oh, then you can write your book!" and when he smiled and answered that it "would be agreeable to know where their bread and rice were to come from while the story was writing," she brought forth from a hiding-place "a pile of gold" — it appears to have been one hundred and fifty dollars — that she had saved from the household weekly expenses. So for the time being anxiety was lessened.

The fact that Hawthorne was glad at heart to be free again comes out in many ways. Something may be due to his wife's bearing the news "better than a man," perhaps, but on the same day it came she is found writing to her mother, "I have not seen my husband happier than since this turning out. He has felt in chains for a long time, and being a man he is not alarmed at being set on his own feet again, — or on his *head* I might say, for that contains the available gold of a mine scarcely yet worked at all." He himself, a few days later, writes to Hillard, "I have come to feel that it is not good for me to be here. I am in a lower moral state than I have been — a duller intellectual one. So let me go; and, under God's providence, I shall arrive at something better." It would not be long before he would be looking back to the last three years, and saying, "The life of the Custom House lies like a dream behind me," in almost the identical words that he used of Boston wharfs and the Brook Farmers. The pendulum of temperament had swung again to the other extreme, and he was now all for the imaginative world once more.

There was, however, to be one sad experience before his new life began. In the midst of these troubles, while he was still writing his vain letters and receiving the vain sympathy of his friends in the injury he had felt, his mother fell into serious illness, and it was plain that the end of her long vigil was near. With that strange impulse which led Hawthorne, out of his sensitive reserve and almost morbid seclusion, to make an open book of his private life, writing it all at large in his journals, he spent the hours of her last days in describing the scenes and incidents of the house in its shadow of death. His wife had the main care of the invalid, and to him was left the charge of the children, Una and Julian, who played in the yard in the warm July weather and were seized with the singular fancy of acting over in their play the scenes of the sick chamber above, while

their father watched them from the window of his
room and wrote down their prattle. Hawthorne
was attached to his mother, and had been a good
son, but there was something now that startled his
nature, perhaps in the unusual nearness in which
he found himself to her life, and he was hardly
prepared for the distress of the circumstances.
His wife wrote, "My husband came near a brain
fever after seeing her for an hour; " and the hour
is the one which Hawthorne himself recorded, in
a passage vividly recalling the tone and character
of those scenes in which Carlyle painted the darker
moments of his own shadow-haunted life: —

"About five o'clock I went to my mother's
chamber, and was shocked to see such an altera-
tion since my last visit. I love my mother; but
there has been, ever since boyhood, a sort of coldness of intercourse between us, such as is apt to
come between persons of strong feelings if they
are not managed rightly. I did not expect to be
much moved at the time, — that is to say, not
to feel any overpowering emotion struggling just
then, — though I knew that I should deeply remember and regret her. Mrs. Dike was in the
chamber; Louisa pointed to a chair near the bed,
but I was moved to kneel down close by my
mother, and take her hand. She knew me, but
could only murmur a few indistinct words; among
which I understood an injunction to take care of
my sisters. Mrs. Dike left the chamber, and
then I found the tears slowly gathering in my

eyes. I tried to keep them down, but it would not be; I kept filling up, till, for a few moments, I shook with sobs. For a long time I knelt there, holding her hand; and surely it is the darkest hour I ever lived. Afterwards I stood by the open window and looked through the crevice of the curtain. The shouts, laughter, and cries of the two children had come up into the chamber from the open air, making a strange contrast with the death-bed scene. And now, through the crevice of the curtain, I saw my little Una of the golden locks, looking very beautiful, and so full of spirit and life that she was life itself. And then I looked at my poor dying mother, and seemed to see the whole of human existence at once, standing in the dusty midst of it."

The next day the children continued the play — they have never left it off — of their grandmother's death-bed, and Hawthorne writes it all down in his journal with minute realism. His genius felt some appeal in it that let him go on unchecked in the transcript of baby-life mocking death in all innocence and unwitting: —

"Now Una is transformed into grandmamma, and Julian is mamma taking care of her. She groans, and speaks with difficulty, and moves herself feebly and wearisomely; then lies perfectly still, as if in an insensible state; then rouses herself and calls for wine; then lies down on her back with clasped hands; then puts them to her head. It recalls the scene of yesterday to me with frightful distinctness; and out of the midst of it little Una looks at me with a smile of glee. Again, Julian assumes the character. 'You're dying now,' says Una; 'so you must lie still,' " — and so the journal goes on through the slow quarter-hours, till it stops when Madame Hawthorne's heart ceased to beat.

The death of his mother removed the last and only reason for Hawthorne's continuing to reside in Salem, but he remained there through the summer and winter. He was hard at work on "The Scarlet Letter," perhaps being more absorbed in it than he ever was in any other of his compositions. It was a time of much trouble in every way. There was sickness in the family, he was himself afflicted with pain, and his wife's sister Elizabeth Peabody seems to have come to the rescue of domestic comfort for the household. O'Sullivan, the kind-hearted editor of the defunct "Democratic Review," bethought himself of his old debt to Hawthorne and sent him a hundred dollars; so the purse was replenished. It was in early winter that the cheerful personality of James T. Fields, the publisher, appeared on the scene, and it was a fortunate hour for Hawthorne that brought such an appreciative, enthusiastic, and faithful friend to his door. Fields was just the man to warm Hawthorne's genius into action, — cordial, whole-souled, and happily not so much a man of letters as to repel him with that alienation which he certainly felt in his contact with authors by profession like Emerson and his other contemporaries. Fields was, too, in a very real sense, the messenger and herald of fame standing at last in the humble doorway of the Mall Street house that had latterly been the scene of such a tangle of human events. The anecdote of what he found there is finely told in his own words: —

"I found him alone in a chamber over the sitting-room of the dwelling; and as the day was cold, he was hovering near a stove. We fell into talk about his future prospects, and he was, as I feared I should find him, in a very desponding mood. 'Now,' said I, 'is the time for you to publish, for I know during these years in Salem you must have got something ready for the press.' 'Nonsense,' said he, 'what heart had I to write anything, when my publishers have been so many years trying to sell a small edition of the "Twice-Told Tales"?' I still pressed upon him the good chances he would have now with something new. 'Who would risk publishing a book for *me*, the most unpopular writer in America?' 'I would,' said I, 'and would start with an edition of two thousand copies of anything you write.' 'What madness!' he exclaimed; 'Your friendship for me gets the better of your judgment. No, no,' he continued; 'I have no money to indemnify a publisher's losses on my account.' I looked at my watch, and found that the train would soon be starting for Boston, and I knew there was not much time to lose in trying to discover what had been his literary work during these last few years in Salem. I remember that I pressed him to reveal to me what he had been writing. He shook his head, and gave me to understand that he had produced nothing. At that moment I caught sight of a bureau or set of drawers near where we were sitting; and immediately it occurred to me that hidden away somewhere in that article of furniture was a story or stories by the author of the 'Twice-Told Tales,' and I became so positive of it that I charged him vehemently with the fact. He seemed surprised, I thought, but shook his head again; and I rose to take my leave, begging him not to come into the cold entry, saying I would come back and see him again in a few days. I was hurrying down the stairs when he called after me from the chamber, asking me to stop a moment. Then quickly stepping into the entry with a roll of manuscript in his hands, he said: ' How, in Heaven's name, did you know this thing was there? As you found me out, take what I have written, and tell me, after you get home and have time to read it, if it is good for anything. It is either very good or very bad, — I don't know which.' On my way up to Boston I read the germ of ' The Scarlet Letter.' "

The romance that was thus captured was not yet in the form which it finally took. Hawthorne had conceived it as a rather longer tale of the same sort that he had previously written, and designed to make it one story in a new collection such as his former volumes had been. He thought it was too gloomy to stand alone, and in fact did not suspect that here was a new kind of work, such that it would put an end forever to his old manner of writing. He intended to call the new volume "Old-Time Legends: together with Sketches, Experimental and Ideal," — a title that is fairly ghostly with the transcendental nonage of his genius, pale, abstract, ineffectual, with oblivion lurking in every syllable. Fields knew better than that. But he gave him something more than advice; he cheered him with his extravagant appreciation, as it seemed to Hawthorne, and invigorated him by a true sympathy with his success. Fields urged that the story be elaborated, filled out, and made into a single volume; and, under this wise suggestion, Hawthorne went to work upon it with renewed interest and with something probably of the power of a new ambition.

His friends, too, had come to his aid with material assistance, and apart from the fact that he was thus enabled to go on with the labor of composition, free from the immediate pressure of poverty and its trials of the spirit, he was stimulated by their confidence and kindness to do all he could for himself. Hillard was the medium of this friendliness, and accompanied the considerable sum of money with a letter, January 17, 1850: —

"It occurred to me and some other of your

friends that, in consideration of the events of the last year, you might at this time be in need of a little pecuniary aid. I have therefore collected, from some of those who admire your genius and respect your character, the enclosed sum of money, which I send you with my warmest wishes for your health and happiness. I know the sensitive edge of your temperament; but do not speak or think of obligation. It is only paying, in a very imperfect measure, the debt we owe you for what you have done for American Literature. Could you know the readiness with which every one to whom I applied contributed to this little offering, and could you have heard the warm expressions with which some accompanied their gift, you would have felt that the bread you had cast upon the waters had indeed come back to you. Let no shadow of despondency, my dear friend, steal over you. Your friends do not and will not forget you. You shall be protected against ' eating cares,' which, I take it, mean cares lest we should not have enough to eat."

Kindly as this letter was, it could only temper what was for Hawthorne a rough and bitter experience; for he had, in intense form, that proud independence in such matters which characterizes the old New England stock. The words he wrote in reply came from the depths of his nature: —

"I read your letter in the vestibule of the Post Office; and it drew — what my troubles never have — the water to my eyes; so that I was glad of the sharply cold west wind that blew into them as I came homeward, and gave them an excuse for being red and bleared.

"There was much that was very sweet — and something, too, that was very bitter — mingled with that same moisture. It is sweet to be remembered and cared for by one's friends — some of whom know me for what I am, while others, perhaps, know me only through a generous faith — sweet to think that they deem me worth upholding in my poor work through life. And it is bitter, nevertheless, to need their support. It is something else besides pride that teaches me that ill-success in life is really and justly a matter of shame. I am ashamed of it, and I ought to be. The fault of a failure is attributable — in a great degree at least — to the man who fails. I should apply this truth in judging of other men; and it behooves me not to shun its point or edge in taking it home to my *own* heart. Nobody has a right to live in the world unless he be strong and able, and applies his ability to good purpose.

"The money, dear Hillard, will smooth my path for a long time to come. The only way in which a man can retain his self-respect, while availing himself of the generosity of his friends, is by making it an incitement to his utmost exertion, so that he may not need their help again. I shall look upon it so — nor will shun any drudgery that my hand shall find to do, if thereby I may win bread."

Four days after this, on February 3, 1850, he finished "The Scarlet Letter." He read the last scene to his wife, just after writing it, on that evening, — "tried to read it, rather," he wrote to Bridge the next day, "for my voice swelled and heaved, as if I were tossed up and down on an ocean as it subsides after a storm. But I was in a very nervous state then, having gone through a great diversity of emotion while writing it for many months." He had, indeed, put his whole energy into the book, writing "immensely," says his wife in the previous autumn, as much as nine hours a day. He now felt the reaction, and besides he had a less healthy regimen of life than hitherto, and had fallen into middle-age habits of lowered physical tone, less active now in his out-door life these last three or four years. He continues in the letter to Bridge, just quoted: "I long to get into the country, for my health latterly is not quite what it has been for many years past. I should not long stand such a life of bodily inactivity and mental exertion as I have lived for the last few months. An hour or two of daily labor in a garden, and a daily ramble in country air, or on the sea-shore, would keep all right. Here, I hardly go out once a week. Do not allude to this matter in your letters to me, as my wife already sermonizes me quite sufficiently on my habits; and I never own up to not feeling perfectly well. Neither do I feel anywise ill; but only a lack of physical vigor and energy,

which reacts upon the mind." "The Scarlet
Letter"[1] was already in the publisher's hands, before the last scene was written, and was rapidly
put through the press. It was issued early in
April in an edition of five thousand copies, which
was soon exhausted; a new edition followed at
once, and Hawthorne's fame was at last established.

"The Scarlet Letter" is a great and unique
romance, standing apart by itself in fiction; there
is nothing else quite like it. Of all Hawthorne's
works it is most identified with his genius in popular regard, and it has the peculiar power that is
apt to invest the first work of an author in which
his originality finds complete artistic expression.
It is seldom that one can observe so plainly the
different elements that are primary in a writer's
endowment coalesce in the fully developed work
of genius; yet in this romance there is nothing
either in method or perception which is not to be
found in the earlier tales; what distinguishes it is
the union of art and intuition as they had grown
up in Hawthorne's practice and had developed a
power to penetrate more deeply into life. Obviously at the start there is the physical object in
which his imagination habitually found its spring,
the fantastically embroidered scarlet letter on a
woman's bosom which he had seen in the Puritan
group described in "Endicott and the Red Cross."

---

[1] *The Scarlet Letter.* A Romance. By Nathaniel Hawthorne.
Boston: Ticknor, Reed and Fields. 1850. 12mo. Pp. iv, 322.

It had been in his mind for years, and his thoughts had centred on it and wandered out from it, tracking its mystery. It has in itself that decorative quality, which he sought in the physical object, — the brilliant and rich effect, startling to the eye and yet more to the imagination as it blazes forth with a secret symbolism and almost intelligence of its own. It multiplies itself, as the tale unfolds, with greater intensity and mysterious significance and dread suggestion, as if in mirrors set round about it, — in the slowly disclosed and fearful stigma on the minister's hidden heart over which he ever holds his hand, where it has become flesh of his flesh; in the growing elf-like figure of the child, who, with her eyes always fastened on the open shame of the letter on her mother's bosom or the hidden secret of the hand on her father's breast, has become herself the symbol, half revealed and half concealed, is dressed in it, as every reader remembers, and fantastically embodies it as if the thing had taken life in her; and, as if this were not enough, the scarlet letter, at a climax of the dark story, lightens forth over the whole heavens as a symbol of what cannot be hid even in the intensest blackness of night. The continual presence of the letter seems to have burnt into Hawthorne's own mind, till at the end of the narrative he says he would gladly erase its deep print from the brain where long meditation had fixed it.   In no other work is the physical symbol so absorbingly present, so reduplicated, so much alive in

itself. It is the brand of sin on life. Its concrete vividness leads the author also by a natural
compulsion as well as an artistic instinct to display
his story in that succession of high-wrought scenes,
tableaux, in fact, which was his characteristic
method of narrative, picturesque, pictorial, almost
to be described as theatrical in spectacle. The
background, also, as in the early tales, is of the
slightest, no more than will suffice for the acting
of the drama as a stage setting sympathetic with
the central scene, — a town, with a prison, a meet-
ing-house, a pillory, a governor's house, other
habitations on a street, a lonely cottage by the
shore, the forest round about all; and for occasion
and accessories, only a woman's sentence, the incidental death of Winthrop unmarked in itself, a
buccaneering ship in the harbor, Indians, Spanish
sailors, rough matrons, clergy; this will serve, for
such was Hawthorne's fine economy, knowing that
this story was one in which every materialistic element must be used at its lowest tone. Though
the scene lay in this world, it was but transitory
scaffolding; the drama was one of the eternal life.

The characteristic markings of Hawthorne's
genius are also to be found in other points. He
does not present the scene of life, the crowd of
the world with its rich and varied fullness of interest, complexity of condition and movement, and
its interwoven texture of character, event, and fate,
such as the great novelists use; he has only a few
individual figures, and these are simplified by being

exhibited, not in their complete lives, but only in that single aspect of their experience which was absorbing to themselves and constituted the life they lived in the soul itself. There are three characters, Hester, the minister, and the physician; and a fourth, the child, who fulfills the function of the chorus in the old drama, in part a living comment, in part a spectator and medium of sympathy with the main actors. In all four of these that trait of profound isolation in life, so often used before in the earlier tales, is strongly brought out; about each is struck a circle which separates not only one from another, but from all the world, and in the midst of it, as in a separate orb, each lives an unshared life. It is inherent, too, in such a situation that the mystery that had fascinated Hawthorne in so many forms, the secrecy of men's bosoms, should be a main theme in the treatment. He has also had recourse to that method of violent contrast which has been previously illustrated; on the one hand the publicity of detected wrongdoing, on the other the hidden and unsuspected fact; here the open shame and there the secret sin, whose sameness in a double life is expressed by the identity of the embroidered letter and the flesh-wrought stigma. But it is superfluous to illustrate further the genesis of this romance out of Hawthorne's art and matter in his earlier work, showing how naturally it rose by a concentration of his powers on a single theme that afforded them scope, intensity, and harmony at

once. The new thing here is the power of his genius to penetrate, as was said above, deep into life.

The romance begins where common tales end.
The crime has been committed; in it, in its motives, circumstances, explanation, its course of
passion and human tide of life, Hawthorne takes
no interest. All that is past, and, whatever it
was, now exists only as sin; it has passed from
the region of earthly fact into that of the soul,
out of all that was temporal into the world where
eternal things only are. Not crime, not passion,
not the temptation and the fall, but only sin now
staining the soul in consequence is the theme; and
the course of the story concerns man's dealing
with sin, in his own breast or the breasts of others.
It is a study of. punishment, of vengeance if one
will; this is the secret of its gloom, for the idea
of salvation, of healing, is but little present and
is not felt; there is no forgiveness in the end, in
any sense to dispel the darkness of evil or promise the dawn of new life in any one of these
tortured souls. The sin of the lovers is not the
centre of the story, but only its initial source; that
sin breeds sin is the real principle of its being; the
minister is not punished as a lover, but as the
hypocrite that he becomes, and the physician is punished as the revenger that he becomes. Hester's
punishment is visibly from the law, and illustrates
the law's brutality, the coarse hand of man for
justice, the mere physical blow meant to hurt and
crush; it is man's social way of dealing with sin,

and fails because it makes no connection with the
soul; the victim rises above it, is emancipated
from its ideas, transforms the symbol of disgrace
into a message of mercy to all who suffer, and
annuls the gross sentence by her own higher soul-
power. The minister's punishment, also, is visibly from the physician, who illustrates man's individual way of dealing with sin in another; but
it is not the minister's suffering under the hand
of revenge working subtly in secret that arrests
our attention; it is the physician's own degener-
acy into a devil of hate through enjoyment of the
sight and presence of this punishment, that stamps
him into the reader's mind as a type of the failure
of such a revenge. "Vengeance is mine, saith the
Lord" is the text here blazed forth. In the
sphere of the soul human law and private revenge
have no place. It is in that sphere that Hester
is seen suffering in the touch of the child, being
unable to adjust the broken harmonies of life; her
incapacity to do that is the ever-present problem
that keeps her wound open, not to be stanched, but
rather breaking with a more intimate pain with the
unfolding of little Pearl's wide-eyed soul. In that
sphere, too, the minister is seen suffering — not
for the original sin, for that is overlaid, whelmed,
forgotten, by the second and heavier transgression
of hypocrisy, cowardice, desertion, — but merely
from self-knowledge, the knowledge that he is
a living lie. The characters, so treated, become
hardly more than types, humanly outlined in fig-

ure, costume, and event, symbolic pictures of states of the soul, so simplified, so intense, so elementary as to belong to a phantasmagoric rather than a realistic world, to that mirror of the soul which is not found in nature but in spiritual self-consciousness, where the soul is given back to itself in its nakedness, as in a secret place.

Yet it is in the sense of reality that this romance is most intense. It is a truthful story, above all; and only its truth could make it tolerable to the imagination and heart, if indeed it be tolerable to the heart at all. A part of this reality is due to the fact that there is a story here that lies outside of the moral scheme in which Hawthorne's conscious thought would confine it; the human element in it threatens from time to time to break the mould of thought and escape from bondage, because, simple as the moral scheme is, human life is too complex to be solved by it even in this small world of the three guilty ones and the child. This weakness of the moral scheme, this rude strength of human nature, this sense of a larger solution, are most felt when Hawthorne approaches the love element, and throughout in the character of Hester, in whom alone human nature retains a self-assertive power. The same thing is felt vaguely, but certainly, in the lack of sympathy between Hawthorne and the Puritan environment he depicts. He presents the community itself, its common people, its magistrates and clergy, its customs, temper, and atmosphere, as forbidding, and

he has no good word for it; harshness characterizes
it, and that trait discredits its ideals, its judgments,
and its entire interpretation of life. Hester, out-
cast from it, is represented as thereby enfranchised
from its narrowness, enlightened, escaped into a
world of larger truth: —

"The world's law was no law for her mind. It
was an age in which the human intellect, newly
emancipated, had taken a more active and a wider
range than for many centuries before. Men of
the sword had overthrown nobles and kings. Men
bolder than these had overthrown and rearranged
— not actually, but within the sphere of theory,
which was their most real abode — the whole system of ancient prejudice, wherewith was linked
much of ancient principle. Hester Prynne im-
bibed this spirit. She assumed a freedom of speculation, then common enough on the other side of
the Atlantic, but which our forefathers, had they
known it, would have held to be a deadlier crime
than that stigmatized by the scarlet letter. In her
lonesome cottage, by the sea-shore, thoughts visited
her, such as dared to enter no other dwelling in
New England; shadowy guests, that would have
been as perilous as demons to their entertainer,
could they have been seen so much as knocking
at her door."

This is the foregleam of the next age, felt in
her mind, the coming of a larger day. Hawthorne
does not develop this or justify it; he only states
it as a fact of life. And in the motive of the

story, the love of Hester and Arthur, much is left dim; but what is discerned threatens to be unmanageable within the limits of the scheme.   Did Hester love her lover, and he love her, through those seven years in silence?   Did either of them ever repent their passion for its own sake?   And when Hester's womanhood came back in its bloom and her hair fell shining in the forest sunlight, and she took her lover, hand and head and form, in all his broken suffering to her affectionate care and caress, and planned the bold step that they go out together across the seas and live in each other's lives like lovers in truth and reality, — was this only the resurrection of a moment or the firm vital force of a seven years' silent passion? Had either of them ever repented, though one was a coward and the other a condemned and public criminal before the law, and both had suffered? Was not the true sin, as is suggested, the source of all this error, the act of the physician who had first violated Hester's womanhood in a loveless marriage as he had now in Arthur's breast "violated in cold blood the sanctity of a human heart"? "Thou and I," says Arthur, "never did so." The strange words follow, strange for Hawthorne to have written, but better attesting his truth to human nature than all his morality: —

"Never, never!" whispered she.   "What we did had a consecration of its own.   We felt it so! We said so to each other!   Hast thou forgotten it?"

"Hush, Hester!" said Arthur Dimmesdale, rising from the ground. "No; I have not forgotten!"

That confession is the stroke of genius in the romance that humanizes it with a thrill that is felt through every page of the stubborn, dark, harsh narrative of misery. It was not a sin against love that had been committed; it was a sin against the soul; and the sin against the soul lay in the lack of confession, which becomes the cardinal situation of the romance solved in the minister's dying acknowledgment. But the love problem is never solved, just as the hate problem in the physician is never solved; both Hester and Roger Chillingworth, one with her mystery of enduring love, the other with his mystery of insatiable hatred, are left with the issue, the meaning of their lives inexplicable, untold. Yet it is from the presence of these elements in the story that something of its intense reality comes.

It remains true, however, that the essential reality lies in the vivid sense of sin, and its experience in conscience. Hawthorne has not given a historical view of New England life; such a village, with such a tragedy, never existed, in that environing forest of the lone seacoast; but he has symbolized historical New England by an environment that he created round a tragedy that he read in the human heart, and in this tragedy itself he was able also to symbolize New England life in its internal features. One thing stood plainly out in our home Puritanism, — spirituality; the transcendent sense of the reality of the soul's life with God, its conscience, its perils, and its eternal issue. Spirituality remained the inheritance of the New England blood; and Hawthorne, who was no Puritan in doctrine or sympathy even, was Puritan in temperament, and hence to him, too, spirituality in life was its main element. He took that sin of passion which has ever been held typical of sin against the purity of the soul's nature, and transformed it into the symbol of all sin, and in its manifestation revolved the aspects of sin as a presence in the soul after the act, — the broken law disturbing life's external harmonies but working a worse havoc within, mining all with corruption there, while it infects with disease whatever approaches it from without. It is by its moral universality that the romance takes hold of the imagination; the scarlet letter becomes only a pictorial incident, but while conscience, repentance, confession, the modes of punishment, and the modes of absolution remain instant and permanent facts in the life of the soul, many a human heart will read in this book as in a manual of its own intimate hours.

The romance is thus essentially a parable of the soul's life in sin; in its narrower scope it is the work of the moral intellect allegorizing its view of life; and where creative genius enters into it, in the Shakespearean sense of life in its own right, it tends to be a larger and truer story breaking the bonds of its religious scheme. It has its roots in Puritanism, but it is only incidentally a New England tale; its substance is the most universal experience of human nature in religious life, taking its forms only, its local habitation and name, from the Puritan colony in America, and these in a merely allegorical, not historical manner. Certain traits, however, ally it more closely to New England Puritanism. It is a relentless tale; the characters are singularly free from self-pity, and accept their fate as righteous; they never forgave themselves, they show no sign of having forgiven one another; even God's forgiveness is left under a shadow in futurity. They have sinned against the soul, and something implacable in evil remains. The minister's dying words drop a dark curtain over all.

"Hush, Hester, hush!" said he, with tremulous solemnity. "The law we broke!— the sin here so awfully revealed!— let these alone be in thy thoughts! I fear! I fear! It may be that, when we forgot our God, — when we violated our reverence each for the other's soul, — it was thenceforth vain to hope that we could meet hereafter, in an everlasting and pure reunion."

Mercy is but a hope. There is also a singular absence of prayer in the book. Evil is presented as a thing without remedy, that cannot change its nature. The child, even, being the fruit of sin, can bring, Hester and Arthur doubt, no good for others or herself. In the scheme of Puritan thought, however, the atonement of Christ is the perpetual miracle whereby salvation comes, not only hereafter but in the holier life led here by grace. There is no Christ in this book. Absolution, so far as it is hinted at, lies in the direction of public confession, the efficacy of which is directly stated, but lamely nevertheless; it restores truth, but it does not heal the past. Leave the dead past to bury its dead, says Hawthorne, and go on to what may remain; but life once ruined is ruined past recall. So Hester, desirous of serving in her place the larger truth she has come to know, is stayed, says Hawthorne, because she "recognized the impossibility that any mission of divine and mysterious truth should be confided to a woman stained with sin, bowed down with shame, or even burdened with a life-long sorrow." That was never the Christian gospel nor the Puritan faith. Indeed, Hawthorne here and elsewhere anticipates those ethical views which are the burden of George Eliot's moral genius, and contain scientific pessimism. This stoicism, which was in Hawthorne, is a primary element in his moral nature, in him as well as in his work; it is visited with few touches of tenderness and pity; the pity one feels is not in him, it is in the pitiful thing, which he presents objectively, sternly, unrelentingly. It must be confessed that as an artist he appears unsympathetic with his characters; he is a moral dissector of their souls, minute, unflinching, thorough, a vivisector here; and he is cold because he has passed sentence on them, condemned them. There is no sympathy with human nature in the book; it is a fallen and ruined thing suffering just pain in its dying struggle. The romance is steeped in gloom. Is it too much to suggest that in ignoring prayer, the atonement of Christ, and the work of the Spirit in men's hearts, the better part of Puritanism has been left out, and the whole life of the soul distorted? Sin in the soul, the scarlet flower from the dark soil, we see; but, intent on that, has not the eye, and the heart, too, forgotten the large heavens that ensphere all — even this evil flower — and the infinite horizons that reach off to the eternal distance from every soul as from their centre? This romance is the record of a prison-cell, unvisited by any ray of light save that earthly one which gives both prisoners to public ignominy; they are seen, but they do not see. These traits of the book, here only suggested, have kinship with the repelling aspects of Puritanism, both as it was and as Hawthorne inherited it in his blood and breeding; so, in its transcendent spirituality, and in that democracy which is the twin-brother of spirituality in all lands and cultures, by virtue of which Hawthorne here humiliates and strips the minister who is the type of the spiritual aristocrat in the community, there is the essence of New England; but, for all that, the romance is a partial story, an imperfect fragment of the old life, distorting, not so much the Puritan ideal — which were a little matter — but the spiritual life itself. Its truth, intense, fascinating, terrible as it is, is a half-truth, and the darker half; it is the shadow of which the other half is light; it is the wrath of which the other half is love. A book from which light and love are absent may hold us by its truth to what is dark in life; but, in the highest sense, it is a false book. It is a chapter in the literature of moral despair, and is perhaps most tolerated as a condemnation of the creed which, through imperfect comprehension, it travesties.

With this book Hawthorne came into fame; but his fellow townsmen were ill pleased to find some disrepute of their own accompanying his success. It is surely to be regretted that this was the case; and, effective as his sketch of the Custom House is, one feels that Hawthorne stooped in taking his literary revenge on his humble associates by holding them up to personal ridicule. The tone of pleasantry veils ill feeling, which is expressed without cover in a letter he wrote to Bridge a day or two before he left the town: —

"As to the Salem people, I really thought that I had been exceedingly good-natured in my treatment of them. They certainly do not deserve good usage at my hands after permitting me to be deliberately lied down — not merely once, but at two several attacks, on two false indictments — without hardly a voice being raised on my behalf; and then sending one of the false witnesses to

Congress, others to the Legislature, and choosing another as the mayor.

"I feel an infinite contempt for them — and probably have expressed more of it than I intended — for my preliminary chapter has caused the greatest uproar that has happened here since witch-times. If I escape from town without being tarred and feathered, I shall consider it good luck. I wish they would tar and feather me; it would be such an entirely novel kind of distinction for a literary man. And, from such judges as my fellow-citizens, I should look upon it as a higher honor than a laurel crown."

He had said his farewell in the too famous sketch, with an ill grace, shaking the dust of his native place from his feet, and frankly taking upon himself the character of the unappreciated genius, which is seldom a becoming one. The passage fitly closes this chapter in which his nativity, for better or worse, is most apparent.

"Soon my old native town will loom upon me through the haze of memory, a mist brooding over and around it, as if it were no portion of the real earth, but an overgrown village in cloud-land, with only imaginary inhabitants to people its wooden houses, and walk its homely lanes, and the unpicturesque prolixity of its main street. Henceforth it ceases to be a reality of my life. I am a citizen of somewhere else. My good townspeople will not much regret me; for — though it has been as dear an object as any, in my literary efforts, to be of some importance in their eyes, and to win myself a pleasant memory in this abode and burial-place of so many of my forefathers — *there* has never been, for me, the genial atmosphere which a literary man requires, in order to ripen the best harvest of his mind. I shall do better amongst other faces; and these familiar ones, it need hardly be said, will do just as well without me."

VI.

LITERARY LABORS.

IN the late spring of 1850 Hawthorne removed his family and household goods to the little red cottage amid the Berkshire Hills which was to be a nature's hermitage to him for the next year and a half. It was a story-and-a-half building, rude and simple, on a great hillside, commanding a view of a small lake below and of beautiful low mountain horizons. Here began again that secluded happy family life which had belonged to the Old Manse, and he was perhaps happier than he had ever been. The home had the same internal look as of old, for he had brought with him the relics of family furniture, the oriental objects from over sea that were heirlooms from his father, and the Italian Madonnas, the casts and paintings with which his wife delighted to surround the home-life in an atmosphere of artistic adornment and suggestion; and, as the quarters were very small, the effect was one of mingled homeliness and refinement. Bridge soon joined them, and devoted himself in a practical way to making things shipshape, providing necessary closets and shelves out of packing boxes, and generally eking out the interior arrangements with a sailor's ready ingenuity. Outside there was a barnyard, and a two-story hencoop to be put to rights, with its brood of pet chickens each with its name, — Snowdrop, Crown Imperial, Queenie, Fawn, and the like decorative appellations. The two children, Una and Julian, were in a paradise. Other friends came, too, to visit or to call. Mrs. Hawthorne soon remarked that they seemed to see more society than ever before. Herman Melville lived near by, at Pittsfield, and became a welcome guest and companion, with his boisterous genuine intellectual spirits and animal strength. Fanny Kemble made an interesting figure on her great black horse at the gate. The Sedgwick neighbors were thoughtful and serviceable. O'Sullivan reappeared for a moment in all his Celtic vivacity, and Fields, Holmes, Duyckinck, and others of the profession came and went in the summer days. Hawthorne breathed the air of successful authorship at last, and knew its vanities and its pleasures. The mail brought him new acquaintances, and now and then a hero-worshiper lingered at the gate for a look. But as the warm days went by, and the frosts came, he found himself in his old sheltering nook, in a place removed from the world, living practically alone with his wife and children, though the increasing sense of friendliness in the world cheered and warmed him.

He had, however, begun to age. He was forty-six years old, and the last year had told upon

him, with its various anxieties, excitement, and
hard labor with the pen.   He was more easily
fatigued, he was less robust and venturesome, less
physically confident.   He showed the changes of
time.   'On his arrival, "weary and worn," says
his wife, "with waiting for a place to be, to think,
and to write in," he gave up with something like
nervous fever; "his eyes looked like two immense
spheres of troubled light; his face was wan and
shadowy, and he was wholly uncomfortable."   He
soon recovered tone; but though he pleaded that
his mind never worked well till the frosts brought
out the landscape's autumnal colors and had some
similar alchemy for his own brain, it was a needed
rest that he enjoyed while giving and receiving
these early hospitalities in a new country.   He
even found the broad mountain view, with the
lake in its bosom, a distraction which made it
hard for him to write in its presence.   He had
always been used to narrow outlooks from his
windows; even at the Old Manse the scene was
small though open.   With the coming of the fall
days, however, he again took up his writing, and
showed how stimulating to his ambition and ener-
gies the first taste of popularity had been.   Indeed from this time he was more productive than
at any other period, and wrote regularly and suc-
cessfully as he had never before done.   The scale
of the novel gave more volume to his work of itself, and its mere continuity sustained his effort;
moreover the excitement of a new kind of work

was a strong stimulus. He now began to write novels, differently studied and composed from his earlier stories, more akin to the usual narrative of fiction. "The Scarlet Letter," a work of pure imagination, was the climax of his tales, the furthest reach of his romantic allegorizing moral art in creation; but he now undertook to utilize his experience and observation in the attempt to delineate life in its commoner and more realistic aspects of character and scene. He began "The House of the Seven Gables" in September and finished it early in January. He wrote regularly, but the story went on more slowly than he had hoped, requiring more care and thought than "The Scarlet Letter," because the latter was all in one tone, while here there was variety. He had to wait for the mood, at times; but the composition was really rapid, and seemed slow only because he was used to the smaller scale of effort. The book was at once sent to press and published in the spring.[1]

"The House of the Seven Gables" is a succession of stories bound together to set forth the history of a family through generations under the aspect of an inherited curse which inheres in the house itself. The origin of the curse and of the plot lies in the founder of the family, Colonel Pyncheon, whose character, wrong-doing, and

---

[1] *The House of The Seven Gables.* A Romance. By Nathaniel Hawthorne. Boston: Ticknor, Reed and Fields. 1851. 12mo. Pp. vi, 344.

death make the first act; the second, which is no
more than an illustrative episode and serves to
fill out the history of the house itself, is the tale
of Alice, the mesmerized victim of a later generation, in which the witchcraft element of the first
story is half rationalized; the third part, which
these two lead up to and explain, is the body of the
novel, and contains the working out of the curse
and its dissipation in the marriage of the descendants of the Colonel and the old wizard Maule, from
whose dying lips it had come. The curse itself,
"God will give him blood to drink," is made physical by the fact that death comes to the successive
heirs by apoplexy, an end which lends itself to an
atmosphere of secrecy, mysteriousness, and judgments; but the permanence of those traits which
made the Colonel's character harsh and harmful,
his ambition, will-power, and cruelty, gives moral
probability to the curse and secures its operation
as a thing of nature. There is, nevertheless, a
lax unity in the novel, owing to this dispersion
of the action; and its somewhat thin material in
the contemporary part needs the strengthening
and enrichment that it derives from the historical
elements. The series is united by the uncut
thread of a vengeful punishment that must continue until the original wrong itself shall disappear; but when that happens, the Indian deed
hidden behind the portrait is worthless, the male
line is extinct, and the house itself a thing of the
past. The presence of the past in life, both as

inheritance and environment, is the moral theme, and here it is an evil past imparting misery to whomever it touches. The old house is its physical sign and habitation; the inhabitants are its victims, and in the later story they are innocent sufferers, as Alice had been in the intermediate time.

Such a canvas is one which Hawthorne loved to fill up with the shadowed lights, the melodramatic coloring and fantastic decorativeness of his fancies. The characters are, as always, few. There are but five of them, Hepzibah, Clifford, Phœbe, the daguerreotypist, and the Judge, with the contributory figures of Uncle Venner and little Ned Higgins. They have also the constant Hawthorne trait of great isolation, and live entirely within the world of the story. In sketching them Hawthorne had recourse to real life, to observation, as also in all the contemporary background and atmosphere. The substance and attraction of the novel lie in this fidelity to the life he knew so minutely; for the plot, the crime, the curse, except in their own historical atmosphere, in the Colonel and in Alice's story, interest us but little and languidly. It is, perhaps, not refining too much to see in the novel a closer relationship to those earlier tales and sketches which drew their matter from observation, were less imaginative, more realistic, and belong to a less purely creative art. If "The Scarlet Letter" was the culmination of the finer tales, "The House

of the Seven Gables" is the climax of this less
powerful, but more every-day group of the familiar aspect of country life. It was, possibly, with
some vague sense of this that Hawthorne preferred
this novel as one "more characteristic of my mind,
and more proper and natural for me to write;" it
came from his more familiar self. He was able
to introduce into it that realistic detail concerning
trifles which he delighted to record in his journals; and the minute analysis which in the great
romance he gave to the feelings and inner life of
pain, he here gives rather to the elaboration of
the scene, to external things, to the surface and
texture of the physical elements. He has succeeded consequently in delineating and coloring
a picture of New England conditions with Dutch
faithfulness, and this is the charm of the work.
It appeals, like life and memory themselves, to
the people of that countryside, and goes to their
hearts like the sight of home. To others it can
be only a provincial study, with the attraction of
such life in any land, and for them more dependent on its romantic setting, its moral suggestion,
and general human truth. Those who have the
secret and are of kin to New England, however,
find in the mere description something that en-
dears the book. The life of the little back street,
as it revives in Clifford's childishly pleased senses,
with its succession of morning carts, its scissor-
grinder, and other incidents of the hour; the garden of flowers and vegetables, with the Sunday

afternoon in the ruinous arbor, the loaf of bread
and the china bowl of currants; the life of the
immortal cent-shop, with its queer array, and its
string of customers jingling the bell; the hens,
evidently transported from the great coop of the
Berkshire cottage, but with the value of an event
in the novel, — all these things, with a hundred
other features that are each but a trifle, make up
a glamour of reality that grows over the whole
book like the mosses on the house. In the characters themselves this local realism is carried to
the highest degree of truth, especially in Hepzibah, who in her half-vital state, with her faded
gentility and gentle, heroic heart of patient love,
in all her outer queerness and grotesquely
thwarted life, is the most wholly alive of all of
Hawthorne's characters; in Phœbe, too, though
in a different way, is the same truth, a life entirely real; and, on the smaller scale, Uncle Venner is also to be reckoned a character perfectly
done. Clifford is necessarily faint, and does not
interest one on his own account; he is pitiable,
but his love of the beautiful is too much senti-
mentalized to engage sympathy in the special way
that Hawthorne attempts, and one sees in him
only the victim of life, the prisoner whom the law
mistook and outraged and left ruined; and Holgrave is no more than a spectator, mechanically
necessary to the action and useful in other ways,
but he does not affect us as a character. There
remains Judge Pyncheon, on whom Hawthorne

evidently exhausted his skill in the effort to make him repellent. He is studied after the gentleman who was most active in the removal of Hawthorne from the Custom House, and was intended to be a recognizable portrait of him in the community. Perhaps the knowledge of this fact interferes with the proper effect of the character, since it makes one doubt the truth of it. The practice of introducing real persons into literature as a means of revenge by holding them up to detestation is one that seldom benefits either fiction or truth; it was the ugliest feature of Pope's character, and it always affects one as unhandsome treatment. In this instance it detracts from the sense of reality, inasmuch as one suspects caricature. But taken without reference to the original, Judge Pyncheon is somewhat of a stage villain, a puppet; his villainy is presented mainly in his physique, his dress and walk, his smile and scowl, and generally in his demeanor; it is not actively shown, though the reader is told many sad stories of his misbehaviour; even at the end, in the scene in which he comes nearest to acting, the plot never gets further than a threat to do a cruel thing. In other words it is a portrait that is drawn, not a character that is shown in its play of evil power actually embodying itself in life. He is the bogy of the house, the Pyncheon type incarnated in each generation; and when he sits dead in the old chair, he seems less an individual than the Pyncheon corpse. In the long chapter which serves as his requiem, and in which there is the suggestion of Dickens not in the best phase of his art, the jubilation is somewhat diabolic; it affects one as if Hawthorne's thoughts were executing a dance upon a grave. The character is too plainly hated by the author, and it fails to carry conviction of its veracity. Yet in certain external touches and aspects it suggests the hypocrite who everywhere walks the streets, placid, respectable, sympathetic in salutations, but bearing within a cold, gross, cruel, sensual, and selfish nature which causes a shudder at every casual glimpse that betrays its lurking hideousness. The character is thoroughly conceived, but being developed by description instead of action, seems overdone; prosperity has made him too flabby to act, and kills him with a fit as soon as he works himself up to play the rôle.

After all, the story in its contemporary phase is but a small part of the novel, which does not much suffer even if the Judge in his youthful, hard-hearted, cowardly crime and the victim in his æsthetic delicacy are both ineffective in making the impression the author aimed at. The real scene is the singularly trivial and barren life of the old house, where nothing takes place but the purchase of a Jim Crow, a breakfast of mackerel, a talk about chickens, gossip with Uncle Venner, and the passing of a political procession in the street; and one too easily forgets the marvelous art which could make such a life interesting and stimulating

and engaging to the affections, even with the aid
of Hepzibah and Phœbe in their simpleness. What
makes the happiness of the story is to be found
in these details, and in the century-old atmosphere
which Hawthorne has generated about them, com-
pounding into one element the witchcraft memories, the foreign horizons, the curse in the house,
the threadbare gentility, the decay material and
spiritual, the odor of time, all of which he had
absorbed from his Salem life; thence it came that
he was able to give to New England its only imaginative work that has ancestral quality. All
this, too, is distilled from the soil. Hawthorne
felt in his own life the weight of this past; its
elements were familiar and near to him, so that
his own family legend imparts coloring to the tale
and gives him sympathy with it; and in leaving
Salem it was from such a past that he desired to
be free. He expresses himself, in these matters,
through Holgrave, in his democratic new life urg-
ing Hepzibah to abandon gentility and be proud
of her cent shop as a genuine thing in a practical
and real world, — she would begin to live now at
sixty, such was his narrowness of youthful view;
but the democratic sentiment is Hawthorne's.
So, too, in his rhetorical impeachment of the past,
though the passage is meant to summarize the
point of view of reform, there is an emphasis such
as sincerity gives: —

"'Shall we never, never get rid of this Past?'
cried he, keeping up the earnest tone of his pre-

ceding conversation. 'It lies upon the Present like a giant's dead body! In fact, the case is just as if a young giant were compelled to waste all his strength in carrying about the corpse of the old giant, his grandfather, who died a long while ago, and only needs to be decently buried. Just think a moment, and it will startle you to see what slaves we are to bygone times, — to Death, if we give the matter the right word!'

"'But I do not see it,' observed Phœbe.

"'For example, then,' continued Holgrave, 'a dead man, if he happen to have made a will, disposes of wealth no longer his own; or, if he die intestate, it is distributed in accordance with the notions of men much longer dead than he. A dead man sits on all our judgment-seats; and living judges do but search out and repeat his decisions. We read in dead men's books! We laugh at dead men's jokes, and cry at dead men's pathos! We are sick of dead men's diseases, physical and moral, and die of the same remedies with which dead doctors killed their patients! We worship the living Deity according to dead men's forms and creeds. Whatever we seek to do, of our own free motion, a dead man's icy hand obstructs us! Turn our eyes to what point we may, a dead man's white, immitigable face encounters them, and freezes our very heart! And we must be dead ourselves before we can begin to have our proper influence on our own world, which will then be no longer our world, but the world of

another generation, with which we shall have no
shadow of a right to interfere. I ought to have
said, too, that we live in dead men's houses; as,
for instance, in this of the Seven Gables!'"

This is in the form of dialogue; but Hawthorne's
own attitude toward reform is clearly disclosed in
the analytic passages in which he discusses Holgrave, though it is observable that he embodies no
adverse criticism upon it in the character itself,
as he was to do in his next novel. He appears
to take the same view of reform that is sometimes
found in respect to prayer, that it has great sub-
jective advantages and is good for the soul, but is
futile in the world of fact. It was well for Holgrave, he says, to think as he did; this enthusiasm
"would serve to keep his youth pure and make
his aspirations high," and he goes on with his own
judgment on the matter: —

"And when, with the years settling down more
weightily upon him, his early faith should be
modified by inevitable experience, it would be
with no harsh and sudden revolution of his sentiments. He would still have faith in man's brightening destiny, and perhaps love him all the better,
as he should recognize his helplessness in his own
behalf; and the haughty faith, with which he began life, would be well bartered for a far humbler
one at its close, in discerning that man's best directed effort accomplishes a kind of dream, while
God is the sole worker of realities."

This may be profound truth, as it is intended

to be; but it needs no penetration to see here a man whose sympathies with all kinds of those "come-outers" who then multiplied exceedingly in his neighborhood, would be infinitesimal. He had not, however, yet engaged with this problem so closely as he was to do. So far one would discern only that fatalistic and pessimistic trait indicated by "The Scarlet Letter" and found in "The House of the Seven Gables" in the hard conclusion that there was no remedy for the harm that had been done in the long past. The curse was done with now, it is true, by the marriage of Phœbe and Holgrave, but for Clifford and Hepzibah there was no amends for the lives the dead Judge had ruined by the aid of an imperfect and blundering human law; they were wrecks, so Hawthorne represents it, — they had missed life's happiness and were now in hospital, as it were, till they should die; but in their lives evil had been triumphant, had made them innocent victims, and for this there was neither help nor compensation. The irremediableness of the breach that sin makes in the soul had been preached in "The Scarlet Letter;" here is the other half of the truth, as Hawthorne saw it, the irremediableness of the injury done to others. So far as the book has ethical meaning it lies in the implacability of the uncanceled wrong lingering as a curse, destroying the bad and blasting the good descendants of the house, and presenting the mystery of evil as something positive, persisting, and unchecked in its career. The moral element, nevertheless, lies well in the background and is overlaid with romantic and legendary features; its hatefulness in the main story is not the principal theme; and the novel pleases and succeeds, not by these traits, but by its humble realism, its delicate character-drawing, and that ancestral power which makes it the story of a house long lived in.

On finishing this work Hawthorne took that rest which he always required after any great intellectual exertion, and spent the time with his children and wife. His second daughter, Rose, was born in the spring. A happier childhood seldom gets into books than that which appears in the reminiscences of this small family, whether they were in Salem, or Berkshire, or Liverpool. Hawthorne lived much with his children, and he had the habit of observing them minutely and writing down the history of their little lives in his journals. All winter their play and recreation, their sayings and adventures and habits, diversified the Berkshire days; they thrived on "the blue nectared air," and had rosy cheeks and abounding spirits, and their heads were stuffed with fairy tales. The year was a glorious one in Julian's memory, and the page he makes of it may be taken as a leaf of his father's life at home, disclosing his daily life and home-nature, as it was through years of domestic happiness. Hawthorne, indeed, is never so attractive as when seen with the light of his children's eyes upon him: —

"He made those spring days memorable to his children. He made them boats to sail on the lake, and kites to fly in the air; he took them fishing and flower-gathering, and tried (unsuccessfully for the present) to teach them swimming. Mr. Melville used to ride or drive up, in the evenings, with his great dog, and the children used to ride on the dog's back. In short, the place was made a paradise for the small people. In the previous autumn, and still more in the succeeding one, they all went nutting, and filled a certain disused oven in the house with such bags upon bags of nuts as not a hundred children could have devoured during the ensuing winter. The children's father displayed extraordinary activity and energy on these nutting expeditions; standing on the ground at the foot of a tall walnut-tree, he would bid them turn their backs and cover their eyes with their hands; then they would hear, for a few seconds, a sound of rustling and scrambling, and, immediately after, a shout, whereupon they would uncover their eyes and gaze upwards; and lo! there was their father — who but an instant before, as it seemed, had been beside them — swaying and soaring high aloft on the topmost branches, a delightful mystery and miracle. And then down would rattle showers of ripe nuts, which the children would diligently pick up, and stuff into their capacious bags. It was all a splendid holiday; and they cannot remember when their father was not their playmate, or when they ever desired or imagined any other playmate than he."

The spirit of such a fatherhood, and all this delight in the children's world, was distilled for the great multitude of other children in "The Wonder - Book" and its sequel "Tanglewood Tales." From very early in his career he had written charming childhood sketches, of which "Little Annie's Ramble" and "Little Daffydowndilly" are easily recalled; and his association with his wife's sister, Elizabeth Peabody, had directed his attention particularly to literature for children, and "Grandfather's Chair" had been the result. Whenever he fell into discouragement in respect to the earning capacity of his pen, his first thought was that he would write children's books for a living. For some time he had meditated a volume which should adapt the classical tales of mythology to the understanding and interests of such children as his own, and he now put the plan in execution. He began "The Wonder-Book" with the summer, and finished it at one effort in six weeks of June and July; the ease with which he accomplished the task indicates how pleasurable it was, and well adapted to his sympathies and powers; and the result was very successful, a book of sunshine from cover to cover. It[1] was published in the fall, and was followed

---

[1] *A Wonder-Book for Girls and Boys.* By Nathaniel Hawthorne, with Engravings by Baker from designs by Billings. Boston: Ticknor, Reed and Fields. 1852. 16mo. Pp. vi. 256.

after an interval by its second part, "Tanglewood Tales."[1]

A multitude of children have loved these books, for whom their very names are a part of the golden haze of memory; and, in view of the association of Hawthorne's genius and temperament with quite other themes and the darker element in grown lives, this band of children make a kind of halo round his figure. Whether the thing done should have been so done, whether Greek should have been turned into Gothic, is a foolish matter. To please a child is warrant enough for any work; and here romantic fancy plays around the beautiful forms and noble suggestion of old heroic and divine life, and marries them to the hillside and fireside of New England childhood with the naturalness of a fairy enchantment; these tales are truly transplanted into the minds of the little ones with whose youngest tendrils of imagination they are intertwined. To tear apart such tender fibres were a poor mode of criticism, for the living fact better speaks for itself; and, in the case of the present writer, whose earliest recollection of the great world of literature, his first dawn-glimpse of it, lying in dreamy beauty, was Bellerophon's pool, the memory is potent and yields an appreciation not to be distilled in any other alembic. Few facts are more fixed in his memory than that

[1] *Tanglewood Tales for Girls and Boys.* Being a Second Wonder-Book. By Nathaniel Hawthorne, with Fine Illustrations. Boston: Ticknor, Reed and Fields. 1853. 16mo. Pp. 336.

he was the child who watched the pool for the tall boy with the shining bridle who was his strange friend from another world. If to wake and feed the imagination and charm it, and fill the budding mind with the true springtime of the soul's life in beautiful images, noble thoughts, and brooding moods that have in them the infinite suggestion, be success for a writer who would minister to the childish heart, few books can be thought to equal these; and the secret of it lies in the wondering sense which Hawthorne had of the mystical in childhood, of that element of purity in being which is felt also in his reverence for womanhood, and which, whether in child or woman, was typical of the purity of the soul itself, — in a word, the spiritual sense of life. His imagination, living in the child-sphere, pure, primitive, inexperienced, found only sunshine there, the freshness of the early world; nor are there any children's books so dipped in morning dews.

On finishing "The Wonder-Book" Hawthorne devoted himself to life with Julian for three weeks, during the absence of the rest of the family on a visit, and wrote a daily account of it with such fullness that this history would fill a hundred pages of print. Some passages have been published, and they illustrate how this amusement had taken the place of the earlier note-books which recorded his observations of ordinary and even trivial life round about him. There may be some wonder that a mind of Hawthorne's powers should

find its play in such literary journalizing, and
the inference is ready that, when not at work in
imagination, he was mentally unoccupied; his intellectual interests were, however, always limited in
scope, and his readings in the evening to his wife
were confined to pure literature; outside of such
books he apparently had no intellectual life, and
his thoughts and affections found their exercise in
the domestic circle just as his eyes were engaged
with the look of the landscape, the incidents of
the road, and the changes of the weather. His
capacity for idleness was great, and as his vigor
had already somewhat waned his periods of repose
were long. He undertook no new work during
the summer, but prepared for the press a new
volume of tales, "The Snow Image," [1] which was
ready by the first of November and was soon

---

[1] *The Snow Image and other Twice-Told Tales.* By Nathaniel
Hawthorne. Boston: Ticknor, Reed and Fields. 1852. 12mo,
brown cloth. Pp. 273. The contents and source of the tales
were as follows: The Snow Image, *International Review*, No-
vember, 1850; The Great Stone Face, *National Era*, January
24, 1850; Main Street, *Æsthetic Papers*, 1849; Ethan Brand,
Dollar Magazine, May, 1851; A Bell's Biography, *Knickerbocker
Magazine*, March, 1837; Sylph Etherege, Boston *Token*, 1838;
The Canterbury Pilgrims, Boston *Token*, 1833; No. I, Old
News, *New England Magazine*, February, 1835; No. II, The Old
French War, March, 1835; No. III, The Old Tory, May, 1835;
The Man of Adamant, Boston *Token*, 1837; The Devil in Manu-
script, *New England Magazine*, May, 1835; John Inglefield's
Thanksgiving, *Democratic Review*, March, 1840; Old Ticonderoga,
Democratic Review, February, 1836; The Wives of the Dead,
Boston *Token*, 1832; Little Daffydowndilly, *Boys' and Girls'
Magazine*, Boston, 1843; Major Molineux, Boston *Token*, 1832.

afterwards issued. It is made up of stories and
sketches out of old periodicals, which had not been
gathered in the former collection, some of them
dating from the beginning of his career. Three,
however, were later in composition, and were perhaps among those which he had thought of binding up with "The Scarlet Letter," had that been
issued according to his original plan as one of
several new tales. These three were "The Great
Stone Face," from "The National Era," January
24, 1850, "The Snow Image" from "The International Magazine," November, 1850, and "Ethan
Brand; a Chapter from an Abortive Romance,"
from "Holden's Dollar Magazine," May, 1851;
they were all published with the author's name.
These stories require no comment, as the types to
which they belong are well marked. They were,
in reality, his last trials of his art as a teller of
tales.

Late in November, the family again removed
to a new dwelling-place. The inland air had
proved, it was thought, less favorable to health
than was expected, and except in the bracing
months of mid-winter Hawthorne found it ener-
vating. He had been, however, very happy in
Berkshire, as happy probably as it was in his nature to be, and the distant beauty and near wild-
ness of the country had been attractive; the house,
nevertheless, was very small, and he fretted at its
inconveniences, not in a disagreeable way, but
desiring to have a house and home of his own

among more familiar scenes and within reach of the sea; he regarded the new move as a makeshift, and settled in West Newton, a suburb of Boston, where his wife's family lived, until he should purchase a place of his own. The change from the winter picturesqueness of Berkshire was marked, but the village was of the usual New England type and his surroundings were not essentially different from those he was accustomed to at Concord and Salem.

West Newton was near to Roxbury and the scenes of his rural experience at Brook Farm; but he hardly needed to refresh his memory of the places and persons that had been so much a part of his life ten years before. Brook Farm, as an experiment in the regeneration of society, had run its course, and was gone; but much that was characteristic of it externally was now to be transferred to the novel Hawthorne had in hand as his next work. "The Blithedale Romance"[1] was written during the winter, and was finished as early as May, 1852, when it was at once issued. It is the least substantial of any of his longer works. It lacks the intensity of power that distinguishes "The Scarlet Letter," and the accumulated richness of surface that belongs to "The House of the Seven Gables," due to the overlaying of story on story in that epitome of a New England family history. "The Blithedale Romance," on the con-

[1] *The Blithedale Romance.* By Nathaniel Hawthorne. Boston: Ticknor, Reed and Fields. 1852. 12mo, cloth. Pp. viii, 288.

trary, has both less depth and less inclusiveness; and much of its vogue springs from the fact of its being a reflection of the life of Brook Farm, which possesses an interest in its own right. Hawthorne used his material in the direct way that was his custom, and transferred bodily to his novel, to make its background and atmosphere, what he had preserved in his note-books or memory from the period of his residence with the reformers. The April snowstorm in which he arrived at the farm, his illness there, the vine-hung tree that he made his autumnal arbor, the costume and habits, the fancy-dress party, the Dutch realism of the figure of Silas Foster, and many another detail occur at once to the mind as from this origin; his own attitude is sketched frankly in Miles Coverdale, and the germs of others of the characters, notably Priscilla, are to be found in the same experience. The life of the farm-house, however, is not of sufficient interest in itself to hold attention very closely, and the socialistic experiment, after all, is not the theme of the story; these things merely afford a convenient and appropriate ground on which to develop a study of the typical reformer, as Hawthorne conceived him, the nature, trials, temptations, and indwelling fate of such a man; and to this task the author addressed himself. In the way in which he worked out the problem, he revealed his own judgment on the moral type brought so variously and persistently under his observation by

the wave of reform that was so strongly characteristic of his times.

The characters are, as usual, few, and they have
that special trait of isolation which is the birthmark of Hawthorne's creations. Zenobia, Priscilla, and Hollingsworth are the trio, who, each in
an environment of solitude, make the essence of
the plot by their mutual relations. Zenobia is set
apart by her secret history and physical nature,
and Priscilla by her magnetic powers and enslave-
ment to the mesmerist; Hollingsworth is absorbed
in his mission. It is unlikely that Hawthorne
intended any of these as a portrait of any real
person, though as the seamstress of Brook Farm
gave the external figure of Priscilla, it may well
be that certain suggestions of temperament were
found for the other two characters among his impressions of persons whom he met. Neither Zenobia nor Priscilla, notwithstanding the latter's
name, are essentially New England characters;
in each of them there is something alien to the
soil, and they are represented as coming from
a different stock. Hollingsworth, on the other
hand, is meant as a native type. The unfolding
of the story, and the treatment of the characters, are not managed with any great skill. Hawthorne harks back to his old habits, and does so
in a feebler way than would have been anticipated.
He interjects the short story of The Veiled Lady,
for example, in the middle of the narrative, as he
had placed the tale of Alice in "The House of the

Seven Gables," but very ineffectively; it is a pale narrative and does not count visibly in the progress of the novel, but only inferentially. He uses also the exotic flower, which Zenobia wears, as a physical symbol, but it plays no part and is only a relic of his old manner. The description of the performance in the country hall seems like an extract from one of the old annuals of the same calibre as the Story-Teller's Exhibition. Mesmerism is the feebler substitute for the old witchcraft element. In a word, the work is not well knit together, and the various methods of old are weakly combined. One comes back to the moral situation as the centre of interest; and in it he exhibits the reformer as failing in the same ways in which other egotists fail, for he perceives in the enthusiasm of the humanitarian only selfishness, arrogance, intolerance in another form. Hollingsworth, with the best of motives apparently, since his cause is his motive, as he believes, is faithless to his associates and willing to wreck their enterprise because it stands in his way and he is out of sympathy with it; he is faithless to Priscilla in so far as he accepts Zenobia because she can aid him with her wealth, and on her losing her wealth he is faithless to her in returning to Priscilla; he has lost the power to be true, in the other relations of life, through his devotion to his cause. One feels that Hollingsworth is the victim of Hawthorne's moral theory about him. It is true that at the end Hawthorne has secured in the character that tragic reversal which is always effective, in the point that Hollingsworth, who set out to be the friend and uplifter and saviour of the criminal classes, sees at last in himself the murderer of Zenobia; but this is shown almost by a side-light, and not as the climax of the plot, perhaps because the reader does not hold him guilty in any true sense of the disaster which overtakes Zenobia. In its main situation, therefore, the plot, while it suggests and illustrates the temptations and failures of a nature such as Hollingsworth's, does not carry conviction. Description takes the place of action; much of Zenobia's life and of Hollingsworth's, also, is left untold in the time after Coverdale left them; as in the case of Judge Pyncheon, the wrong-doing is left much in the shadow, suggested, hinted at, narrated finally, but not shown in the life; and such wrong-doing loses the edge of villainy. It might be believed that Hollingsworth as a man failed; but as a typical man, as that reformer who is only another shape of the selfish and heartless egotist sacrificing everything wrongfully to his philanthropic end, it is not so easily believed that he must have failed; it is the absence of this logical necessity that discredits him as a type, and takes out of his character and career the universal quality. This, however, may be only a personal impression. The truth of the novel, on the ethical side, may be plainer to others; it presents some aspects of moral truth, carefully studied and probably observed, but they seem very partial aspects, and too incomplete to allow them, taken all together, to be called typical. The power of the story lies rather in its external realism, and especially in that last scene, which was taken from Hawthorne's experience at Concord on the night when he took part in rescuing the body of the young woman who had drowned herself; but with the exception of this last scene, and of some of the sketches that reproduce most faithfully the life and circumstances of Brook Farm, the novel does not equal its predecessors in the ethical or imaginative value of its material, in romantic vividness, or in the literary skill of its construction. The elements of the story are themselves inferior; and perhaps Hawthorne made the most of them that they were capable of; but his mind was antipathetic to his main theme. His representation of the New England reformer is as partial as that of the Puritan minister; both are depraved types, and in the former there is not that vivid truth to general human nature which makes the latter so powerful a revelation of the sinful heart.

Hawthorne had purchased at some time during the winter, while at work upon this novel, the house at Concord that he named The Wayside. It had belonged to Mr. Alcott, and was an ordinary country residence with about twenty acres of ground, part of which was a wooded hillside rising up steeply back of the house, which itself stood close to the road. The family took possession of this new home early in June, and it soon took on the habitual look of their domicile, which, wherever it might be, had a character of its own. Mrs. Hawthorne, as usual, was much pleased with everything, and wrote an enthusiastic account of its prettiness and comfort, though no important changes were then made in the house itself. She describes the "Study," and the passage, which is in a letter to her mother, gives the very atmosphere of the place: —

"The study is the pet room, the temple of the Muses and the Delphic shrine. The beautiful carpet lays the foundation of its charms, and the oak woodwork harmonizes with the tint in which Endymion is painted. At last I have Endymion where I always wanted it — in my husband's study, and it occupies one whole division of the wall. In the corner on that side stands the pedestal with Apollo on it, and there is a fountain-shaped vase of damask and yellow roses. Between the windows is the Transfiguration [given by Mr. Emerson]. (The drawing-room is to be redeemed with one picture only, — Correggio's Madonna and Christ.) On another side of the Study are the two Lake Comos. On another, that agreeable picture of Luther and his family around the Christmas-tree, which Mr. George Bradford gave to Mr. Hawthorne. Mr. Emerson took Julian to walk in the woods, the other afternoon. I have no time to think what to say, for there is a dear little mob around me. Baby looks fairest of fair to-day. She walks miles about the house."

No words but her own do justice to the happiness of her married life. She worshiped her husband, who always remained to her that combination of adorable genius and tender lover and strong man that he had been ten years before when they were wedded. He had been on his part as devoted to her, and especially he had never allowed the burden of poverty to fall upon her in any physical hardship. In the absence of servants, for example, he himself did the work, and would not permit her to task herself with it. He was never a self-indulgent man, except toward his genius; he had early learned the lesson of "doing without," as the phrase is, and she describes him as being "as severe as a Stoic about all personal comforts" and says he "never in his life allowed himself a luxury." Her testimony to his household character is a remarkable tribute, nor does it detract from it to remember that it is an encomium of love: —

"He has perfect dominion over himself in every respect, so that to do the highest, wisest, loveliest thing is not the least effort to him, any more than it is to a baby to be innocent. It is his spontaneous act, and a baby is not more unconscious in its innocence. I never knew such loftiness, so simply borne. I have never known him to stoop from it in the most trivial household matter, any more than in a larger or more public one. If the

Hours make out to reach him in his high sphere, their wings are very strong. But I have never thought of him as in time, and so the Hours have nothing to do with him. Happy, happiest is the wife who can bear such and so sincere testimony to her husband after eight years' intimate union. Such a person can never lose the prestige which commands and fascinates. I cannot possibly conceive of my happiness, but, in a blissful kind of confusion, live on. If I can only be so great, so high, so noble, so sweet, as he in any phase of my being, I shall be glad."

This was written in the Berkshire days, but it represents her habitual feeling at all times; and now, in the pleasant society of Concord and among the scenes which were endeared to their memory as those of their early married life, this strain of happiness often overflows in her letters like a flood of sunshine. "All that ground," she writes of the neighborhood of the Old Manse, "is consecrated to me by unspeakable happiness ; yet not nearly so great happiness as I now have, for I am ten years happier in time, and an uncounted degree happier in kind. I know my husband ten years better, and I have not arrived at the end; for he is still an enchanting mystery, beyond the region I have discovered and made my own. Also, I know partly how happy I am, which I did not well comprehend ten years ago."

One scene, out of scores that are contained in her correspondence, is too pretty and characteristic to miss, and, besides, serves by a single glimpse to give the home life of this new Concord sojourn with great vividness, yielding — what is the hardest of all to obtain in such intimate views — its quality, like a tone of color. It describes Hawthorne's return from a three weeks' absence at the Isles of Shoals during which he had also attended his class reunion at Bowdoin: —

"I put the vase of delicious rosebuds, and a beautiful China plate of peaches and grapes, and a basket of splendid golden Porter apples on his table; and we opened the western door and let in a flood of sunsetting. Apollo's 'beautiful disdain' seemed kindled anew. Endymion smiled richly in his dream of Diana. Lake Como was wrapped in golden mist. The divine form in the Transfiguration floated in light. I thought it would be a pity if Mr. Hawthorne did not come that moment. As I thought this, I heard the railroad-coach — and he was here. He looked, to be sure, as he wrote in one of his letters, 'twice the man he was.' "

Earlier in the summer this happy home had been shadowed by the tragedy of the death of Hawthorne's sister, Louisa, who was lost in a steamship disaster on the Hudson. Like all such natures, Hawthorne took his griefs hard and in loneliness; but in such a home healing influences were all about him, and even such a sorrow, which he deeply felt, could only add another silence to his life.

His summer work, to which he had turned with reluctance and had rapidly finished by the end of August, was the campaign biography of Franklin Pierce, his life-long friend, who was now a candidate for the Presidency. It is a brief but sufficient book,[1] done well though without distinction, and it holds no real place among his works. Much adverse criticism has, however, been made upon him for writing it at all. It is thought that as a man of letters he lost dignity by using his skill for a political end, and also that as a Northerner he placed himself upon the wrong side in the important public questions then coming to a great national crisis. This is an unjust view. It has already become plain, in the course of the story of his life, that he was not a reformer nor in any real sympathy with reform. He was not only not an abolitionist, which in itself, in view of the closeness of his association with the friends of the cause, argues great immobility in his character; he was, on the contrary, a Democrat in national politics, and took the party view of the slavery question, not with any energy, but placidly and stolidly, so far as one can judge. In fact he took little or no interest in the matter. There was no objection in his mind to writing the biography because of Pierce's political position; he did not hesitate on that score. He did not hang back, on the other hand, because he felt that he could

[1] *Life of Franklin Pierce.* By Nathaniel Hawthorne. Boston: Ticknor, Reed and Fields. 1852. Pp. 144. 12mo.

not tell the truth about his friend in a book
pledged to see only the good in him. He was as
honest as the granite, so far as that is concerned;
and he respected as well as loved his friend, and
was quite willing to serve him by showing his
life and character as he knew them. He had no
intention to deceive any one by a eulogy. He
indulged in no illusions about Pierce, nor about
any of his other friends. He was, in fact, an
unsparing critic of men's characters, and he had
a trait, not rare in New England, — a willingness
to underrate men and minimize them. His fellow-citizens are not natural hero-worshipers; to
them "a man is a man, for a' that," with an
accent that levels down as well as up. Hawthorne
had to the full this democratic, familiar, deroga-
tory temper. Pierce was to him a politician, just
as Cilley had been, and for politicians as a class
he had a well-defined contempt. He believed
Pierce to be a man of honor, sagacity, and tact,
a true man, not great in any way, but quite the
equal of other men in the country and fit in ability, experience, and character to be President, if
his fellow-citizens desired him to serve in that
office. The biography Hawthorne wrote contains
no conscious untruth. It cannot be thought that
Hawthorne compromised with himself either with
regard to the national question involved or to the
personal character of the candidate. His reluctance to write the book had no deeper root than
a dislike to seem to be paid for doing it by an
office. He knew that Pierce would provide him

with a lucrative post in any case; and the public would say that office was his pay. The prospect of this situation was so irksome to him that he decided beforehand to refuse the office, since he preferred rather to do that than to decline the request of his friend to oblige him with his literary service at such a crisis of his career. It is unjust to Hawthorne to suppose that the act had any political complexion, or was anything else than a mere piece of friendliness, natural and proper in itself; his association with the political group, of which Pierce was one, did not proceed from principle, but was an accident of college companionship; the fact is, however strange it may seem, he had no politics, but stood apart from the great antislavery cause just as he did from the transcendental philosophy; neither of these two main movements in the life of his times touched him at all in a personal way. It belongs to the shallowness of his objection to undertake the biography, his dislike to take office as a kind of pay, that it was easily removed. Fields very sensibly persuaded him that he should not neglect so favorable an opportunity to provide for his wife and children, who had no support but his life. When the newly elected President, therefore, offered him the best office in his gift, the Liverpool consulate, Hawthorne decided to take it. The nomination was confirmed March 26, 1853; and, after sending "Tanglewood Tales" to the press, which had been his winter's work, he prepared to leave Concord for a long residence abroad.

VII.

LIFE ABROAD.

HAWTHORNE left the Wayside home with a good deal of regret for its quiet happiness, and yet with pleasant anticipations of the opportunity of seeing foreign countries. He had the roaming instinct; and, though he had almost completed fifty years of life, its satisfaction had been of the slightest. It is necessary to recall how very little he had seen of the world in order to appreciate at all the way in which England and Italy looked to his middle-aged eyes, the points in which they failed to appeal to him as well as those in which they arrested his interest. With all his love, or at least sentiment, for the sea, this was the first voyage he had made, and finding himself a good sailor he enjoyed it immensely. It was the next thing to commanding a ship himself upon his ancestral element, and he felt the mystery and distance and that vague impression of indefinite time that belong to the ocean atmosphere, — the wish to sail on and on forever. In Liverpool, where he arrived in July, he was plunged at once into a confused mass of new impressions and also into the very mundane duties and surroundings of the consulate.

The narrative of his European experiences in every aspect is fully told in the book of reminiscences " Our Old Home," which he published after his return, and in the voluminous note-books kept in his English, French, and Italian sojourns; and this long story is still further enlarged and varied by the letters of the family, and the recollections of his friends. It can be read in detail, and except as a story of detail it has very little interest. The essential point which belongs to his biography is to see how Hawthorne bore himself, the general impression made on him, the ways in which his character came out, in these novel circumstances. At first, he found the office itself very much an old story. In fact, as a matter of routine and a part of daily external affairs, the life of the consulate was that of the Boston coal wharf and the Salem Custom House over again. He repeated the history of these early experiences to the letter, except that he was no longer ridden with the idea that he must go to work in a material, every-day task in order to be a man among men; he was free from that delusion, but at the same time he welcomed the change of life. Politics had already begun to take on that unpleasantness for a Northern man of his affiliations which could make even so dull a participant as he was, in his sluggish conservatism, very uncomfortable; he had felt its rude censures and misapprehensions of delicate personal relations — such as existed between himself and President Pierce —

disagreeably near at hand; and he was glad to get
away from his native land, upon which before a
year had passed he looked back with the feeling
that he never desired to return to it. He did not
enjoy England so much, however, as this might
seem to indicate; and, especially, he did not enjoy his work, for, notwithstanding his philosophy of the usefulness of manual toil and regular
occupation of an unliterary kind, the touch of
work always disenchanted his mind at once. He
liked it no better than on the two previous occasions at Boston and Salem; it bored and wearied
him, and just as before, though he does not now
complain of the fact, it put an end to his literary
activity, paralyzed and sterilized his genius as·
completely as if it had blasted him with a
curse. The difficulty of serving two masters,
though it is sometimes thought to be a service
peculiarly fitted for men of letters, was illustrated
in Hawthorne's career in many ways and on several occasions, but nowhere more plainly than in
the period of his five years of atrophy from the
time he entered the consulate till the composition
of "The Marble Faun." He wrote vigorously in
his note-books, from time to time, but such composition was the opiate it had always been for his
higher imaginative and moral powers, and exercised only his faculty of observation. The fact
that he does not complain of this state of affairs
is due probably to his growing weariness of higher
literary effort, the true power of his genius, which

now had only an ebbing physical force for its basis. He was too much engaged in affairs, and too tired, to write; but he was not displeased to have so good an excuse, and perhaps his ambition was already really satisfied by the success he had achieved, and he felt the spur less.

Altogether, the first and lasting impression made by his account of his life at Liverpool is that he was the same discontented employee who had chafed against circumstances before, and had not changed his mind with the skies over him. The expression of his moods has the old touch of irritability, too, in its excess of language, its air of confiding something that one would not say aloud, its half-conscious pettishness. In March, 1854, he writes to Bridge, in this character, though here possibly it is the presence of politics that is the disturbing factor: —

"I like my office well enough, but any official duties and obligations are irksome to me beyond expression. Nevertheless, the emoluments will be a sufficient inducement to keep me here, though they are not above a quarter part what some people suppose them.

"It sickens me to look back to America. I am sick to death of the continual fuss and tumult and excitement and bad blood which we keep up about political topics. If it were not for my children I should probably never return, but — after quitting office — should go to Italy, and live and die there. If Mrs. Bridge and you would go, too, we might form a little colony amongst ourselves, and see our children grow up together. But it will never do to deprive them of their native land, which I hope will be a more comfortable and happy residence in their day than it has been in ours. In my opinion, we are the most miserable people on earth.

"I wish you would send me the most minute particulars about Pierce — how he looks and behaves when you meet him, how his health and spirits are — and above all, what the public really thinks of him — a point which I am utterly unable to get at through the newspapers. Give him my best regards, and ask him whether he finds his post any more comfortable than I prophesied it would be."

Another year's experience completed his dissatisfaction, and it had reached the familiar acute stage, as early as July, 1855, when he indited that well-known note to Mr. Bright, "the tall, slender, good-humored, laughing, voluble" English friend, who had done everything in the world to make him happy: —

DEAR MR. BRIGHT, — I have come back (only for a day or two) to this black and miserable hole.
Truly yours,
NATH. HAWTHORNE.

There spoke the man, as if the sun had photographed him. It is true that he had a particular occasion for black spirits at the moment, inasmuch as the law reducing the emoluments of the office had just gone into effect, in consequence of which the wages of his slavery were much reduced. He was now very much disposed to resign. He had saved enough money to free his mind from any anxiety for the future, since he thought he could live on what he had with the exercise of economy; the health of Mrs. Hawthorne was somewhat impaired, and it was necessary to arrange a change of residence for her; and he was thoroughly weary of his English surroundings. The President offered him a post in the American Legation at Lisbon, but he declined to consider it; and finally the matter was settled by Mrs. Hawthorne spending the winter at Lisbon with O'Sullivan, who was minister there, while Hawthorne himself retained the consulate and remained in Liverpool, keeping Julian with him while the other two children accompanied their mother. Mrs. Hawthorne, after a delightful visit, returned much improved in health, and it was not until the autumn of 1857 that Hawthorne retired from office, after Buchanan became President.

As a consul Hawthorne discharged his duties with fidelity and efficiency, and was in every way a satisfactory officer. He was diligent and attentive in business affairs, and he was especially considerate of the numbers of distressed citizens who naturally drifted into his care and notice, and was always conscientious and generous in dealing with them, while the burden was a heavy charge. The only matter that stands out notably in his official action is his interest in the inhumane treatment of sailors on American ships, and just before he left office he sent a long dispatch to his government in respect to it. His reflections on the subject, which are apposite and sensible enough, are of less interest biographically than a few sentences upon himself in this philanthropic character, which he wrote to his sister-in-law: —

"I do not know what Sophia may have said about my conduct in the Consulate. I only know that I have done no good, — none whatever. Vengeance and beneficence are things that God claims for Himself. His instruments have no consciousness of His purpose; if they imagine they have, it is a pretty sure token that they are *not* His instruments. The good of others, like our own happiness, is not to be attained by direct effort, but incidentally. All history and observation confirm this. I am really too humble to think of doing good! Now, I presume you think the abolition of flogging was a vast boon to seamen. I see, on the contrary, with perfect distinctness, that many murders and an immense mass of unpunishable cruelty — a thousand blows, at least, for every one that the cat-of-nine-tails would have inflicted — have resulted from that very thing. There is a moral in this fact which I leave you to deduce. God's ways are in nothing more mysterious than in this matter of trying to do good."

This is the same voice that was heard in "The House of the Seven Gables" and "The Blithedale Romance," and shows how deep-seated was Hawthorne's antipathy to conscious philanthropy, and doubtless he meant Elizabeth Peabody as she read it to lay it to heart as an abolitionist.

If Hawthorne observed much cruelty among the crews of American ships, he must have accepted it as a part of the general misery of the world with as much philosophy as he was master of, while he did his duty with regard to it according to his opportunities. He was well liked by the sea captains who came in contact with him. He had, indeed, a good previous training, inasmuch as his terms of service in the Custom House had made him familiarly acquainted with this seafaring type, to which he was also akin. He met the American captains not only at his office, but at the boarding-house of Mrs. Blodgett, where they resorted in numbers, and where he himself lived at various times, and during the whole period of his wife's absence in Portugal. This house is described by himself as strongly impregnated with tar and bilge-water, and the men as very much alive. He admired them, and thought they contrasted very favorably with Englishmen in vitality, and he liked to be with them. Just as he had associated happily and on equal terms with similar men whom he had known in his own country, and made good-fellowship with them at Salem, he now was a welcome and companion-

able member of this hardy group, which his son
Julian remembered in its general look and quality, and describes in a smoking-room scene that
makes this side of Hawthorne more lifelike than
it appears elsewhere: —

"The smoking-room was an apartment barely
twenty feet square, though of a fair height; but
the captains smoked a great deal, and by nine
o'clock sat enveloped in a blue cloud. They
played euchre with a jovial persistence that seems
wonderful in the retrospect, especially as there
was no gambling. The small boys in the house
(there were two or three) soon succeeded in mas-
tering the mysteries of the game, and occasionally
took a hand with the captains. Hawthorne was
always ready to play, and used to laugh a great
deal at the turns of fortune. He rather enjoyed
card-playing, and was a very good hand at whist;
and knew, besides, a number of other games,
many of which are now out of fashion, but which
he, I suppose, had learned in his college days.
Be the diversion or the conversation what it
might, he was never lacking in geniality and good-
fellowship; and sparkles of wit and good humor
continually came brightening out of his mouth,
making the stalwart captains haw-haw prodi-
giously, and wonder, perhaps, where his romances
came from. Nevertheless, in his official capacity,
he sometimes made things (in their own phrase)
rather lively for them; and it is a tribute to his
unfailing good sense and justice, that his enforce-
ment of the law never made him unpopular."

Christmas Day was an occasion of special festivity at this boarding-house, and that of 1855 was unusually distinguished in its annals by the presence of Hawthorne and the legend of the merry-making about him which his friend Bright put into his clever rhymes of the "Song of Consul Hawthorne." Whether in his office, or at the boarding-house, or going about the docks at Liverpool, "Consul Hawthorne" was evidently a very typical New Englander abroad, and popular with his own people. He had laid the author off, and was as purely a practical man of nautical affairs as would be found in any shipping office in the city; and it needed no close observer to see that the native element in him was of a very obstinate and unmalleable nature.

It has been suggested that Hawthorne was afraid of liking English people better than an American ought, as he says he suspects Grace Greenwood did: —

"She speaks rapturously of the English hospitality and warmth of heart. I likewise have already experienced something of this, and apparently have a good deal more of it at my option. I wonder how far it is genuine, and in what degree it is better than the superficial good feeling with which Yankees receive foreigners, — a feeling not calculated for endurance, but a good deal like a brushwood fire. We shall see!"

He had abundant opportunity to see, for he was very kindly received by the society which it was

natural for him to mingle with, and several of his
hosts were untiring in their efforts to please him
and render him comfortable. He was by no
means incapable of social intercourse, notwithstanding his retired habits; the capacity had never
been developed by early breeding or by later necessity, and though on his return home, the change
in him was noticeable, even under the influence
of his foreign travels he remained a silent, difficult, and evasive person in society. When he was
among his own old and familiar friends, such as
Bridge or Pierce, or with new companions whom
he accepted into his circle, such as Fields, he was
open enough and took his share genially and sometimes jovially, as well as when he was with the
American sea captains or his old associates in
Salem; but the touch of social formality, the
presence of a stranger, the ways and habits of
conventionality shut him up in impenetrable reserve and made him temporarily miserable. In
England, however, he was compelled to meet and
be met in the ordinary intercourse of men and
women, and he fared much better than might
have been anticipated. Very greatly to the surprise of his friends he proved an excellent after-
dinner speaker, not only on the public occasions
where the sense of his official station as a representative of his country would have spurred him
to acquit himself well, but also at private parties
and in purely personal relations. Like many
silent men he was a good listener, and his sensi-

tiveness and mental alertness gave the impression
of more sympathy than perhaps he felt. He made
himself agreeable, at all events, and he submitted
to an amount of human fellowship that was aston-
ishing to himself. The novelty of the society he
entered, doubtless, attracted him, and fed his
curiosity, as it certainly was an excitement to his
wife. They had lived all their lives in a community so much simpler in all the furnishings of
refined living, so much less characterized by the
material luxuries of wealth, than this in which
they now found themselves, that the mere sight of
the houses, dinners, and liveries was a new experience, and they observed them like country cous-
ins. The manners of this society, also, arrested
their attention. It was inevitable that Hawthorne
should maintain an aloofness from all this, nevertheless, with the natural democratic questioning
of the reality of the courtesy, the propriety of the
system, the kind and quality of the social results.
He felt the appeal that this life made, he per-
ceived its fitness to the soil, he saw it as a growth
that belonged in its place; but he was thoroughly
glad that there was nothing like it in his own
country. There is not the slightest hint in any
word of his that he regarded himself as an ambas-
sador of friendship in a foreign country or thought
that it was any part of his duty to cultivate international good feeling: he felt himself politically,
socially, fundamentally, an alien in England, and
he preferred to be so; what first struck him were

those obvious differences that distinguish the two peoples, and these remained most prominently in his mind. He was a stranger when he landed at Liverpool, and he never suffered the least tincture of naturalization while he was in the country.

This attitude determines the point of view in his notes and reminiscences. He was an observer, close and accurate and interested; but he had not that sympathy which seeks to understand, to interpret, to justify what one sees, and to put one's self in accord with it. He had his standards already well fixed, and his limitations which he was not sufficiently aware of to desire to escape. He had, too, the critical spirit which is a New England trait, and with this went its natural attendant, the habit of speaking his mind. In writing down his impressions of English manners and institutions and people, he behaved exactly as he had done in his records of similar things at home; there was no difference in his method or in the character of what he said; he was telling what he saw with that indifference to how it would strike other people which comes near to being unconsciousness. He was a good deal surprised when he discovered that the English did not relish what he said; he protested that he had done them more than justice, that they were too easily hurt, and as for hating them, he adds, "I would as soon hate my own people." There is no ill-nature in "Our Old Home;" there is only the clearly expressed, bare, unsympathetic statement of what

he had seen, touched here and there with that
irony and humor which were apt to mix with his
view of men and things. So the people at Salem
had thought he did them injustice in his sketch of
his native home, and he in turn had told them
that he had treated them very considerately, without enmity or ill feeling of any kind, and in fact
what he had written "could not have been done
in a better or kindlier spirit nor with a livelier
effect of truth." He had written of England in
precisely the same way, with that remorseless adherence to his own impression which was second
nature to him, and with that willingness to see
the wrong side of things that he disliked, to minimize human nature when it bored him, and to get
a grim humor out of his victims, which was also
a part of his endowment. In all this, as in some
other parts of Hawthorne's personality, there is
a reminder of Carlyle. The hard judgment he
wrote down of Margaret Fuller, for example, and
the humorous extravagance of his visit to Martin
Tupper, are not to be paralleled except in Carlyle's reminiscences; there was the same unflinching rigor, the same cold obtuseness, the same
half-wearied contempt for what excited their humor
in both men. In his vexation of spirit Hawthorne
is especially suggestive of some discomfortable
cousinship between them; and he was often vexed
in spirit. He was, it would seem, especially burdened by the material comfort of England, in
which he found a grossness but little consonant

with his own taste and spirit, and he made of this the type of things English, as it is easy to do: —

"The best thing a man born in this island can do is to eat his beef and mutton and drink his porter, and take things as they are; and think thoughts that shall be so beefish, muttonish, portish, and porterish, that they shall be matters rather material than intellectual. In this way an Englishman is natural, wholesome, and good; a being fit for the present time and circumstances, and entitled to let the future alone!"

The ascetic and intellectual element, which was large in his ideal past, was revolted by these things, just as the democratic instincts of his nature were shocked by the aristocratic system of society with its social results. He was, too, always in a certain sense homesick; not that he was anxious to go home or looked forward to his return with great pleasure, but he was a man out of place, and had lost the natural harmonies between the outer and the inner life. He had taken a house at Rock Park, a suburb of Liverpool, but he could not make a home out of it, and his account of his residence there gives the whole interior atmosphere of his English stay.

"I remember to this day the dreary feeling with which I sat by our first English fireside and watched the chill and rainy twilight of an autumn day darkening down upon the garden, while the preceding occupant of the house (evidently a most unamiable personage in his lifetime) scowled inhospitably from above the mantelpiece, as if indignant that an American should try to make himself at home there. Possibly it may appease his sulky shade to know that I quitted his abode as much a stranger as I entered it."

It is plain to see that he rather endured than enjoyed English life, notwithstanding the true pleasures he found and the kind friends he made. He was a stranger, taking a stranger's view and with much suspicion of his surroundings, anticipating something hostile in them and forestalling it with his own defenses not too friendly in aspect; in a word he was a foreigner, and he never lost the sense of being in a country not his own, to which he felt superior in all essential matters.

Some regret has been expressed that he did not come into closer contact with English literary life, and especially with the more famous writers of the day. He did not even make the acquaintance of Dickens, Thackeray, Tennyson, Carlyle, George Eliot, to name the most important, nor was he really introduced to the best intellectual life of England at all. He met several second-rate writers, and he knew the Brownings more particularly in Italy. It is not likely, however, that much was lost by this failure to get into touch with the great masters of his own art or with English thinkers and poets in general. Hawthorne had never cared for such society in his own country, and it was probably by his own choice that he missed the literary sets in London. The distaste that he felt for society seems to have taken an aggravated form where his own craft was concerned, whether through self-consciousness, or the memory of his years of obscurity, or for whatever reason; perhaps he had known authors enough at Concord and had no spirit of adventure left in that direction. His own genius was solitary, and in his friendships literary sympathy had no share, for he neither received nor gave it; in fact, if he became familiar with an author, such as Thoreau or Ellery Channing or Herman Melville, it was with the man, not the author. The terms on which he stood with Longfellow and Emerson are those on which, at the happiest, he might have met Thackeray, Tennyson, or Carlyle; but, though speculation must be vain, it is far more probable that he would have found little congeniality with any one of the three. Lord Houghton appears to have made an effort to take him about, but with so little success that he thought Hawthorne had taken a dislike to him. As it was, Hawthorne saw quite enough, and more than he desired, of literary England; it was mostly weariness to him.

It must be acknowledged that the manners and institutions of the country, and its people for the most part, were little to Hawthorne's taste, and he showed this in his book about them; but, for all that, he found the country interesting and often lovely in its picturesque antiquity and softnesses of light and color, and he appreciated to the full the literary and historical sentiment that most appeals to Americans of like education and breeding. He made many excursions in different parts of England, and visited Scotland and the Isle of Man, and he lingered in many towns and villages and was disposed to haunt old places with a pilgrim devotion. He loved the face of the country, too, and notwithstanding its misted and dreary skies, especially over Liverpool, he found some good words for its weather, its seasons, its long days, and all its out-door look. He went about with the mind and senses of a tourist, satiating his instincts for minute and detailed observation and writing it all down; in a spirit, too, of enjoyment and discovery; and out of this satisfaction of his inveterate habits of observing and noting and walking about with no other end in view, just as if he were taking an autumn stroll in Salem, came the felicity of the English notes, which after all deductions is very great in its own field of delicate sentiment and realistic grasp and the atmosphere of a mind. Hawthorne was thoroughly happy in indulging his wandering propensity in such voyages of discovery; especially in London he found a city that satisfied his idea of it, and he seems to have busied himself there for days and weeks in merely going about from point to point and seeing the spectacle of its vast and varied life. Hawthorne's English experiences will, perhaps, be best realized, if he is thought of apart from literature, as a man much identified with the shipping interests and commercial society of Liverpool, and attending to this business rather doggedly and wearily, not especially liking the place or the people, whose ways and notions he was instinctively against, being himself a settled New Englander of a strong race type; and yet, besides this, a man who managed in his four years' residence to see a great deal of the length and breadth of England, as a summer tourist might visit its shrines on pilgrimage. This describes his life, nevertheless, only from the outside; as soon as one opens his note-books, his personality changes the impression, and pervades even his least sympathetic pages with a human quality that wins on the reader in spite of all reservations, and one sees how in the face of his prejudices and limitations England was saved to him by his literary faculty, the interests, susceptibilities, and powers that were his as a man of letters. One finds in his experience, too, besides the consul and the man of letters, a kindly and simple manhood of a more primitive element, the human heart in its own original right, as in the well-known incident of the workhouse child who was so strangely drawn to him. Of the humane actions, however, of which any record remains, none is so honorable as his considerateness, generosity, and conscientiousness in his correspondence with Delia Bacon, whom he endured and befriended with infinite patience and delicacy; the letters which he wrote to her show his character in a very noble light, and bring out one side of his life which has little illustration, his habitual thoughtfulness for the weak.   One recalls his care for his Brook Farm friend Farley at Concord, for example; and all his relations with what one may call the wayside acquaintance of life were to his honor.

One other incident must also find a place here, which completes an earlier story and rounds out his own conception of integrity.   On coming to Liverpool he had incurred heavy expenses, but six months of his more fortunate days had not gone by before he sent to Hillard the money which his friends had given to him in his sore need at Salem while he was writing "The Scarlet Letter."   His own words best express the feelings which led him to make this restitution: —

LIVERPOOL, December 9, 1853.

DEAR HILLARD, — I herewith send you a draft on Ticknor for the sum (with interest included) which was so kindly given me by unknown friends, through you, about four years ago.

I have always hoped and intended to do this, from the first moment when I made up my mind to accept the money.   It would not have been right to speak of this purpose before it was in my power to accomplish it; but it has never been out of my mind for a single day, nor hardly, I think, for a single working hour.   I am most happy that this loan (as I may fairly call it, at this moment) can now be repaid without the risk on my part of leaving my wife and children utterly destitute. I should have done it sooner; but I felt that it would be selfish to purchase the great satisfaction for myself, at any fresh risk to them. We are not rich, nor are we ever likely to be; but the miserable pinch is over.

The friends who were so generous to me must not suppose that I have not felt deeply grateful, nor that my delight at relieving myself from this pecuniary obligation is of any ungracious kind. I have been grateful all along, and am more so now than ever. This act of kindness did me an unspeakable amount of good; for it came when I most needed to be assured that anybody thought it worth while to keep me from sinking. And it did me even greater good than this, in making me sensible of the need of sterner efforts than my former ones, in order to establish a right for myself to live and be comfortable. For it is my creed (and was so even at that wretched time) that a man has no claim upon his fellow-creatures, beyond bread and water and a grave, unless he can win it by his own strength or skill. But so much the kinder were those unknown friends whom I thank again with all my heart.

This money must have been the first he had saved, and he could now spare it from his income. In the four years that he held the consulate he had held to his main purpose of laying by a competency, and when he resigned, on August 31,

1857, his mind was at ease with regard to the future for himself and his family. His gratitude for this late won independence, humble as it was, must have been deeply felt, as is apparent from his letters at the time; a great weight had been lifted from his spirit, and his happiness was such as only a man with his ideas of personal independence could realize. He proposed now to linger in Europe for some time longer; and when he was relieved from his duties in the fall he went with the family through France to Italy, hoping that the southern winter would be of benefit to Mrs. Hawthorne's still uncertain health.

Life in Italy proved far more agreeable than it had been in England, and there were periods in it when Hawthorne enjoyed as great happiness in the placid course of the days as he ever experienced. For the first time in his life he was free from the necessity of labor, and he had recently escaped from that practical business of affairs and daily duties which was always irksome to him. The change, too, from the dark skies of England and its grimy Liverpool materialism to an atmosphere of sun and warmth and artistic beauty was itself enough to reanimate his spirit; and he found at once some congenial society, and not a few who seemed to him like old friends. He appears for the first time in his life really to live with other people, not as an occasional visitant coming out of his hermitage, but as one of themselves. He sought out Story, who was an old neighbor at Salem, though he had known him only slightly, and under his guidance he mixed with the American artists then in Rome, — Miss Hosmer, Thompson, Ropes, and Miss Lander, — as well as with others of the foreigners resident there, Miss Bremer, Mrs. Jameson, and Bryant among the rest; and he became good friends with Motley and his family, whose companionship he enjoyed in a very natural, frank way. The picturesque ruins of Rome, its gardens and fountains and the sky and air appealed to him, as if to new senses or at least to senses newly awakened and developed; and he was sensibly attracted by the artistic works on every hand. He was not wholly uncultivated in art, though his æsthetic sense had been rather a hope than a reality all through his life. He had written to his wife before marriage, nearly twenty years ago, "I never owned a picture in my life; yet pictures have been among the earthly possessions (and they are spiritual ones too) which I most coveted;" and in his tales there is a recurring reference to pictures as a part of his imaginative world. The influence of his wife's artistic tastes in his home life had also been a kind of preparation for appreciation of the masterpieces, many of which had long been familiar to his eyes and thoughts in reproductions. In his Boston days he use to visit such collections of pictures as were accessible to him, and he knew sculpture somewhat through casts. Such cultivation, however, was at best a very limited and incomplete preparation, and did not preserve him from the tourist's weariness of galleries. He had wished in London that the Elgin marbles had all been reduced to lime. There was something pictorial in his genius, but painting was slower to give up its secrets to him than sculpture, which, being a more abstract art and simpler in intention, as well as nearer to the living form, made the easier appeal to him. He did not respond to Italian painting very perfectly at the best, and his education hardly proceeded farther than an appreciation of the softer and brighter works of Guido and Raphael, nor did he ever free himself from the intellectual prepossessions of his mind. He did not become even an amateur in art, and he probably knew it; he had begun too late to enter that world; and he contented himself with a moral sympathy, an apprehension of idea and feeling, rather than the seeing eye and understanding heart by which one takes possession of the artistic world as a free citizen there. It was not an important matter, however; his comments on art have only a personal interest, lighting up his own nature; but, within his limits, he enjoyed a new and great experience, one that illumined and softened his mind, in his wanderings about the galleries and churches and his sittings in artists' studios. The contemporary and native world of Italy he attended to but very little, noting its picturesque aspects somewhat, but taking the slightest interest in its people; if he had felt a barrier between

himself and the English, here was a gulf of difference that it was hopeless to attempt to pass over,
and he left the Italians in the inaccessible foreign-
ness in which he found them.

The first four months were spent at Rome, in
this gradual opening of his mind to the new impressions of the city, so fascinating to his imagination, and in establishing himself and his family
in the new society of their daily life.   Late in
May, 1858, they went north by the carriage road,
and settled at Florence in the Casa Bella, near
Casa Guidi, where the Brownings were, and not
far from Powers's studio.   In August they took
possession of the old villa of Montaüto on the
hill of Bellosguardo, near the city, which is so
closely associated with Hawthorne's Italian days
as the tower of Monte Beni.   Here he began to
write "The Marble Faun," shutting himself up
for an hour or two every day in the stern effort,
as he describes it, of coming "to close grip with
a romance which I have been trying to tear out
of my mind."   The scene of his labors was quite
remote, such a place as he liked to have to write
in, and he was undisturbed unless it were by the
Spiritualism of the Browning villa, where Mrs.
Browning was a believer; and, perhaps under the
influence of this association, Mrs. Hawthorne
showed more plainly her natural inclination to a
more than curious interest in the phenomena.
She was, indeed, somewhat a believer in the
power of communication with the spiritual world,

and its near presence and influence in our lives. The seclusion of the villa of Montaüto was very grateful to Hawthorne, and he writes of it to Fields with almost a home-feeling, as if he had again found a lodging place at least for his wandering Penates: —

"It is pleasant to feel at last that I am really away from America — a satisfaction that I never really enjoyed as long as I stayed in Liverpool, where it seemed to me that the quintessence of nasal and hand-shaking Yankeedom was gradually filtered and sublimated through my consulate, on the way outward and homeward. I first got acquainted with my own countrymen there. At Rome, too, it was not much better. But here in Florence, and in the summer-time, and in this secluded villa, I have escaped out of all my old tracks, and am really remote. I like my present residence immensely. The house stands on a hill, overlooking Florence, and is big enough to quarter a regiment, insomuch that each member of the family, including servants, has a separate suite of apartments, and there are vast wildernesses of upper rooms into which we have never yet sent exploring expeditions. At one end of the house there is a moss-grown tower, haunted by owls and by the ghost of a monk who was confined there in the thirteenth century, previous to being burnt at the stake in the principal square of Florence. I hire this villa, tower and all, at twenty-eight dollars a month; but I mean to take it away bodily and clap it into a romance, which I have in my head, ready to be written out."

The kind of life that was led by the family is more vividly sketched by his daughter in her reminiscences of the time, and her pages afford the only full companion picture to those of the Old Manse and the Berkshire cottage, and to some extent supply the lack of that autobiographic background to "The Marble Faun" which the reader misses in Hawthorne's own preface.

"The walls of the hall and staircase were of gray stone, as were the steps which led echoingly up to the second story of the house. My sister exclaims in delight concerning the whole scene: ' This villa, — you have no idea how delightful it is! I think there must be pretty nearly a hundred rooms in it, of all shapes, sizes, and heights. The walls are never less than five feet thick, and sometimes more, so that it is perfectly cool. I should feel very happy to live here always. I am sitting in the loggia, which is delightful in the morning freshness. Oh, how I love every inch of that beautiful landscape!' The tower and the adjacent loggia were the features that preëminently sated our thirst for suggestive charm, and they became our proud boast and the chief precincts of our daily life and social intercourse. The ragged gray giant looked over the road-walls at its foot, and beyond and below them over the Arno valley, rimmed atop with azure distance, and touched with the delicate dark of trees.

Internally, the tower (crowned, like a rough old king of the days of the Round Table, with a machicolated summit) was dusty, broken, and somewhat dangerous of ascent. Owls that knew every wrinkle of despair and hoot-toot of pessimism clung to narrow crevices in the deserted rooms, where the skeleton-like prison frameworks at the unglazed windows were in keeping with the dreadful spirits of these unregenerate anchorites. The forlorn apartments were piled one above the other until the historic cylinder of stone opened to the sky. In contrast to the barrenness of the gray inclosures, through the squares of the windows throbbed the blue and gold, green and lilac, of Italian heavens and countryside. . . .

"Some of the rooms at Montaüto I studiously avoided. The forlorn cavern of a parlor, or ballroom, I remember to have seen only once. There was a painful vacuum where good spirits ought to have been. Along the walls were fixed seats, like those in the apse of some morally fallen cathedral, and they were covered with blue threadbare magnificence that told the secrets of vanity. Heavy tables crowded down the centre of the room. I came, saw, and fled. The oratory was the most thrilling place of all. It opened out of my sister's room, which was a large, sombre apartment. It was said to attract a frequently seen ghost by the force of its profound twilight and historic sorrows; and my sister, who was courageous enough to startle a ghost, highly approved of this corner of her domain. But she suddenly lost her buoyant taste for disembodied spirits, and a rumor floated mistily about that Una had seen the wretched woman who could not forget her woes in death. In ' Monte Beni' this oratory is minutely pictured, where ' beneath the crucifix . . . lay a human skull . . . carved in gray alabaster, most skillfully done . . . with accurate imitation of the teeth, the sutures, the empty eye-caverns.' Everywhere the intense picturesqueness gave material, at Montaüto, for my father's romance."

Amid such surroundings the new romance was sketched out, but not very much progress could have been made with it. In October the family returned to Rome by way of Siena, where some happy days were spent with Story, — a town which impressed Hawthorne almost temperamentally, standing apart in his mind with Perugia. "A thoughtful, shy man," he says, "might settle down here with the view of making the place a home, and spend many years in a sombre kind of happiness." At Rome they settled again in the Piazza Poli, and entered on the winter days with much happiness, feeling acquainted now and partly at home in the city. But a misfortune came to them in the illness of Una, who was taken with Roman fever, and her life was despaired of. Hawthorne always took his sorrows hard, and he suffered much in this period of anxiety, enduring in his stoic way the heavy pressure; happily the doctor proved mistaken in his confidence that the child would die, and though her illness was long, she gradually recovered strength. It was during her convalescence that Pierce came to Rome, and Hawthorne found in his friendship a great support and comfort. It is plain that Pierce was the only man that Hawthorne loved with his full heart, and he had come to recognize the great place this friendship held in his life. His loyalty to Pierce was a true tribute, and its expression does honor to both men: —

"I have found him here in Rome, the whole of my early friend, and even better than I used to know him; a heart as true and affectionate, a mind much widened and deepened by the experience of life. We hold just the same relation to one another as of yore, and we have passed all the turning-off places, and may hope to go on together, still the same dear friends, as long as we live. I do not love him one whit the less for having been President, nor for having done me the greatest good in his power; a fact that speaks eloquently in his favor, and perhaps says a little for myself. If he had been merely a benefactor, perhaps I might not have borne it so well; but each did his best for the other, as friend for friend."

The illness of Una had thrown a shadow over these last days at Rome, and it was in any case necessary to take her away. In a characteristic outburst Hawthorne writes to Fields: —

"I bitterly detest Rome, and shall rejoice to bid it farewell forever; and I fully acquiesce in all the mischief and ruin that has happened to it, from Nero's conflagration downward. In fact, I wish the very site had been obliterated before I ever saw it."

They left Rome late in May and went by sea to Marseilles, and after a rapid journey up the Rhone and to Geneva went by Paris to London. The return to England was somewhat like home-coming, and during this second residence Hawthorne shows a more sympathetic and contented spirit. He determined to finish his romance here, and settled first at Whitby and afterwards at Redcar, and still later he migrated to Leamington; but the romance was mainly put into shape at Redcar, where the necessary conditions of solitude were best realized. He lived very much as when he had written his other works at home, writing in the morning and spending the rest of the day with the children out of doors on the sands. He finished the book on November 8, and it was published early the following spring.[1]

Hawthorne came to the writing of "The Marble Faun" after his genius was matured, with his temperament fully ripened, his intellectual and moral and artistic nature consonant in its varied play, and at the height of his literary powers.

[1] *The Marble Faun*, or the Romance of Monte Beni. By Nathaniel Hawthorne, author of "The Scarlet Letter." Boston: Ticknor and Fields. 1860. 12mo. 2 vols., pp. 283; 288.

The story is in one sense a culmination, and it is perhaps his most complete expression of life; but it is less characteristic of him, less peculiarly his own, than the American tales, notwithstanding its greater breadth, its finer beauty, and its more profound mystery. In method he develops nothing new; the scheme, the manner, the tone are the same already made familiar. He had recourse to his life abroad for the realism of the scene, and took out of his note-books and memory the whole visible world of his romance, precisely as he had formerly utilized the New England village life and the Brook Farm experience. He has drunk in the charm of Italy and absorbed the picturesque and artistic atmosphere of Rome and its religious impressiveness; he has taken most delicately and harmoniously into his sensitive temperament the loveliness and the power of both the world of the past and the world of art, and he renders them back in description as they were mirrored in himself; the stir of Roman life, its antiquity, its still and immutable forms of picture and sculpture, are given back with full sympathy and as clearly as the autumn woodland of the old Puritan town in his first romance; and this realism, for such it is notwithstanding its glamour, is the substance of the tale, though it is all surface, just as was the case with "The House of the Seven Gables." He has done for Rome and Italy what he there did for Salem, different as the effect may seem, owing to the greater nobility and dignity of the material.

He has also in the management of the story confined himself, as was his wont, to a few characters, Donatello, Miriam, Hilda, and Kenyon, each strictly isolated in peculiar individuality, and offering the opportunity for powerful contrasts; and he has allowed his imagination to find its spring in the symbolism of a physical object, here the marble statue of the faun, and let his moral scheme evolve out of the brooding of his thought upon the spiritual thing thus suggested for the play of meditation. The plot itself, though more definitely disclosed in its main incident of crime, which is made central in the narrative, is of the simplest sort, and no more than enough to provide corporal fact sufficient to give the body of event and situation; and, for the rest, the story both before and after is left wholly vague, the mystery of Donatello's fate repeating the mystery of Miriam's past. In this he showed again his indifference to what became of his characters when they had fulfilled their function artistically; he had no human sympathy with their personal fortunes. This peculiarity is only another phase of the fact that crime itself did not interest him in its mortal career. The use he found in crime was only as the means by which sin was generated in the soul; and his concern was with the latter, not the former.

He has projected on such a background and out of such a group of characters an analytic study of the nature of evil, and this is his main theme, overlaid as it is with all the decorative beauty of

his interpretation of Italy. He had formerly set
forth the history of sin in the heart, taking the
evil for granted and reflecting upon it as a thing
given; he now looks backward and is engaged
with the genesis of sin in a natural man, the coming
of sin into the world of nature; and yet this is
not all, but he endeavors to think about the meaning of evil, the reason for sin's existence, the old
problem fundamental in thought about the spiritual life. It cannot be regarded as a matter on
which he came to any satisfactory conclusion or
even uttered any novel reflections; and it is this
that gives its lack of firmness to the work on the
ethical side. Donatello is made into a living soul
of a higher capacity by his experience of crime;
but Hawthorne suggests that evil serves a good
purpose in this only with much reluctance, and indeed he may almost be said to reject this explanation. Donatello became "a sadder and a wiser
man," and with that old phrase the issue for him
seems to be summed. It is noticeable that, as in
"The Scarlet Letter," there is no question of how
this soul that has come into a miserable consciousness is to be healed; and it is remarkable that the
only consolation the Church can give is vouchsafed
by Hawthorne to the heretic Hilda, but not to the
child of its own bosom. Hawthorne, if he indicates through Kenyon his ideas, seems to advise,
as elsewhere, letting the dead past bury its dead
while Donatello and Miriam should go on to what
self-sacrificing life they can find. Unsatisfactory

as the story is, merely as a tale, it is less vague
than the central truth, the moral theme which it
embodies. The truth is that after all, in the
ethical sphere of the story, Hawthorne has given
no more than his meditations, very much at random, upon sin as it appears in the world of nature, and the way in which his chosen characters
react under its influence. Hilda is as innocent
as Donatello, but her soul frees itself from the
contact; and Miriam is as guilty, yet she alone is
unaffected by the crime in her essential nature, so
far as appears. She is the most vital character in
the book, having touches in her of both Hester
and Zenobia; the three women are all of one
kind in their different environment, and Miriam is
the most human of the three, — strong, assertive,
practical as they all are, and also entirely resource-
less in their tragedies.

The romance is not of a kind to sustain very
firm critical handling, for its structure is thus
weak, not merely in the plot but in its ethical meaning; if the former is left unwrought, so the latter
is left unclarified. The power of the work lies
rather in its artistic effects, independent of any
purpose Hawthorne had in writing; his genius was
creative in its own right, and when he had once
brought the background, the characters, and the
idea together, they in a certain sense took life
and built up their own story, while his hand
linked picture to picture in the unfolding scene,
with a free play of sentiment, fancy, and medita-

tion round about them. Intense points show out, as if by an inner and undesigned brilliancy. The companionship of Donatello, full of the freshness and laughter of the early world, with Miriam tracked by her own terrible secret, is itself a startling situation, and the effecting of their union by a crime, which paralyzes the love of one while it creates the love of the other, is the work of a master imagination. Hilda in her dove-cote, keeping the perpetual lamp burning at the Virgin's shrine and taking into her heart the lovely pictures of old time as a pool reflects heaven in its quiet depths, is a figure of sensitive purity, rendered symbolically, with the same truth and delicacy as Donatello, though so opposed in contrast to his natural innocence blighted and stained; even the quality of mercilessness, which Hawthorne gave her out of his own heart, she turns to favor and to prettiness, till it seems to belong to her as a part of her chastity of nature. The reduplication of the characters in the world of art about them, though it is frequently resorted to by Hawthorne, does not grow monotonous; but by this method he rather animates the external world, as if picture and statue and tower had absorbed life and were permeated with its human emotion. The faun is, perhaps, a somewhat hard symbol, and needs to be vitalized in Donatello before its truth is felt to be alive; but the drawing that reproduces the model as the demon's face, the sketches of Miriam portraying a woman's revengeful mischief, the sights that Donatello and Kenyon shape out of the sunset, the benediction of the statue of the pontiff, the evasive eyes of Beatrice felt in Hilda, Donatello, and Miriam, are instances of borrowed or attributed life, which illustrate how constantly and effectively Hawthorne uses this means of expression, and it is the chief means by which he has integrated and harmonized the various material into a whole artistically felt. It is an error, however, to force his interpretation too far, as in the attempt to see in the Beatrice portrait a shadow of Miriam's mystery; if such a thought crossed his mind, it left no record of itself, and he was as ignorant as others of Miriam's actual past, one may be sure. That unwillingness to be gazed upon, of which he makes so much, recurring to it again and again and most pointedly in Donatello, was the simplest and primary symbol to him, apparently, of the shock of sin, whether it were in the victim like Beatrice or the participant like Donatello or the spectator like Hilda. In Miriam it is less felt, because to her the knowledge of evil had come in her earlier career.

It is in rendering this spiritual shock, disturbing the very seat of life, that Hawthorne best succeeds in the moral part of his subject; and it is by awakening some answering vibration in his readers that he imparts to the romance that universal interest which makes it rank so high as it does in the literature of the soul's life. He was not, however, very apt in the mechanics of his art, and in lieu of structure such as a man of far less faculty might be an adept in, he finds in his imagined tale a principle of life itself; his work is seldom well reasoned, but it has vital germs of thought, emotion, and action, and these are loosed into activity and grow of themselves, and he fosters and develops them in his richly brooding mind. So, here, the spiritual shock, which is the central spring of the romance, is allowed to transmit itself in every direction, and he lays bare its workings. It is saddest in Donatello in the moment when he heard the cry of the falling wretch, when he turned cold at Miriam's touch, when he lost his kinship with the wild creatures he loved; and it is fixed in his unquiet, evasive eyes. One loves Donatello, and of no other character of Hawthorne can it be said that it wins affection; and one wishes that, if he must have a soul, he might have come into it in some way of natural kindness dissociated from a moral theory. This theory — and here is the one discord — is, after all, felt to be an exotic in the Italian air. Donatello has been puritanized, and though the character may be a perfect symbolic type, it has nothing racial in it; and to be racial was Donatello's charm. It is the same wherever the story is taken up; it is charming as an artistic work, but when one begins to think about it, the method of approach is proved to be wrong because it solves nothing and ends in futility. It is throughout a Puritan romance, which has wandered abroad and clothed itself in strange masquerade in the Italian air. Hawthorne's personality pervades it, like life in a sensitive hand. It is the best and fullest and most intimate expression of his temperament, of the man he had come to be, and takes the imprint of his soul with minute delicacy and truth. It is a meditation on sin, but so made gracious with beauty as to lose the deformity of its theme; and it suffers a metamorphosis into a thing of loveliness. To us it is in boyhood our dream of Italy, and in after years the best companion of memory; it is also a romance of nature and art, and of the mystery of evil, shot through with such sunshine gleams, with the presence of pure color and divine forms, as to seem like the creations of that old mythic Mediterranean world which, though it held shapes of terror, was the most beautiful land that the imagination has ever known.

VIII.

LAST YEARS.

HAWTHORNE reached Concord, on his home journey, late in June, 1860, and took possession of the Wayside almost unobserved. He had intended to improve the house and grounds, and set about the task; the well-known tower, in memory of the tower of Montaüto, was added for his study, and some other changes were made, but his funds, which were diminished by an unfortunate loan, were insufficient to enable him to do all he desired. He was welcomed by his old Concord friends, and began again the agreeable village life he had formerly known; but he mingled more on equal terms with other people than had been his custom before his foreign residence had forced him into some share of society. He went not infrequently to the Saturday Club in Boston, and though always a silent and reserved person in such gatherings, his enjoyment of these occasions was as great as he could ever derive from literary companionship, and many of the members were old and familiar acquaintances. It was at home, however, that he spent his days, working in his study over his writing, and pacing the footpath on the hill-ridge back of his house, and from time to time going to the seaside at Beverly or in Maine with his son Julian for a companion. His health was not so firm as it had been. A change seems to have fallen on him with some suddenness on his return to America; for some years, ever since the hard winter of "The Scarlet Letter" at Salem, he had complained of fatigue in writing and of lassitude and slowness of mind; after the winter in Rome he felt this with new weariness, as he says when he practically ended his note-books in Switzerland, not having the vital impulse to continue them, and in the intervening time he had completed "The Marble Faun;" now he began perceptibly to lose physical force, to grow thin, and to lack energy. He wrote a good deal, sitting down to his desk and "blotting successive sheets of paper as of yore;" but with little satis-faction to himself.

The times were unfavorable to peace of mind and the quiet of literary occupation. Secession began soon after he arrived, and war followed in the spring with that outburst of passionate devo-tion to the Union which was transforming all his neighborhood into a camp and sending all the youth of his people to the battle southward. To Hawthorne, being in such imperfect sympathy with this feeling and the causes which gave it passion, the war was only vexation and disas-ter, with much meaninglessness, foolishness, use-lessness, however he might try to look at it with

Northern eyes.   In nothing is his natural detach-
ment from life so marked as in this incapacity to
understand the national life in so supreme a crisis
and under the impulse of so profound a passion.
He stood aloof from it, unmoved in his superan-
nuated conservatism, as abroad he had stood aloof
from the English life wrapped in his imperturb-
able New England breeding.   He was obliged to
take some stand in his own mind, and he naturally went with his own State, never having been
really an American, on the national scale, but
only a New Englander, as he confessed.   During
his life at Liverpool, four years before, he had
made up his mind which side he would be on, when
the prospect of war began to loom up as a possibility, and wrote briefly to Bridge about it: —

"I regret that you think so doubtfully (or,
rather, despairingly) of the prospects of the
Union; for I should like well enough to hold on
to the old thing.   And yet I must confess that I
sympathize to a large extent with the Northern
feeling, and think it is about time for us to make
a stand.   If compelled to choose, I go for the
North.   At present we have no country — at
least, none in the sense an Englishman has a
country.   I never conceived, in reality, what a
true and warm love of country is till I witnessed
it in the breasts of Englishmen.   The States are
too various and too extended to form really one
country.   New England is quite as large a lump
of earth as my heart can really take in.

"Don't let Frank Pierce see the above, or he would turn me out of office, late in the day as it is. However, I have no kindred with, nor leaning towards, the abolitionists."

In the first flush of the war he felt the contagion of the patriotic thrill, and was with his friends a "war Democrat;" but his mind was filled with reservations. On May 26, 1861, he again writes to Bridge: —

"The war, strange to say, has had a beneficial effect upon my spirits, which were flagging woefully before it broke out. But it was delightful to share in the heroic sentiment of the time, and to feel that I had a country, — a consciousness which seemed to make me young again. One thing as regards this matter I regret, and one thing I am glad of. The regrettable thing is that I am too old to shoulder a musket myself, and the joyful thing is that Julian is too young. He drills constantly with a company of lads, and means to enlist as soon as he reaches the minimum age. But I trust we shall either be victorious or vanquished before that time. Meantime, though I approve the war as much as any man, I don't quite understand what we are fighting for, or what definite result can be expected. If we pummel the South ever so hard, they will love us none the better for it; and even if we subjugate them, our next step should be to cut them adrift. If we are fighting for the annihilation of slavery, to be sure it may be a wise object, and offer a tangible result, and the only one which is consistent with a future union between North and South. A continuance of the war would soon make this plain to us, and we should see the expediency of preparing our black brethren for future citizenship by allowing them to fight for their own liberties, and educating them through heroic influences. Whatever happens next, I must say that I rejoice that the old Union is smashed. We never were one people, and never really had a country since the Constitution was formed."

Six months later he writes again with nearly the same point of view, accepting in fact the theory of disunion as the only possible result: —

"I am glad you take such a hopeful view of our national prospects so far as regards the war; but my own opinion is that no nation ever came safe and sound through such a confounded difficulty as this of ours. For my part I don't hope, nor indeed wish, to see the Union restored as it was. Amputation seems to me much the better plan, and all we ought to fight for is the liberty of selecting the point where our diseased members shall be lop't off. I would fight to the death for the northern slave States and let the rest go."

It is this despair of the Union that characterizes his attitude throughout, and with it goes also an absence of belief in the Union; but one feels that he is not deeply interested in the matter for its own sake. Thus after another interval he again writes to Bridge, February 14, 1862: —

"Frank Pierce came here and spent a night, a week or two since, and we mingled our tears and condolences for the state of the country. Pierce is truly patriotic, and thinks there is nothing left for us but to fight it out, but I should be sorry to take his opinion implicitly as regards our chances in the future. He is bigoted to the Union, and sees nothing but ruin without it; whereas I (if we can only put the boundary far enough south) should not much regret an ultimate separation."

The next month Hawthorne visited Washington and saw the edges of the conflict, and he wrote out his impressions of men and of the scenes in his article "Chiefly about War Matters," which was published in "The Atlantic Monthly" for July, 1862. The text was sufficiently unsympathetic with the times to trouble the editor's mind, and Hawthorne, to ease the situation, added explanatory comments of his own as if from an editorial pen. The article shows conclusively how little Hawthorne had been affected, how completely he stood out of the national spirit, being as mere an observer of what was going on as at any time in his life and expressing his own view from time to time with entire obliviousness, as in the passages on Lincoln and on John Brown, of everything except his own impression. The judgment he passes on John Brown illustrates, too, better than pages of comment, his mental attitude in politics, its excuses and its limitations: —

"I shall not pretend to be an admirer of old John Brown, any farther than sympathy with Whittier's excellent ballad about him may go; nor did I expect ever to shrink so unutterably from any apothegm of a sage, whose happy lips have uttered a hundred golden sentences, as from that saying (perhaps falsely attributed to so honored a source), that the death of this blood-stained fanatic has 'made the Gallows as venerable as the Cross!' Nobody was ever more justly hanged. He won his martyrdom fairly, and took it firmly. He himself, I am persuaded (such was his natural integrity), would have acknowledged that Virginia had a right to take the life which he had staked and lost; although it would have been better for her, in the hour that is fast coming, if she could generously have forgotten the criminality of his attempt in its enormous folly. On the other hand, any common-sensible man, looking at the matter unsentimentally, must have felt a certain intellectual satisfaction in seeing him hanged, if it were only in requital of his preposterous miscalculation of possibilities."

Whatever one may think of this as the truth of common-sense, its publication in the summer of 1862 in Massachusetts showed an impenetrable self-possession in the author, and it is doubtless true, as has been said, that no other Northern man could have written such an article as this, so disengaged from the realities, the passion and prejudices of the time, so cold in observation and so impartial in feeling, so free from any participation in the scene.

It was during the winter of this year and the spring of 1863 that Hawthorne renewed his literary work by contributing to "The Atlantic Monthly" the papers afterwards published as "Our Old Home."[1] The contents of this volume have already been spoken of, and it need only be remarked here that some allowance may fairly be made for their tone and manner on the score of the depression of the time, arising from Hawthorne's increasing ill-health as well as from public confusion. The one memorable incident connected with the new book is the adherence of the author to his design of dedicating it to Franklin Pierce, to whom indeed it fitly belonged. Fields, however, was doubtful how the public would look on a compliment paid to the unpopular ex-President, and on communicating his views to Hawthorne he received this answer: —

"I thank you for your note of the 15th instant, and have delayed my reply thus long in order to ponder deeply on your advice, smoke cigars over it, and see what it might be possible for me to do towards taking it. I find that it would be a piece of poltroonery in me to withdraw either the dedication or the dedicatory letter. My long and intimate personal relations with Pierce render the

[1] *Our Old Home.* A Series of English Sketches. By Nathaniel Hawthorne. Boston: Ticknor and Fields. 1863. 12mo. Pp. 398.

dedication altogether proper, especially as regards this book, which would have had no existence without his kindness; and if he is so exceedingly unpopular that his name is enough to sink the volume, there is so much the more need that an old friend should stand by him. I cannot, merely on account of pecuniary profit or literary reputation, go back from what I have deliberately felt and thought it right to do; and if I were to tear out the dedication, I should never look at the volume again without remorse and shame. As for the literary public, it must accept my book precisely as I think fit to give it, or let it alone."

Hawthorne's decision was in the line of his character, and the dedication itself was in excellent taste.

The imaginative work of these last years was considerable in bulk, but it was never brought to any perfection; and though it has been published, the entire mass of it is only a bundle of more or less rough or uncompleted sketches and studies. It is comprised in the group of half-wrought tales, "The Ancestral Footstep," "Septimius Felton," "Dr. Grimshawe's Secret," and "The Dolliver Romance," which are all various shapes of the one work that Hawthorne was trying to evoke from his mind. They are interesting illustrations of the operation of his imagination, of his methods of thought, construction and elaboration, and in general of the manner in which a romance might grow under the hand; but there is little probability, so far as can be judged, that Hawthorne ever before worked in this experimental and ineffectual way. He had sketched an English romance "The Ancestral Foot-Step," in 1858, before his Italian experiences, and laid it aside. It was after his return to Concord that he again took up the scheme, and he attempted to join it with another plan involving a different idea. The four states in which the romance exists are the results of his various efforts, but in none of them is it anything more than inchoate. The idea on the English side of the story sprang from the imprint of a bloody foot-step at the foot of the great staircase at Smithell's Hall; on the American side it sprang from a tradition which Thoreau reported about the Concord house, to the effect that a man had lived there in the Revolution who sought the elixir of life. But neither of these two topics developed satisfactorily. The physical type which had served Hawthorne so well hitherto no longer responded to his art; neither the bloody footstep, nor the flower that grew upon the grave, which was after all only a fungus and not the real flower of life, had any story in them, either alone or together, and the figure of Sylph, who embodies allegorically this graveyard flower, has no power to win credence such as other, earlier, symbolic characters had won. The power of narration, the rich surface of romantic art, the character of the physician and the child, the scene of the Revolutionary morning, the English chamber, the white-haired old man,

the treasure chest with its secret of golden hair,
— all these things are in one or another of these
studies, and there is much loveliness of detail;
but there is no vitality in any of these; that element of life which has been spoken of before, as
the germinal power in Hawthorne's imaginative
work, is gone; here are only relics and fragments,
the costume and settings, the figures, the sentiment, the beauty of surface, the atmosphere of
romance, but the story has refused to take life.
Whether it was due to Hawthorne's failing powers
or to inherent incapacities of the theme, is immaterial; he was not to finish this last work, and he
knew it.   He had gone so far as to give Fields the
promise of "The Dolliver Romance," as if it were
in that form that he meant to reduce the whole;
but he did so with no confidence, as appears from
his successive notes: —

"There is something preternatural in my reluctance to begin.   I linger at the threshold, and
have a perception of very disagreeble phantoms to
be encountered if I enter. . . . I don't see much
probability of my having the first chapter of the
Romance ready as soon as you want it.   There are
two or three chapters ready to be written, but I am
not robust enough to begin, and I feel as if I
should never carry it through."   And he writes
again: " I am not quite up to writing yet, but
shall make an effort as soon as I see any hope of
success.   You ought to be thankful that (like most
other broken-down authors) I do not pester you

with decrepit pages, and insist upon your accepting them as full of the old spirit and vigor.   That
trouble, perhaps, still awaits you, after I shall have
reached a further stage of decay.   Seriously, my
mind has, for the present, lost its temper and its
fine edge, and I have an instinct that I had better keep quiet.   Perhaps I shall have a new spirit
of vigor, if I wait quietly for it; perhaps not."

In February, 1864, he advises that some notice
be given the readers of the magazine that he cannot furnish the promised romance, and he tries to
touch the subject with humor, but it is too plain
that his spirits are ill at ease: —

"I hardly know what to say to the public about
this abortive romance, though I know pretty well
what the case will be.   I shall never finish it.
Yet it is not quite pleasant for an author to an-
nounce himself, or to be announced, as finally
broken down as to his literary faculty. . . . I
cannot finish it unless a great change comes over
me; and if I make too great an effort to do so, it
will be my death; not that I should care much
for that, if I could fight the battle through and
win it, thus ending a life of much smoulder and
a scanty fire in a blaze of glory.   But I should
smother myself in mud of my own making. . . .
I am not low-spirited, nor fanciful, nor freakish,
but look what seem to me realities in the face,
and am ready to take whatever may come.   If I
could but go to England now, I think that the
sea-voyage and the ' old Home ' might set me all
right."

At the end of March he started south with Ticknor, in hopes of some improvement by the change of air and scene; his companion, who was expected rather to have the care of Hawthorne, was himself taken ill and suddenly died in Philadelphia. The shock to Hawthorne in his state of health was a great one, and he returned home excited and nervous. He failed rapidly, and his family and friends became anxious about him, though they did not anticipate the suddenness of the end. In the middle of May Frank Pierce proposed that they should go to the New Hampshire lakes and up the Pemigewasset, by carriage, and Hawthorne consented. He bade his wife and children good-by, and was perhaps convinced that he would never return; whatever thoughts were in his mind, he kept silence concerning them. The narrative of the journey, with its end, is given by Pierce in a letter to Bridge: —

"I met H. at Boston, Wednesday (11th), came to this place by rail Thursday morning, and went to Concord, N. H., by evening train. The weather was unfavorable, and H. feeble; and we remained at C. until the following Monday. We then went slowly on our journey, stopping at Franklin, Laconia, and Centre Harbor, and reaching Plymouth Wednesday evening (18th). We talked of you, Tuesday, between Franklin and Laconia, when H. said — among other things — ' We have, neither of us, met a more reliable friend.' The conviction was impressed upon me, the day we left Boston, that the seat of the disease from which H. was suffering was in the brain or spine, or both; H. walked with difficulty, and the use of his hands was impaired. In fact, on the 17th I saw that he was becoming quite helpless, although he was able to ride, and, I thought, more comfortable in the carriage with gentle motion than anywhere else; for whether in bed or up, he was very restless. I had decided, however, not to pursue our journey beyond Plymouth, which is a beautiful place, and thought, during our ride Wednesday, that I would the next day send for Mrs. Hawthorne and Una to join us there. Alas! there was no next day for our friend.

"We arrived at Plymouth about six o'clock. After taking a little tea and toast in his room, and sleeping for nearly an hour upon the sofa, he retired. A door opened from my room to his, and our beds were not more than five or six feet apart. I remained up an hour or two after he fell asleep. He was apparently less restless than the night before. The light was left burning in my room — the door open — and I could see him without moving from my bed. I went, however, between one and two o'clock to his bedside, and supposed him to be in a profound slumber. His eyes were closed, his position and face perfectly natural. His face was towards my bed. I awoke again between three and four o'clock, and was surprised — as he had generally been restless — to notice that his position was unchanged, — exactly the same that it was two hours before. I went to his bedside, placed my hand upon his forehead and temple, and found that he was dead. He evidently had passed from natural sleep to that sleep from which there is no waking, without suffering, and without the slightest movement."

The funeral took place at Concord on May 24, 1864, and he was buried in Sleepy Hollow; on his coffin lay his unfinished romance, and his friends stood about the open grave, for he was almost the first of the distinguished group to which he belonged to lay down the pen. Emerson and others whose names have been frequent in this record now lie with him in that secluded spot, which is a place of long memory for our literature. His wife survived him a few years and died in London in 1871; perhaps even more than his genius the sweetness of his home life with her, as it is so abundantly shown in his children's memories, lingers in the mind that has dwelt long on the story of his life.

INDEX

GEORGE E. WOODBERRY was an American man of letters in his own right. A frequent contributor to the *Atlantic Monthly* and the *Nation*, he served as literary editor of the *Boston Post* before moving on in 1891 to begin a thirteen-year tenure as Professor of Literature at Columbia University. His works include an impressive array of critical biographies, literary essays and poems.

RICHARD POIRIER, the Marius Bewley Professor of English at Rutgers University, is a member of the American Academy of Arts and Sciences, and the recipient of the achievement award in criticism from the American Academy of Arts and Letters. His works include *The Comic Sense of Henry James*, *A World Elsewhere: The Place of Style in American Literature*, *The Performing Self*, and *Robert Frost: The Work of Knowing*.